D0869649

Executive Target

by PETE BYER

Mary, I know it took longer than I thought - but here it is!
I hope you're proud.

Cover Design by Brian Wren. Wilmington, NC

ISBN: 978-1-54396-224-6 (Print)
ISBN: 978-1-54396-225-3 (eBook)

Prologue

An envelope addressed to President James Whitcomb's daughter, Kristina, arrived at the White House.

The envelope was from the *New York Chronicle*, a publication viewed by Whitcomb loyalists as a thorn in the side of the administration. The editors and reporters of the *Chronicle* had it out for President Whitcomb since he had decisively defeated the Democratic presidential nominee, Senator Elizabeth Warren, another terrible campaigner on the "first woman president" plank, and her vice president-nominee, "Pajama Boy" from the 2013 Obamacare advertising campaign.

President Whitcomb's career contravened everything for which the *Chronicle* stood. Whitcomb was a decorated war hero; his staff frequently circulated what became a famous photo of Whitcomb, obviously bloodied, carrying a wounded black crewman out of his downed helicopter in Iraq. Before being elected president, Whitcomb had been a corporate attorney who became a successful and moderate Republican governor in New Jersey, a decidedly blue state. His rise to prominence was aided by the overwhelming popularity of his two bestsellers, *Hillary Clinton and the End of Feminism* and *The Myths of Global Warming*. Aside from adding substantially to his bank account, the books served to increase his favorability ratings among conservative and moderate voters across the nation.

During his two terms in Trenton he was able, with much wailing and gnashing of teeth, to move towards a balanced budget, reach an accommodation with public employee unions over the pension crisis, introduce significant public education reforms and reclaim some inner cities, although Camden remained an intractable problem. His popularity had been unmatched by any governor of either party. His refusal to block Democratic legislation outlawing gestation crates in New Jersey, while causing a short-term setback in the Iowa caucuses, solidified his popularity in the state and reinforced his stature across the country as a candidate of unquestioned integrity.

Even his divorce early in his first term did not have a lasting negative impact on his image.

Kristina, known as Krissy, was set to graduate from NYU in the spring. She loved the school and being in New York City. The large urban environment gave her a degree of anonymity and independence while also being convenient for either parent to visit. She was a focused student, scheduled to graduate with a BA in political science with honors distinction. It had not yet been formally announced what her plans for after graduation would be, and while she had her choice of postgraduate programs from which to choose, she wasn't quite sure what she wanted to do. However, after receiving acceptances to every program to which she applied and several long conversations with a professor with whom she had become close, her two best friends and her parents, she had made her decision two weeks earlier.

Krissy was visiting the White House for a long weekend, so the president's personal aide, Pat Howley, known as PJ, was able to deliver the envelope to her. Krissy read the enclosed graduation card and went looking for her father. She was unable to speak to him immediately because he was meeting with foreign dignitaries in the Treaty Room. She did the next best thing and texted PJ, asking him to make sure that her father made time for her later that day.

When the President finally made it to the Family Quarters later that afternoon, Krissy ran to her father, wide-eyed and grinning ear to ear. "I have a job for this summer!" she announced.

Her father, who had experienced easier days in the White House, was delighted to be in the presence of his exuberant daughter. She made him forget, at least momentarily, the dire warnings of Russian and Chinese military aggression that the Chairman of the Joint Chiefs had given him that morning. Krissy handed him the elaborate graduation card and stood back for his reaction. Inside the card, with the standard "Happy Graduation to the Graduate" greeting, was a handwritten note on expensive stationary:

Dear Kristina,

> *Congratulations on your upcoming graduation and your recent decision to attend Columbia's Graduate School of Journalism. We have many alumni and alumnae from*

that outstanding school here on staff. As you may know, it happens to be my alma mater. We all recall our days at "J-School" fondly.

I would be very pleased and honored if you would consider a position this summer in our intern program. You will be exposed to some of the finest journalists in the world plying their chosen trade. Our summer interns have had exciting and wonderful experiences in our program, and some are now on staff at the Chronicle today.

We hope you will give us serious consideration.

Warmest regards,
Jake Rosen
Publisher
New York Chronicle

"Well…that's wonderful, honey," the president stammered.

"I'm going to call mom and let her know. This is so exciting!"

As his daughter left, Whitcomb absorbed what had just transpired. The country's leading bastion of progressive ideology in the media, long known for its anti-Republican stance in general, and the policies of this president in particular, was inviting a close family member into its employ.

The White House had not yet announced Krissy's decision to attend Columbia. Only the closest of the president's inner circle and a few family members were privy to that information.

How had the *Chronicle* found out?

* * * * *

Jake Rosen logged off his computer and turned to look out his window at the lights of Manhattan's West Side. He always tried to end his workday this way—all calls returned, all emails answered, the next day's schedule finalized; he wanted today's work completed so he could have a clear head to spend time thinking—thinking strategically, thinking long term, thinking big.

He would have "Uneasy lies the head that wears the crown" tattooed on his arm if he wasn't so afraid of needles. Instead, the phrase, written on a cocktail napkin (by him), sat in a frame on his desk. Indeed, Jake carried a heavy burden, but he embraced it without hesitation. Being the publisher of the *New York Chronicle* was what Jake had been born to do. His family had owned the *Chronicle* for generations, back to the middle of the nineteenth century. His grandfather, Abe, began at the *Chronicle* when the paper had been located in a dingy warehouse on the Lower East Side with used printing presses, second hand desks and a staff who couldn't always count on receiving their weekly paychecks. Under Abe's leadership, the *Chronicle* evolved into a daily publication loved by its readers and often condemned, despised and feared by its subjects. As the paper's prestige grew, so did its domestic and international bureaus, number of feature writers and Pulitzer prizes.

Jake's father, Morty, started at the *Chronicle* as a copy boy and learned the newspaper business from the ground up. Morty had worked for the paper during breaks from public high school and City College. After graduation, he took a job at a Chicago newspaper, determined to chart his own path in the newspaper world. For three years he covered funerals, the police beat, local politics and became a lifelong Cubs fan. However, the calling to work in the family business inexorably brought him back to New York and the *Chronicle*. Upon his return, Morty started as a junior reporter and rose through the ranks, earning the respect and admiration of its staff. Many longtime staffers fondly remembered the unassuming son of the publisher who had performed his copy boy duties without mentioning his last name.

Morty eventually became the *Chronicle's* executive editor and his father's right-hand man. Together they molded the *Chronicle* into the premier progressive publication in the United States. Its coverage of local, state, national and international politics and governments, business, entertainment and culture (everything except sports; the *Chronicle's* sports bureau seemed to be an afterthought) was unmatched. Politicians sought the *Chronicle's* endorsement, business leaders cringed if their companies were the subjects of negative articles and Broadway producers waited on pins and needles for their shows' reviews to be published on opening night. The *Chronicle's* power to influence government policies, political party platforms, societal trends, scientific debates and cultural movements became unrivaled in the media.

Abe and Morty understood that the *Chronicle's* ability to shape the public's perception of events was a power to be nurtured and used with great restraint and discretion. By the 1990s the two old-style newspaper men had shepherded the *Chronicle* to a level of prominence that was hard to imagine when Abe started at the paper in that Lower East Side warehouse.

Abe died shortly after the turn of the century, and Morty succeeded his father in position. After Morty's incapacity due to a stroke, the *Chronicle's* helm fell to Jake.

Jake had also decided at a young age to follow his father and grandfather into the family business. He worked as a copy boy during high school at Collegiate and college at Yale. However, unlike his father, Jake did not feel the need to set his own course. He was happy to join the *Chronicle* immediately after finishing graduate school. As for learning the newspaper business from the bottom up, that was not Jake's path. He had no qualms taking a staff reporter position, which typically requires several years' experience, when he walked in the door. He was initially assigned to the Metro bureau and covered local stories. After a brief stint in that bureau, he reported on national and international politics. He worked in the Washington, DC bureau for a few years, covering the White House and a presidential campaign.

Jake made no secret of his ambition to succeed his father, and most staffers at the *Chronicle* saw the writing on the wall. He often shared bylines with other reporters who had done most, if not all, of the background investigation of the subject at hand. Other reporters helped Jake rewrite poorly drafted articles, referred leads or directed sources to contact him. Staff who had the foresight to help Jake early in his career at the *Chronicle* did so hoping that such favors would be returned in the not too distant future.

They guessed right.

Jake wasn't unintelligent or lazy. He had a plan but "working his way up the ladder" was not part of that plan. He respected and admired both his grandfather and father and was grateful to them for giving him the opportunity to work at the *Chronicle*. He felt they had not fully appreciated the power to be wielded for good behind the masthead of the *Chronicle*. He was determined to take the *Chronicle* to heights greater than those achieved by his forebears.

As expected, Jake quickly rose to the upper echelon of the *Chronicle* and began to exert his influence. Because of Morty's departure from the *Chronicle*, his loyal lieutenants felt they had no choice but to support Jake as he maneuvered himself into the publisher's corner office adjacent to the newsroom. They put up with "good" Jake, that is, the one who congratulated administrative assistants on their birthdays, sent flowers to the wakes of employees' relatives and shared unused tickets to sporting events and Broadway shows with the staff. When this Jake conducted meetings, a give and take existed among the participants. Saul Slowinski, the executive editor, and Harry O'Rourke, the deputy executive editor, had free rein to select the stories to appear on the front page above the fold. O'Rourke and the assistant editors determined staff assignments, feature articles and expensive and lengthy investigative pieces with minimal intrusion. "Good" Jake sought to report the news in an objective, non-judgmental fashion; to select stories based on newsworthiness and relevance to the *Chronicle*'s readers; and to highlight issues believed significant to voters, union members and the middle class.

However, while it was important for the *Chronicle* to report the "news," Jake also believed that the *Chronicle* had an obligation to lead the cause of liberal, progressive righteousness. The *Chronicle*'s readers had to be guided to the "Truth," which was obvious to Jake and the "Council," a group of like-minded senior advisors at the *Chronicle*.

This Truth was that a strong central government was needed to limit the excesses of the American people and to redistribute the wealth concentrated in the hands of a small group of individuals and their families. First and foremost, the wealthy had to pay their fair share of taxes. Children had to be told what to eat, study and how to play based on government funded studies. Businesses had to be regulated so that equal pay for the sexes and a living wage, as determined by the government, were the norms. Excess business profits, as calculated by the government, had to be taxed. Health care had to offer comprehensive coverage, including free birth control and unrestricted abortions. Regulations had to be imposed on Wall Street so that no firm became too big to fail and no executive too rich to jail. Those year-end bonuses Wall Street bankers and hedge fund managers routinely received had to be taxed.

American business, academia, military and government merely tolerating racial, gender and ethnic diversity was not enough; rather, such diversity in all aspects of society, at all levels, and at all times must be embraced as a primary goal.

Industries had to cease any operations that added to anthropogenic climate change and the undeniable and inevitable cataclysmic effects of such change. Alternative energy sources, sustainable industries and initiatives and technological advances to reduce greenhouse gases had to be developed and funded by increased taxes on existing businesses, identified by the government, that contributed to climate change.

Opponents of such goals, whether climate change deniers, abortion opponents or bakers who wouldn't make wedding cakes for gay couples, had to be marginalized, isolated and rendered powerless – and if need be, crushed.

And the wealthy had to be taxed.

The preeminence of the *Chronicle*, nurtured by his grandfather and father, had left Jake presiding over a treasured progressive institution whose influence was felt across cultural, political and socio-economic confines. Jake's turn to harness the *Chronicle's* influence and transform the newspaper into the tip of the spear in the battle to instill this Truth throughout the United States had arrived.

Now, using all of the resources he had marshalled in the last few years, Jake was ready to set in motion his plan to drag America out of the virtual insane asylum it had unwittingly entered in November 2016.

* * * * *

Bobby Manzi hated driving into Manhattan. When he was in his early twenties, he hadn't cared for the Manhattan club scene that many of his friends found so appealing. The cover charges and drinks were expensive. It always seemed that the better looking a girl was, the more stuck up she was. Most of the time, when he eventually told a girl he was from Staten Island, she said she had to go to the bathroom, and that was the last he saw of her. Once a girl asked if his father was a corrections officer; Staten Island was one big prison, wasn't it? Now, approaching forty, he was a doting father to his twin sons, Primo and Secondo, and he took them to Knicks games at the

Garden like his father had with him and his sister. He took them to Yankees games, too; he didn't mind the Bronx.

But Manhattan was full of suits, yellow cabs and idiot tourists who actually rode bicycles to get around. Who was dumber, Manzi wondered, the tourists who risked life and limb jousting with those yellow cabs or the politicians who thought riding bikes in Manhattan traffic was a good idea? Getting over the Verrazano-Narrows Bridge was a hassle since he had to wait in the cash lane. An E-ZPass would make life easier, of course, but then the feds could track him. Parking was a pain and he always had trouble understanding the illegal immigrants who seemed to work at every parking garage or lot. Except for the few good restaurants remaining in Little Italy, food in Manhattan was overpriced and the portions were small and served by "actors" trying to make it on Broadway.

As a union leader, he frequently visited his "crew" who helped run his electrician and carpenter union locals. Seeing these guys, some of whom went to grammar school with him at St. Cecilia's, almost made the trip into Manhattan worthwhile. Vito "Not for Nothing" Paterno, the crew chief, Ray "Karate Kid" Siconolfi and Tony "I Don't Let My Wife Do That on Account of Those Lips Kiss My Kids" Delmonica comprised the crew. Manzi was known as "Three Balls."

But today he was not going to spend much time with his boys. Today he was meeting with one of his least favorite people, but one who paid Manzi very well for the periodic special services Manzi was able to provide. The routine for their meetings was always the same: Manzi went to the midtown electricians' local office, bullshitted with the staff, then walked down to the basement and through the little-known passageway that led to the *New York Chronicle's* underground parking garage. If any feds had followed him from Staten Island that day, they would be sitting two blocks away watching his car in a parking lot.

*　*　*　*　*

"God, I love my job."

How many people can actually say that about their work? Not many, thought Secret Service Special Agent Jamal McDaniels as he sprinted the last hundred yards of his daily early morning run through the streets of Washington, DC. His route took him from his apartment in Southwest near the Wharf development to the Washington Monument to do push-ups, sit-ups and squats for twenty minutes. He would continue past the World War II Memorial, around the Korean and Vietnam War Memorials, to the Jefferson Memorial and then back to his apartment. Rain or shine. Hot or cold. Winter, summer, spring or fall. The run was part of his daily routine, and he loved it. He saw DC at its best. No tourists, panhandlers or millennial scum carrying briefcases and talking on phones. At that time of the day he could look Lincoln in the face and say a quiet prayer as he ran past the war memorials. These runs were his form of decompression or meditation and better than any weed he had tried as a teenager.

McDaniels enlisted in the Army as a pudgy junior college graduate determined to set himself straight. He had been an athlete in high school but never felt the camaraderie that he experienced while in the Army. The training was challenging, both physically and mentally, but he loved every minute of it. Once he understood the drill sergeants and their ultimate goals, the constant yelling didn't bother him. He enjoyed learning to fight and defend himself. He overcame his initial skittishness handling guns and became an expert marksman. He enjoyed the infantry training and was disappointed when it ended. While Ranger School was the most difficult two months of his life, he was never prouder of himself than when he graduated and received that tab.

He did three tours in the Middle East: one in Iraq and two in Afghanistan. He never spoke of his time overseas with people who had not served in the military; they would never understand what he did-had to do-over there.

After eight years in the Army, his last tour overseas and rising to the rank of staff sergeant, McDaniels decided to leave the military. He took a year off and traveled across the country and decided that law enforcement would suit him best. He believed that he would thrive in a structured, quasi-military environment; civilian life didn't offer enough discipline. He discussed his options with some military friends who introduced him to several federal and local law-enforcement officers. He applied to the Secret Service. He received points for his military service, was physically qualified and passed a battery of physiological exams. His first assignment was in Atlanta, where he excelled at his job, rose rapidly through the ranks and was accepted in the Presidential Protection Division.

He knew he was serving a worthwhile cause protecting POTUS. The protection detail received routine briefings from the Secret

Service Intelligence Division (and occasionally from the FBI and the CIA) describing possible plots against POTUS and other high-level government officials and buildings. If the public only knew how many people out there hated America and wanted to kill Americans, no matter those Americans' political affiliation, color, religion or profession, but just as long as they were Americans, controversy over the NSA, drone strikes or domestic surveillance would disappear. If America only knew....

Chapter 1

"Good morning, Mr. President."

"Good morning, PJ. Anything happen overnight I need to know about?"

James Whitcomb was in the third year of his term as president of the United States. He learned early in his presidency that many days began with unexpected news of events occurring in unknown corners of the world which would effectively cancel that day's schedule. Pat Howley was Whitcomb's personal aide and usually the first person he saw each morning after his valets. PJ's mood this morning in the Oval Office was buoyant, so Whitcomb knew this day was not going to start off with a crisis *du jour*.

"No, Mr. President, we had a quiet night. Today's schedule is on your desk. We're working on a fairly tight one today, sir. Not much room to deviate from what we have you set for. Shall I order you some breakfast?"

Whitcomb appreciated PJ's quiet efficiency and upbeat demeanor. Compared to many in the White House, his eagerness to serve was genuine, his ego non-existent; he wasn't waiting for the president's term to end so he could write a book about *his* time in the White House. PJ's father, Patrick John F.X. Howley, Sr., was the "dean" of Wall Street general counsels and had been Whitcomb's longtime client and friend. Whitcomb had known PJ since he was a teenager and given PJ his first job out of college as a staff member while Whitcomb had been governor of New Jersey.

"Sure, PJ," Whitcomb replied. "Some coffee, fruit and a muffin should do it. Would you ask Denis to come see me as soon as he gets in?"

"Sure thing, Mr. President."

Denis Lenihan was Whitcomb's chief of staff and best friend. Whitcomb's former law partner, Lenihan held the same position during most of Whitcomb's two terms as governor. Lenihan had a hard edge about him that Whitcomb sometimes lacked. Lenihan was not afraid to make the difficult decisions on policy or personnel often required of a chief executive. He was also unfailingly loyal to Whitcomb, which led outsiders, particularly the liberal media, to assume he was simply a "yes" man, unthinkingly carrying the Whitcomb flag, no matter what the issue or national interest might be. However, Lenihan was not hesitant to express a view contrary to Whitcomb's, to highlight the administration's missteps or to guide the president toward a decision that he might otherwise be reluctant to make when the two men were alone.

Moreover, although a Washington neophyte, Lenihan quickly adjusted to the ways and means of the nation's capital. While Whitcomb's presidential campaign portrayed him as an outsider, free of Capital Beltway corruption, influence and money, Lenihan knew a successful and productive presidency would require the cultivation and maintenance of good relations with Washington insiders on Capitol Hill, in the press and on K Street. Lenihan already possessed superior analytical and negotiating skills from years working as a transactional attorney representing Wall Street investment banks. He coupled those skills with the aggressiveness garnered from the bare-knuckle politics for which New Jersey is known, not to mention street brawls in the Vailsburg section of Newark where Lenihan had grown up. He had now elevated those skills so as to gain the grudging respect of the Washington *cognoscenti*.

Executive and judicial appointments and relations with both houses of Congress, the Pentagon and other offices in the Executive Branch went smoother with Lenihan's guiding hand. He would never be confused with the Ham Jordans and Don Regans of past administrations.

The president went behind his desk. He hadn't slept well the night before. Lenihan walked in with the president's campaign manager, Don Mangini. Mangini had run the campaign of one of Whitcomb's opponents in the Republican primary race that ended much closer than expected. Looking back, Whitcomb and Lenihan recognized how well Mangini had managed their opponent's campaign. With Whitcomb's blessing, Lenihan approached Mangini after the Inauguration to solicit him to join the administration. Mangini accepted a position as Lenihan's assistant chief of staff and had proved invaluable in helping the administration craft policies as well as navigate the serpentine paths of Washington politics. Whitcomb's and Lenihan's growing reliance on Mangini allowed him entry into the president's inner sanctum.

"Good morning, Mr. President," both men said.

"Good morning, gentlemen. Please, grab some coffee."

After pouring themselves some coffee, Lenihan and Mangini sat on a couch as the president moved from behind his desk to join them. Mangini had a look of concern on his face as he addressed the President. "Mr. President, we're meeting this afternoon with the campaign staff, but I wanted to give you a heads up on some issues that are concerning me."

"Are they the same issues that kept me awake last night?" Whitcomb asked in an irritated voice.

"Well, sir, if those issues were the blow-up of the Israeli-Palestinian peace talks, the Democrats' announcement of their opposition to your budget proposals and the reaction of Reverend Hood to the withdrawal of the Wainsworth nomination, I can see why you have bags under your eyes."

Whitcomb turned toward his chief of staff. "Denis, I thought we had smoothed things over with the good reverend and his legions. We were never going to get Wainsworth's nomination out of committee. We fought the good fight, but there comes a time when you have to step back, lick your wounds and look to the next battle."

Nathan Wainsworth had been the administration's nominee for the vacant Secretary of Education position. The last time

Wainsworth had been in a classroom was thirty years before when he taught high school English in Georgia for two years after college. He met his future wife and, after marriage, joined his father-in-law's textbook publishing company. He eventually took over the company and became a significant financial contributor to Republican politicians and causes. He also championed the publishing of several books used to teach creationism in grade schools throughout the South. Wainsworth became the darling of several Southern Republican and Democrat senators, not to mention Reverend Josiah Hood, the leader of one of the largest Evangelical congregations in the South. Reverend Hood prodded his Congressional allies, who in turn lobbied the administration to appoint Wainsworth to the education post.

However Wainsworth's popularity proved to be nonexistent outside the South. The more Reverend Hood and his supporters pushed for Wainsworth's nomination, the more negative publicity was generated by teacher unions, church-state separatists and liberal bloggers. When the bulk of the Senate saw that his nomination was not well received by the rest of the country, his support quickly evaporated.

After the administration was forced to withdraw his nomination earlier in the week, the White House was inundated with phone calls and emails from members of Reverend Hood's vast congregation. Lenihan did his best at damage control. Since this was one issue on which the liberal mainstream media and blogosphere agreed with the administration, the discontent expressed over the White House's decision was not widely reported by the media or on Twitter. Nevertheless, Lenihan was concerned.

"With your permission, sir, I'd like to have Don reach out to Reverend Hood and see what we can do to calm him and his supporters down. We are going to need him in the election. He has to be on our side if we're going to get the religious right vote."

"Sure, that's a great idea, Denis," the president said, turning toward Mangini. "Don, do whatever you can to turn the volume down on this. Don't promise him anything yet. Let's see what a visit from a senior White House staff member does to get us back in his good graces."

"Understood, Mr. President," Mangini said as he stood up to leave. "I'm sure that the good reverend will like nothing better than to hear from a lapsed Catholic like me what God's will is for this country."

After Mangini left, Lenihan grabbed another cup of coffee and sat down next to the president. "Jim, I'm concerned about your reelection, and you should be too. The setbacks Don mentioned are real, and they're not going away anytime soon; the timing couldn't be worse. I think you have to develop a mindset that you're going to be in the fight of your life. Election Day will be here sooner than you think, and you can't sit back now and rest on your laurels."

"Laurels? What laurels? You would think from reading the *Chronicle* and listening to a few of my future opponents that I've been sitting on my hands for the last two years."

Whitcomb had fairly thick skin when it came to the criticism he received from the media, Democrats and bloggers. Whitcomb was even able to tolerate this new breed of Internet do nothings, the "vloggers." How millennials could make ranting into a computer camera while sitting in their unkempt bedrooms into a legitimate profession baffled Whitcomb.

Moreover, Whitcomb continued to be harangued by supporters of former President Trump, still venting over Trump's decision to not seek a second term after his historic and unprecedented defeat of Hillary Clinton and the mainstream media in 2016. This was inexplicable to Whitcomb since it was Trump's decision alone to not seek reelection. In hindsight, the signs to keen political observers were there. While Trump did achieve some significant successes, the process of governing while dealing under the constraints of an opposition party, an independent judiciary, independent counsel investigations and the sustained assault of the liberal media clearly frustrated the volatile real estate developer and businessman; he had never faced such personal, mean spirited and almost continuous opposition while conducting his business affairs. His announcement only weeks before the Iowa caucuses that he would not seek a second term opened the field for the Republican nomination. Whitcomb, a lawyer, war hero and popular two-term Republican governor of a blue state, was happy to step in.

The Whitcomb administration continued and even improved some of the policies and legislation enacted by the Trump administration in such areas as health care, education, immigration and criminal justice reform. In other areas, such as energy policy, the Whitcomb administration was able to set its own course.

President Whitcomb's stature had also risen due to his consistent stand against the political correctness that had infiltrated so much of American culture. When he was invited to give the commencement address at his *alma mater*, Rutgers University, during his first year in Washington, the university administration was petitioned to withdraw the invitation by chairs of the multicultural and gender studies departments, including women's studies, black studies, LGBTTQQFAGPBDSM studies and socialist party studies, to name a few. The petition was supported by the Students Against White Privilege, Students Against Israel, Students For Palestine, Students Against American Exceptionalism and the Students for Sexual Experimentation. Even the parents of the men's lacrosse team protested Whitcomb's selection; they still remember Whitcomb, who played third base at Rutgers, once describing lacrosse as "a sport for rich white kids who can't play high school baseball."

Unlike other conservative commencement speakers who experienced similar opposition at other schools, President Whitcomb indicated he intended to appear and fully participate in the graduation ceremonies.

During the president's speech, several faculty stood up and left the stage. A small group of students stood and began chanting. However, they were shouted down by graduates of the Rutgers' baseball team, the ROTC cadets who cheered for the president, himself a former Navy ROTC cadet who became a Marine helicopter pilot, and the parents of the Asian Pacific students. The speech continued otherwise uneventfully.

During his second year in office, the administration announced the participants in the White House summer internship program. One was a student at Duke who had been falsely accused of sexually assaulting a female student and successfully sued the school to regain admission along with monetary damages and a written apology from the school president and eighty faculty members. The second was the former editor at the newspaper published by the Conservative Student Union at the University of Wisconsin. He had been removed from his position by the school administration at the behest of a small but vocal group of students after authoring an article reviewing President Trump's one term as president entitled "Donald 'Built That Wall' Trump: The Greatest American Ever?"

President Whitcomb believed he was having a successful first term, cruising into his reelection campaign facing a field of nondescript and unimpressive potential Democratic challengers. "Look, Denis," the president said to his now somber chief of staff, "if we can focus on the positives and the real accomplishments of this administration, we'll have a great story to tell the voters. I know that we can sell this administration to the people who matter, the ones who supported me two years ago and the ones who'll support me in the next election. Screw the media."

At this point, PJ Howley walked in the Oval Office with a waiter from the White House Mess with the president's breakfast. Howley assisted the waiter as he set up the breakfast on a side table. The waiter served the president breakfast and Lenihan another cup of coffee. The chief of staff grinned as he looked at his old friend. "I know you too well, Mr. President. I suspected that would be your reaction. I've already started preparations for a national tour. We'll get you out of Washington and in front of friendly crowds on military bases, solidly Republican districts, county fairs and have you eat a fried turkey leg or something like that. You'll have the opportunity to make your case to real Americans in the heartland who will be happy to hear your message. We'll make sure that your speeches get distributed nationwide. We'll have you highlight different policies and programs at each stop. We'll get your message out to the people directly."

"Great idea, Denis, I love it. I know you sometimes think I'm too impulsive, but I don't see any downside to this."

"I agree, Mr. President. I don't see the need to run this by consultants or focus groups. Mangini agrees with me, by the way."

"That's the best news I've had this week," the president said. "We've had some good road shows in the past. We can do it again. Set up a meeting with the speech writers. I've already got a few ideas of what I want to address."

"Will do, Mr. President," Lenihan said and left the Oval Office relieved. Now that they had agreed on a plan of action, Lenihan was ready to get to work. As for the president, he was at his best when he had a framework with set goals and definitive timeframes. Whitcomb felt rejuvenated and was ready to take on his opponents, whether they be coastal elites, the mainstream media or Internet trolls.

Chapter 2

Jake Rosen had summoned the Council to his conference room for a meeting.

The Council was Rosen's sounding board and his confidants, and sometimes the only ones at the *Chronicle* who could control Rosen's periodic bursts of anger and paranoia toward perceived enemies or simple incompetents, in other words, "bad" Jake. No one at the *Chronicle* would soon forget the junior sportswriter who had the temerity to submit an article for publication a few years ago that questioned why the longtime head basketball coach at Jesuit University in Washington, DC only recruited black players. The rest of the student body of Jesuit University primarily consisted of rich white kids from prominent East Coast Catholic high schools. The Archangels were usually a top-twenty team and routinely made the NCAA championship tournament. Notwithstanding the notoriety of the coach and his program, no sportswriter for the *Chronicle* had ever sought to explore the reason why the coach rarely, if ever, recruited white players and in most seasons the team's roster consisted exclusively of black players.

The article came to Rosen's attention because Marty Lavelle, a longtime *Chronicle* employee and the sports bureau chief, was on vacation. Lavelle would not have permitted the article to leave his desk. After reading the article, Rosen could be heard screaming throughout the newsroom "Who cares about this?", "What difference does it make?", "Who is this asshole reporter?", and "Jesuit University has a basketball team?" The only sport Rosen followed was soccer; hence the reason the *Chronicle* was the only major United States newspaper to regularly cover international soccer matches in non-World Cup years. He called the young reporter to his office for a closed-door meeting after which the reporter, visibly shaken, took the rest of the day off. The article was quickly killed. Two weeks later, the reporter was stopped by the police while driving to a party at another *Chronicle* staffer's home in Brooklyn. He was arrested when cocaine was found in his car. He denied knowledge or ownership of the cocaine but eventually took a leave of absence to handle the matter. He was never heard from again.

Marty Lavelle did not take a vacation for the next three years.

Another time, Rosen sent an internal memo, rumored to have actually been authored by the head of the New York City teachers' union, to the *Chronicle* staff praising public education and describing the *Chronicle's* support for public schools, particularly those in urban areas. The memo indicated staffers should complete the attached form listing which public schools their children attended so that the *Chronicle* could support the schools by donating issues of the paper, books for libraries, providing speakers for career days, etc. The memo further indicated employees whose children attended public schools could apply for interest-free loans for summer camps, college scholarships sponsored by the *Chronicle* and other tuition support when their children went to college. The memo concluded with a comment to the effect that Rosen felt it was incumbent upon the *Chronicle* and its employees to fully support public education in the United States.

The memo indicated that children of employees who attended private schools were not eligible to participate in the program.

The irony of the fact that neither Rosen nor his two children attended public schools was lost on him but not on *Chronicle* staffers. Those who lived in Brooklyn, Queens, Hoboken, Jersey City and Washington, DC, to name a few, and who sent their children to private or Catholic schools told their supervisors they were going get new jobs at *Chronicle* rivals or move to the suburbs and then get jobs at *Chronicle* rivals. Under no circumstances would these *Chronicle* staffers be sending their precious children to the public schools in their urban neighborhoods.

When confronted with the mass exodus of reporters and other staffers, Slowinski and O'Rourke pleaded with Rosen to reconsider the program, which he did only after being urged to do so by the Council.

The Council, as they named themselves, was a select group known only to each other. When Rosen became publisher, he sought out like-minded people on the *Chronicle* staff who shared his vision to expand the newspaper's influence.

Rosen's first recruit was Francis Ritzie, the *Chronicle's* longtime theater critic turned columnist. The supremely confident (others might say pompous) journalist, author and social critic had become Rosen's closest and most trusted advisor, a "first among equals" on the Council. Ritzie often brought events or issues to Rosen's attention that he believed the *Chronicle* should address. Ritzie was quick to second any appropriate initiative decreed by Rosen; Ritzie's silence during any of Rosen's proposals served as a signal to the other Council members that perhaps Rosen had gone a little too far. Ritzie had considered impractical or ill-advised Rosen's plans for federally maintained and publicly available lists of names and addresses of gun owners and gender quotas for private sector and government jobs, for example.

Ritzie continued to view the George W. Bush victory in 2000 as simple election theft, a point which he never let his readers forget (even today the mere mention of "hanging chads" caused his left eye to twitch involuntarily). He also focused on what he argued were the failures of the Bush administration in prosecuting the Iraq and Afghanistan wars. His attacks on the Republican neocons who pontificated in favor of the wars and nation building received significant support from *Chronicle* readers.

Hillary Clinton's presidential campaign invigorated Ritzie as his columns reflected his enthusiastic support for the presumed first female president. However, with her defeat by Donald Trump, the fire that burned in Ritzie during the second Bush's presidency was, like for many progressives, extinguished. Except for the repeated attacks on the white people who voted for Trump ("'deplorables'- oh, Hillary was *so* right about that" Ritzie was often heard to say after his third rosé), Ritzie and many of his colleagues in the media could not accept President Trump's victory. The devastation of the Clinton loss, after all the support the media had given her, was felt in progressive circles through President Trump's entire term.

Somehow, however, with Whitcomb's election, Ritzie was able to rejuvenate himself and his sense of duty to the progressive cause. He requested that Rosen assign a team of reporters, led by Ritzie, to dig into Whitcomb's background. Ritzie envisioned this team having the same success as the teams he led during the Bush presidency. Rosen readily agreed to Ritzie's proposal and met regularly with him to discuss the progress of the "Alpha team," as it was known within the Council. The Alpha team's findings served, in part, as the catalyst for Rosen's plot against Whitcomb.

Tom Freeman was a reporter, columnist and author who covered the Middle East, international economics and globalization. He also devoted numerous columns to climate change and the projected consequences should the human race fail to reduce greenhouse gases. For Freeman, Clinton's stunning defeat aroused feelings of anger and betrayal for the ineptness of the campaign, James Comey and those damn emails, the blue-collar whites who put Trump in office and the Russian hackers. Freeman frequently lectured his readers on the need for the United States and other Western countries to reduce the effects of climate change by reducing oil consumption, developing alternative energy sources and eliminating the most egregious producers of carbon emissions, such as coal-fired power plants. He traveled the world, interviewing individual government leaders, local politicians and businessmen, tribal leaders, war widows and former child soldiers. He had an uncanny ability to draw inescapable conclusions supporting the underlying thesis of his particular column from these individual interviews.

He often attended Council meetings via a secure teleconference link from his spacious home in the Washington, DC suburbs. Some observers have noted that Freeman never interviewed anyone from local utilities on the environmental impact of heating and air conditioning his 11,000-square-foot house.

Paul Enrony was an economist's economist. An Ivy League trained college professor and author, and a former in-house economist for Fortune 500 companies, his columns were routinely cited as authority by liberal commentators. He frequently dealt with economic issues on a macro level, which he preferred. Most readers didn't really understand such esoteric economic topics, and critics were reluctant to take him on over issues such as aggregate supply and demand, structural unemployment or total labor productivity. He particularly liked to lecture government officials about fiscal policy or, more precisely, his perception of errors in the government's fiscal policies.

Enrony had been left deflated by Clinton's defeat. He took a sabbatical from the *Chronicle*, traveled and tried to write a book. His working title was *The End of the Civilized World We Once Loved* but he was unable to complete it. Every time he typed out President Trump's name, his hands trembled, he began to sweat profusely and his tongue swelled. His longtime Upper West Side therapist confided to him that she had many other patients with similar symptoms; she named the condition "Trumpophobia" and obtained a trademark.

The fourth member of the Council was columnist Kris Nickoff. Some political leaders leave such an impression on political observers that they are forever impacted by those exceptional politicians. In Nickoff's case, Bill Clinton was that politician. Nickoff, early in his career, came to understand the way Republicans thought and acted, why they did what they did and their manner of operating. Slaves to the free market theory of economics, tax cuts to benefit the wealthy, and bigger and heavier gas guzzling SUVs, in other words, rich white men looking out for other rich white men. But what Nickoff could never understand, never tolerate and never forgive was the capitulation of nominally liberal politicians to the dark side. Namely, Bill Clinton. NAFTA, workfare, criminal justice reform, don't ask, don't tell; all landed on a list of Clinton failures and betrayals. To have someone Nickoff considered a true believer evolve before his very eyes into a middle-of-the-road, compromising politician, solely concerned with keeping his poll numbers high and appeasing the electorate to ensure a second term, infuriated Nickoff. Therefore, he only supported Hillary's presidential bid through clenched teeth. He viewed Hillary as cut from the same cloth as her husband and rationalized her loss to Trump, at least in part, as political karma.

To Nickoff, most of the world's problems, such as poverty, poor race relations, inner city decay and economic downturns, could be traced to the actions of the rich, Caucasian elites who ruled Western civilization. His initial anger at the non-college educated whites who propelled Trump to the presidency eventually transformed into pity for the poor, stupid white people who were utterly fooled by Trump and his sideshow.

The last, but not the least, member of the Council was Maura O'Reilly, by far the most popular columnist at the *Chronicle*. Known as the scourge of Beltway politicians, the long-legged, twice divorced fiery redhead traveled in Washington social circles as the *grande dame* of the liberal media. She was one of the first female reporters hired by Rosen's father in the Washington bureau and spent her entire career in DC. The maître ds and bartenders in DC's fashionable restaurants and watering holes knew and liked her. She, in turn, was always quick to recognize long-time wait staff and other regulars during her frequent late-night romps through DC.

Her semi-weekly columns were eagerly anticipated by many and read with clenched teeth by more than a few. Her biting sarcasm was mostly directed at conservative Republicans. But not every Democrat was left unscathed. Recently, she had targeted a prominent Democratic Party donor from Illinois who had fired an employee for absences due to the employee's repeated deployments to the Middle East with the Air Force. She also wrote about a Republican Alabama state representative, a married minister with children and vocal opponent of gay marriage, who was arrested in a public restroom with a male prostitute. She most recently authored a scathing expose on a Nevada Democratic senator whose sons, local lawyers, received hundreds of thousands of dollars in legal fees from several real estate developers. They were able to build lucrative commercial properties on formerly undervalued federally owned property they obtained with the unpublicized aid of the good senator.

Like every other liberal in DC, she was stunned by President Trump's victory. But unlike many, she got over it. She was prepared to relentlessly attack Trump for his racism, misogyny, bankruptcies and general inability to resist those 3 AM Twitter rants. But O'Reilly quickly realized that the millennial-driven late-night shows had pushed Trump-bashing to near oversaturation, and she had no desire to join that crowd. So O'Reilly continued to do what she did best: captivate *Chronicle* readers with tales of the imperfections, foibles, indiscretions and occasional indictments of politicians, businessmen, generals and reverends. Her caustic wit never failed to entertain her devoted followers and provide billable hours for image consultants in Washington, New York and elsewhere.

Rosen valued O'Reilly's input and advice as much as any Council member. When he had worked in the DC bureau years ago, he occasionally caught himself watching her in one of those slinky cocktail dresses she favored when leaving the office on Friday nights, but he had never had much luck with shiksas, so he didn't bother chasing that skirt.

Since Rosen was supremely confident in himself, he was only briefly shaken by the Trump victory. Like O'Reilly, Rosen was able to pick himself up and move on. Now, as he completed his review of the information gathered to date regarding his latest project, he was relieved that his most trusted underlings at the *Chronicle* had passed through all seven stages of grief over the Trump victory.

The information that his New Jersey sources gave him over a year ago had seemed incredible at first. However, as Rosen continued to investigate the matter, his belief in the accuracy of the reports caused him to bring Ritzie into the loop. After initially expressing skepticism about the accuracy of the reports, Ritzie had recently come around to Rosen's view that the rumors and allegations disclosed in the reports warranted further scrutiny. With Ritzie's agreement, Rosen was now ready to present his findings to the full Council, together with his plan of action.

Rosen made his opening remarks. "Thank you all for coming tonight. The purpose of this meeting is to present to you a proposal I have worked on for the past several months with Fran's able assistance. We've been looking into the administration in Washington and the current occupant of the White House." Maura O'Reilly shot Paul Enrony a knowing glance, which Enrony acknowledged with a wink. "Through the efforts of Fran's Alpha team and others, we have come upon some information that we believe we can use to great effect. I can only emphasize to you that what I am about to share with you cannot leave this room. If knowledge of our use or possession of this information were to somehow become public, there would be significant negative repercussions for the *Chronicle*. Your utmost discretion is required.

"Let me begin at the beginning."

Chapter 3

Rob Manzi left the union offices and made his way to Jake Rosen's car in the *Chronicle's* garage. His driver, one of the biggest Irishmen Manzi had ever met (probably ex-NYPD; he could see the bulge in his jacket), opened the door to the town car for Manzi. Rosen appeared shortly and entered his car. He poured them each a scotch. Manzi was not much of a scotch drinker but was acquiring a taste for Rosen's brand. Still, he had no delusions about his relationship with Rosen. Rosen was a book smart, white shoe Jew who looked down on Manzi and his Staten Island Italian roots, but Manzi could tell that Rosen pretty much looked down on everyone. On the flipside, Manzi knew that Rosen needed a street-smart guy like him to complete the odd jobs that had to be done every now and then.

Manzi was meeting with Rosen to report the status of his current job, which wasn't the type of "job" his family did twenty to thirty years ago for Rosen's family; although still known as the toughest Italian on Staten Island, Manzi hadn't broken anyone's bones in several years. In many ways, this job for Rosen was similar to operations Manzi had conducted for others: get to know the target, find the target's weakness, and either put them in a compromising position to make them uncomfortable or place them completely at ease. In either scenario, the information sought eventually makes its way out, trickling at first, but eventually flowing like water over a waterfall. In this case, the target had a weakness for Asian women and a need to impress these women with his vast array of inside information. Luring this target in actually hadn't taken Manzi too long. He had reliable acquaintances in a New York high-end escort service who also operated in the DC area. They arranged for the target to meet his soon-to-be-girlfriend in a local spot he visited almost daily. Then, as usual, nature took its course.

This meeting was going to be short and sweet. Manzi didn't have much to report. As expected, the subject was passing information to his girlfriend. Most of it was useless, but every so often he received a tidbit that Manzi knew Rosen would lap up.

"So my friend, what news have you for me from the nation's capital," Rosen said as he sipped his drink.

"Well, boss, things are moving in the direction we anticipated. Little PJ is now so cunt-struck he must walk around his office all day with a hard on, thinking of his lovely little girlfriend waiting for him. When he finally gets to see her, he can't wait to tell her what his day was like at the White House. She, of course, is suitably impressed. After sex and a few lines of coke, he cannot stop telling her about everything that he saw, talked about or heard others talking about."

"And the girl?"

"No problem there. She's used to having politicians, lobbyists or visiting businessmen take her out for a fancy dinner at a high-end restaurant, then going back to a hotel room and getting smacked around, doing all sorts of crazy things, mostly tied up. Having her get that job in the local coffee shop, making her dress like a millennial, that was brilliant, boss (it was actually Manzi's idea, but he let Rosen take the credit). She's in heaven. She'll do this as long as we want."

"And the New Jersey rumors?"

"I gotta hand it to you, boss, you're onto something there. The more I look into this the more there is to see. Your instincts on this are pretty good. Each time I speak to a source, he gets me to another source, and another. We're not at the end of the road yet, but we are reaching a point when you are going to be able to put some perfume, makeup, and a skirt on this, and you will be good to go."

Rosen never appreciated Manzi's humor. Manzi was okay with that. Rosen didn't find the situation funny. He said, "Look, my friend, what we are doing here is very serious. If you screw this up, or if one of your minions does, we both could land in a shit storm, and I am not going to be able to help either of us."

What the fuck is a "minion?" Manzi thought as he said, "Look, boss, I keep telling you, we're in control here. We have cut outs, and-what do they call it in spy movies-plausible deniability. No one knows you, and the only ones who know me I can trust. This Jersey thing is being controlled by my longtime associates, whose father and uncles were my father's and uncles' associates. What we're finding out is something out of their league, and they want to hand this off to us as soon as possible. They like the money we're paying them, but even they are starting to ask more and more questions about what's going on. We told them that we wanted some dirt on businessmen and local pols, so we can get some construction and hauling contracts directed our way. That was brilliant on your part, but it looks like while we're getting the information we want, they're not seeing the revenue from their end. I understand that we have to keep them in the dark, but we are stringing them along, and pretty soon we're going to be out of rope."

Rosen pondered Manzi's comments and hid his impatience with being lectured by someone he viewed as a simple tool. He was not surprised by the information Manzi's New Jersey "cousins" were able to dig up regarding his target. Manzi's information confirmed what Rosen had learned from his sources in New Jersey. The *Chronicle's* tentacles reached into the Garden State via its uglier, fatter younger sister publication, the *Newark Star-Examiner*. The *Chronicle* controlled the *Examiner* like a puppeteer controlling puppets. Rosen pulled the strings from New York, and his underlings in New Jersey did as they were told, such as attack stories on the US military, racial profiling by the state police, crimes committed by Republican politicians and rich Republican businessmen in Bergen, Somerset and Hunterdon Counties not paying their fair share of taxes. The *Examiner* staff knew how to please Rosen and the *Chronicle*.

Rosen was pleasantly surprised that the *Examiner* people were able to uncover what appeared at first as innocuous tidbits of information. Over time, and combined with what Manzi's cousins were able to unearth, the *Examiner's* sleuthing gave Rosen and Fran Ritzie a clear vision of what they had to work with, what they wanted to accomplish and the means to do so. This information gave Rosen and the *Chronicle* the tools they needed to instill in the government, and eventually the country, a different ethos, one focused on equality of condition, reduction in class conflicts by eliminating the wage gap and embrace of the wonderful ethnic, racial and gender diversity of America.

Ever since Rosen envisioned himself in the publisher's office at the *Chronicle,* he had harbored the desire to transform American thought, American culture, the "American way." He recognized some time ago that under his leadership, the *Chronicle* could be the means to effect real changes in America, changes his dear father and grandfather had never dreamed of or even cared about. No, Rosen was clearly the visionary in his family. And now, with the information the Alpha team and Manzi were gathering, those visions were about to be realized.

Chapter 4

Special Agent McDaniels and a team of agents from the protection detail traveled to New York City with POTUS, who was giving a speech at the United Nations, attending a fundraiser on the Upper East Side and having dinner at his daughter's new apartment near Columbia University. A Secret Service advance team had spent the prior week in New York coordinating the trip with the New York field office and the NYPD. The visit to Krissy's apartment was not on the schedule that had been released to the press, nor would it be, although McDaniels fully expected to encounter a contingent of media staking out Nightingale's (Krissy's Secret Service code name) apartment.

Nightingale had moved uptown after her college graduation. Her Secret Service detail had done a thorough job identifying and isolating the few oddballs who found out where she lived and tried sitting on her stoop, in an effort to who knows what. The cameras the Secret Service had surreptitiously installed in several of the surrounding buildings captured a facial image of every person who walked by her apartment building. Her detail noted two men who appeared repeatedly on the street in front of her building. They were identified and investigated; when the Secret Service could not ascertain a reason for them to be in the neighborhood, they were separately and forcefully picked up a few blocks from Nightingale's apartment, taken to a warehouse in Queens, and interrogated for several hours by a team of very large and aggressive agents. Both men saw the error of their ways and were never observed in Nightingale's neighborhood again. This grab and go technique, never publicized by the agency, had proven effective over the years in deterring individuals who took an inordinate interest in the younger members of the First Family.

The speech at the UN had gone well, and thousands of dollars were raised at the fundraiser. The pool reporters travelling with POTUS were simply told that the presidential party was not leaving NYC until later that evening, and they could amuse themselves for a few hours. However, knowing that POTUS's daughter lived in Morningside Heights, several members of the media made their way uptown on the correct assumption that a family gathering was on the agenda. The NYPD had closed the nearby streets leading to Nightingale's apartment building. President Whitcomb arrived a half an hour later. His ex-wife, Kathleen (Secret Service codename "Gentlewoman"), had arrived earlier and was catching up with Krissy. President Whitcomb entered the apartment and warmly embraced his ex-wife. Kathleen's husband had not come, though if he had, it would not have been a problem. He was a good guy who treated Kathleen and Krissy well; Whitcomb was happy that Kathleen had been able to start over and that his daughter had moved on. Despite his differences with his wife, he still loved her, was truly sorry they had split up and considered himself lucky that he now had a great relationship with his ex-wife and daughter (after all, the divorce wasn't Kathleen's fault).

"So, Dad, how do you like my vegetarian chili?" Krissy cheerfully asked. She had always liked baking as a little girl; her Christmas gifts to family and friends when she was young consisted of holiday tins of assorted cookies she and her mother baked in the weeks leading up to Christmas. She could see learning to cook sometime in the future, entertaining friends and family at large, cozy dinners with home-cooked food and plenty of wine. For now, chili, salad and cornbread from a box would have to do.

"Honey it's delicious. Best I've had in a long time. But don't tell me you've become a vegetarian?" Whitcomb looked at his ex-wife and winked. "You know, Hitler was a vegetarian."

Kathleen took a swig of wine and said to her ex-husband, "Stop that Hitler nonsense. If that is the worst lifestyle choice she makes, you should consider yourself lucky." She then filled her glass, laughing to herself about her comeback. She enjoyed seeing her daughter's independence and was planning on having a good time tonight.

"No, Dad, I'm not becoming a vegetarian; I just like vegetarian meals. They're healthy for you. You should give it a try and eat less red meat. Just imagine what it could do for your blood pressure."

Whitcomb felt an internal eye roll come on as flashbacks to tense cabinet meetings and standoffs with hostile foreign leaders flooded his mind. *Sure, it's the red meat that's getting my blood to the boiling point.*

President Whitcomb laughed too. Spending time with his daughter, now that she had moved on from the divorce, was great. They had a solid relationship again, and he enjoyed her company. Krissy accepted that her parents' marriage was over and nothing she could do would bring them back together. Krissy was also happy for her mother and enjoyed being with her mother and stepfather.

All things considered, life was good in the Whitcomb family.

After the three of them shared some stories from Krissy's graduation weekend last month, Whitcomb could no longer hold back. "So tell your mother and me about your internship at the *Chronicle*," the president said as he helped himself to some more of the surprisingly good chili.

"I'm really enjoying it," Krissy replied excitedly. "There's about twenty-five of us all together. A few kids from the Ivies, Notre Dame, Duke, Stanford, schools like that. Everyone is really nice. The first two days were an orientation program. They gave us a tour of the offices and the newsroom. We had presentations made to us by a bunch of bureau chiefs and editors. Fran Ritzie even came and spoke to us." Whitcomb looked at his ex-wife and rolled his eyes.

"Four of us are reporting interns," she continued. "That's what I asked for, and I'm so happy I got accepted in that program. I'm being assigned to the sports bureau for the first few weeks." Whitcomb and his ex-wife exchanged quizzical looks, which Krissy didn't miss. "I know, I know. It's not what I expected either, but we spend a week or two in different bureaus to get exposed to different areas of the paper. I'm actually going to a soccer game Friday night with the reporter who covers soccer. I get to write the first draft of the article that will appear in the paper and on the website. Depending on how well written it is, it may be my first byline!"

At this point, Krissy lowered her head and locked eyes with her father. "Of course, it took everyone a few days to get used to the fact that Margie is always nearby. You know I really like her, Dad, she's always been very nice to me. But couldn't she just wait in the lobby of the building or something?"

Margie O'Hanlon was Krissy's Secret Service escort. Whitcomb laughed as he took a sip of his beer. "Aren't you used to that by now, honey?"

"Well, *I* am," Krissy replied. "But my new coworkers aren't. One girl, who I was starting to be friendly with, asked me if Margie carries a gun. Now she doesn't come near me."

"Look, I'll ask Jerry DeNigris about it," the president responded, meaning the head of the Presidential Protection Division. "But, even though I'm their boss, so to speak, they're going to follow their protocols no matter what I say. So I'm not promising anything."

In an effort to change the subject, the president asked, "Have you met Jake Rosen yet?" He felt almost afraid to hear the answer.

"He came to talk to us during the second day of orientation. Of course, he mentioned me to everyone, as if they all didn't already know I'm your daughter. On the last day of orientation they also had a cocktail party in the newsroom and the interns got to mingle with reporters, editors and the other staff. Somebody pulled me to the side, and there was Mr. Rosen with the executive editor, a few bureau chiefs and Maura O'Reilly. I was so nervous, I didn't know what to say to her. She's so awesome, I love her columns!" Krissy concluded.

"Oh, really," Whitcomb responded, with arched eyebrows and a pained expression on his face.

"I know she gives you a lot of crap, Dad, but, come on, some of it you deserve."

"Oh, really, do I?" the president retorted, with a slightly miffed tone in his voice, as his ex-wife sipped her wine and stifled a laugh. "Just remember one thing during your internship. The most important takeaway from *The Godfather,* one of the all-time greatest movies, is that you don't let strangers know if there is a disagreement within the family. I've told you that before, *la mia bambina,*" the president said as he wagged his finger.

"Yes, Dad," Krissy replied as she rolled her eyes. "You've told me that several times. Don't worry, I won't divulge any family secrets to anyone at the *Chronicle* this summer. "

That got a smirk from of Kathleen.

"Anyway," Krissy continued, "Mr. Rosen was really nice. He said that he hoped I enjoyed the summer at the *Chronicle* and to let him know if I had any questions about how it operates. He said he met you briefly at the White House Correspondents' dinner last year and invited you to the Hamptons for our summer vacation. I told him that we've visited Mr. Howley there a few times but that you've been going to Sea Girt or Spring Lake every summer since you were a teenager, and I didn't think that would ever change."

Krissy put her glass of wine down and looked at her parents, eyes open wide. She took a deep breath. "Maura O'Reilly said if I could help her arrange an exclusive interview with you at the White

House, she would take me with her the next time she interviews a murderous dictator.

"I think she meant it."

"Which one," Kathleen asked, "the interview with your father or the murderous dictator?"

After pausing, Krissy replied "Both." She looked at her parents, who looked at her and each other, and the three of them burst out laughing.

Krissy did not tell her parents about all her experiences at the *Chronicle*. During her second week, a good-looking guy, a few years older, introduced himself. He was a political affairs reporter who was based in New York but traveled the country. He was very friendly and offered to "show her around." He took her to his office and introduced her to other reporters in the political affairs bureau. They all knew who she was, of course, and were outwardly friendly. On Friday that week, he had emailed her that a group was going to a nearby bar for drinks after work and would she care to join them? She went, met some more staffers, listened to their war stories and enjoyed herself.

The next week he took her out to lunch. Over burgers, he talked about the life of a reporter, the highs and lows, how traveling sucks and how controlling your ego when your articles get edited is a must. However, soon the conversation turned to personal issues, such as what's it like for her with divorced parents? He understood; his parents and those of several friends were divorced. He hated the first people his parents dated after their divorce. How did she like the women her father dated? Who did her father socialize with if he wasn't with a woman? What does a divorced man who is the chief executive of a major state, and then a country, do, you know, to relax?

Krissy was initially flattered and appreciative of the attention she was receiving but was not so naive as to open up about her family. Looking back, Krissy recalled that he didn't have any questions about her mother's life after the divorce.

On the following Friday, he emailed her, again saying a group was going out for drinks, this time to a different bar. When she arrived, he was the only *Chronicle* staffer there. When no one showed up after an hour, and after several martinis, he told her there must have been a mix up among the group. By the way, he saw that her father was going to Pittsburgh for a speech; does he have any buddies out there he's going to hang out with after the speech?

She finished her beer, politely said goodbye, and attempted to leave. He grabbed her forearm, saying she should come with him to a great little sushi place near his apartment. When she said thanks but no thanks, his grip tightened. She looked around the bar. She saw her Secret Service escort Margie O'Hanlon staring at them, beginning to rise from her seat, although Krissy had not given the distress signal. She suggested that he remove his hand from her or he would find his name that night on Twitter under the #MeToo hashtag with Harvey Weinstein, Mark Halperin and Mickey Mouse.

The thought of his name, Twitter, and #MeToo in the same sentence almost caused him to wet his pants. He released his hold on Krissy and laughed nervously. Very nervously. Krissy told him to have a nice weekend and left the bar, O'Hanlon following.

She did not see him the rest of her internship. She didn't feel the need to share that incident with her parents.

The First Family had an enjoyable evening. Although he was never a big fan of the media, the president wasn't too upset that his daughter was going to graduate school for journalism. Since she would complete her masters while he was still in office, she certainly would be able to get a job at a reputable publication or network news bureau when she graduated. In the back of his mind, he hoped that after a few years, she would wise up and go into marketing or public relations. He would help any way he could if she needed it. He was confident, however, that she was going to be quite capable of fending for herself after his presidency was over. He just hoped they lived on the same coast, so he could see her whenever he wanted.

Agent McDaniels stood in the lobby of the brownstone with three of his team. Two agents from Nightingale's team were in the hallway outside the apartment. Another two pairs from the New York field office guarded the stairwell one floor above and one floor below Nightingale's apartment. Two sniper teams were located on rooftops across the street and the emergency response team was in two SUVs parked around the block with the communications and medical vans. An NYPD helicopter hovered overhead.

Two blocks away, Bobby Manzi stood behind the police line cordoning off Nightingale's street. *All these cops and feds in the neighborhood. Morningside Heights was never safer.* Manzi kept a low profile. He didn't want some fed to recognize him, although he knew that wasn't likely. FBI surveillance photos of him had little chance of making their way to the Secret Service, given the well-known lack of communication between the two agencies.

He thought that this was a wasted trip because no way was Whitcomb going to sneak away from his wife and daughter on this occasion. From what Manzi had been able to unearth, Whitcomb made his little side trips only when he was away from his home base. In any event, these trips had diminished significantly since he became president. He told this to Rosen, but Rosen told him to go up there anyway in case anything unusual happened. Well, nothing unusual was happening, so Manzi walked to a subway station and headed home to catch the end of the Yankees game.

In a few hours, the team outside Nightingale's apartment notified McDaniels that the party was breaking up. Moving POTUS from a stationary location into public view and then to a major transportation hub via open roadways was always stressful for the protection detail. Now Whitcomb was going to be exposed in city streets with innumerable windows and rooftops, all of which could not be completely monitored. The knot grew in McDaniels's stomach as POTUS and Gentlewomen exited the apartment building, spoke for a few minutes and then got in their cars. Per Secret Service procedure, POTUS's motorcade left first. The fact that people now driving in New York City would be inconvenienced as he traveled through the city didn't bother McDaniels in the least. All he cared about was getting the president back to the White House without an incident.

Thankfully, POTUS was not making one of the little side trips he periodically engaged in while traveling outside of DC. The protection detail was told by staff these were visits with old friends or donors and were not being placed on the president's public schedule. Similarly, occasionally "special guests" visited the White House and stayed for dinner followed by a movie in the theater or bowling in the Truman Lanes. Only necessary information about these guests was given to the Secret Service, so security and screening procedures could be met. These visits didn't happen very often and were not of great concern to the protection detail. After all, this president, unlike some previous White House residents, was very solicitous of the Secret Service and genuinely appreciated their service. He fully understood that they potentially stood between him and a terrorist or an absolute wacko. Consequently, no leaks about these visits from the Secret Service had occurred. As far as McDaniels was concerned, given the burdens of the office, if POTUS wanted to relax with a few old friends, revisit old stories and have a few adult beverages without having to answer questions from the always prying media, he had earned that. As long as the president was not abusive to the detail, followed Secret Service advice when in public and did not take undue risks while outside the White House, McDaniels was content.

That night, Rosen received a text message from one of Fran Ritzie's Alpha team members. Whitcomb had just left Morningside Heights. About 35 minutes later, he received a text from another Alpha team member reporting that Whitcomb was boarding Marine One at the heliport. Rosen poured himself a scotch. He turned on the television in his study to watch an English Premier League match he had recorded earlier. *We didn't catch him...this time. But we will,* he thought, as he watched Manchester United, his favorite team.

Chapter 5

"It is always a pleasure seeing you, Mr. Mayor." Jake Rosen greeted New York City Mayor Robert DeStefano with a warm smile and a firm handshake as he entered Rosen's corner office. Rosen could be extremely cordial when he chose to be. The mayor, all six feet, six inches of him, had arrived, only twenty minutes late for their meeting. He was without his usual coterie of aides; Rosen did not entertain the underlings of people he summoned to his office, and this was well known.

Rosen wasn't particularly fond of this mayor. He viewed DeStefano as a typical New York City politician, that is, humorless, pedantic and, quite frankly, boring. Also, New York City politicians seemed to constantly have a hand out. Especially this mayor. How many fundraisers did he expect the same donors to attend in a given year? How many causes, committees and nonprofits could this mayor be behind? And where was the money going?

But what was most irritating about DeStefano to Rosen was his incessant lecturing about reining in power groups in the City, the need to redistribute wealth, the evil of conservatives and his constant compromising with the very people he should be co-opting and neutering. And always with the homeless. Rosen did his part. The *Chronicle's* Sunshine Fund collected company, employee and public donations to purchase winter coats for the needy, arranged for trips to summer camps for underprivileged children and supported soup kitchens and homeless shelters throughout the city. Rosen did plenty for the homeless. Right now, he had more important concerns. Enough with the homeless.

"It's a pleasure seeing you too, Jake," the mayor cheerfully responded as they shook hands. "I just wanted to thank you for that editorial last week supporting our reeducation centers for municipal employees," DeStefano continued. "We'll be enrolling our first class in the next month or so, and we've hired some great instructors. All the municipal union leaders are behind us. Well, except the cops and firemen. But, then again, they never agree with anything I do. I'll deal with them in time."

DeStefano, at the urging of his activist wife, had the New York City Council pass a bill creating a code of conduct for city employees. Authored by his wife, this bill prohibited "the use of racially, ethnically or culturally insensitive language" toward fellow employees or the public; conduct that failed to treat "historically oppressed persons, such as people of color, indigenous Americans, gays, lesbians and transgender persons, with the proper respect due to such persons" and "any actions, speech, conduct, actions or attitude that could be construed by a third party as culturally insensitive, racist, homophobic, misogynist or offensive to said third party." First time offenders of the code of conduct were required to attend classes run by the city's new Bureau of Reeducation. Instructors from various gender and ethnic studies departments at local universities were recruited to give enlightenment lectures aimed at guiding wayward employees down the path of correct thinking. To pass the class, employees were required to write letters of reflection acknowledging their improper actions and demonstrating their awareness of appropriate conduct.

The new bureau was also tasked with conducting mandatory sensitivity training for middle and senior management municipal employees. These sessions were to deal with topics such as recognizing transgender needs, identifying and denying white privilege as it affects traditionally oppressed persons, helping women succeed in a patriarchal society and the proper use of gender-neutral pronouns.

"Well, that is wonderful, Mr. Mayor," Rosen responded. "I am sure those reeducation centers will prove to be one of the highlights of your administration. Your wife must be very happy. And I am sure the police and fire unions will come around in due time."

At this point, Fran Ritzie walked into the office with Elliot Schneiderputz, the New York State Attorney General. "Good morning, General, and thank you for coming," Rosen said, shaking hands with Schneiderputz.

"Thanks for having me," Schneiderputz replied. "It is always a pleasure to get out of Albany and back to civilization and real bagels, but I'll deny ever saying that if you print it." Turning to DeStefano, Schneiderputz said "Good morning, Robert. Good to see you."

"And good to see you too, Elliot. How are things in Albany? I know I don't have too many admirers up there," the mayor joked awkwardly but not inaccurately. Turning to Rosen, DeStefano said, "This is a pleasant surprise, Jake. You didn't tell me Elliot was going to join us." He then faced Ritzie. "And Fran, by the way, I loved your column last week on that bastard Bush stealing the 2000 election. Boy, that story never gets old."

Well, Mayor, if your office was not such a sieve, and I had confidence that the existence of this meeting would not be leaked, you would have known, Rosen thought but said, "My apologies, Mr. Mayor, but this was a somewhat last minute idea, and I had to do a little scrambling to make sure we could all be here. Let us get started, gentlemen," Rosen continued. "Please be seated, and Fran and I will let you know why we asked you here."

The group moved to the conference table, with Rosen seated at the head. "We have come upon some information that Fran and I would like to share with you. If our information is accurate, and we believe it is very accurate, you both may find it of great use.

"Our sources in Washington have advised that President Whitcomb's staff is preparing for what they are calling 'road shows.' They are planning a series of appearances at multiple venues across the country in the upcoming months. They see this as an opportunity for Whitcomb to get his message out directly to the electorate. Apparently, some of our recent editorials are a cause for concern for the current occupant of the White House. This is the beginning of their reelection campaign.

"Their first appearance, we have learned, will be sponsored by the Westchester County Republican Committee and will take place at the Westchester County Center in about five weeks."

"Right in our backyard," the mayor commented.

"Exactly, Mr. Mayor. And it presents a real opportunity for the two of you to get in front of the administration on national issues that have significant relevance to your supporters locally and across the country, such as the minimum wage.

"This administration continues to oppose any efforts to move forward with a national minimum wage," Rosen continued. "Moreover, at least as far as this administration is concerned, a national living wage is completely off the table. We at the *Chronicle* believe that this road show will enable you and other like-minded persons to confront the administration on these and other issues. You can position yourself and your allies in stark contrast to this administration. Mr. Mayor, this could be an opportunity for you to further project yourself as a national progressive leader. At the same time, we put some speed bumps in the way of their campaign."

"I love the idea, Jake," DeStefano replied. "Given the existence of a minimum wage law in New York, I'm well qualified to speak on that topic. But I can tell you, confidentially, we are now starting to see some issues that may be indirectly related to the minimum wage law here. The Economic Development Corporation has done some studies, which we have not and will not be releasing to the public, showing that places like fast food restaurants and car washes are now automating many of their services. If you can believe it, the owners claim it is actually cheaper to get rid of workers entitled to the minimum wage and replace them with kiosks and computers to take food orders, clean cars and check out purchases at grocery and department stores.

"I'm afraid we are going to see a noticeable drop in minimum wage jobs in the not too distant future in businesses across the city," the mayor continued. "As the technology improves and becomes more widely available, this could become a significant problem in New York and, I imagine, across the country. "

Rosen sat back in his chair and tapped his right knee with his pen as the mayor spoke. Ritzie recognized this as Rosen's typical reaction to being given information about which he already knew. "Well, Mr. Mayor, yes, we here at the *Chronicle* are very aware of the situation. Paul Enrony and his team have completed similar studies. Their results are consistent with what you described. We think we have an answer to that eventuality. Fran?"

"We've come up with an idea to minimize the loss of any jobs due to the technological advances you mentioned," Ritzie began. "As a matter of good business practice, Mr. Mayor, don't you think that businesses should be required to have a minimum number of employees on premises during the hours of operation to ensure the safety of employees and customers? For instance, what if there is a grease fire in the kitchen of a McDonald's or a Burger King? If there aren't some employees in the kitchen at all times, who will ensure that the customers are evacuated, and the fire gets put out? Who will service elderly customers or recently arrived undocumented immigrants who will be unfamiliar with or uncomfortable using the new technology?

"Car washes use thousands of gallons of water daily contaminated with detergents. Who will ensure those pollutants are properly disposed of? What if a drain in the middle of the car wash line gets clogged? Who will be there to notice and fix it before polluted water spills over to adjoining properties?

"And what about cashiers and clerks? They are guaranteed meal and bathroom breaks. There have to be enough employees on premises at all times to make sure that employees are treated humanely," Ritzie concluded.

"A possible solution to the issues Fran has raised is to have legislation passed requiring businesses to have a minimum number of employees on the job," Jake said. "Mr. Mayor, you and your allies on the city council can draft legislation requiring the Economic Development Corporation to conduct a study of the city's businesses to determine the minimum number of employees required to operate in a safe and responsible manner. The study can be funded by a small, one-time surcharge on businesses that utilize minimum wage workers. Based on the findings of the study, you can set a minimum number of workers tied to weekly or monthly gross revenue that can be fine tuned, depending on the nature of the particular business."

"That sounds very, very doable," DeStefano responded. "I like the idea of the surcharge, so we won't have to have this study impact my budget. I'll get my staff working on that pronto."

"What can I do to help out, Jake?" Schneiderputz asked. "I'm afraid I am not much of an economist."

"You are not an economist, General, but you are a prosecutor with both civil and criminal prosecutorial powers. Our thoughts here, General, are that trade associations, companies, their lobbyists and paid experts have promulgated an economic falsehood for years, if not decades, about the minimum wage. For your convenience, we have compiled a list of these groups."

Ritzie handed folders to DeStefano and Schneiderputz.

"They continue to claim that raising the minimum wage results in loss of jobs and higher teenage unemployment, the list goes on. However, ninety-seven percent of economists now believe that incremental increases in the minimum wage do not have a negative impact on employment. In other words—"

Schneiderputz interrupted the *Chronicle's* publisher with a large grin. "In other words, Jake, the science is settled? Now, that's something I understand!"

"Yes, the science is settled. These companies and their enablers continue to oppose the implementation of a minimum wage on a national basis and in those states that have not passed one. Their arguments have been discredited, yet they continue to obstruct laws that would have an immediate positive impact on low-wage workers and their families across the nation."

"If that is the case, gentlemen," Schneiderputz interjected in a formal tone, "it appears to me that those companies and their supporters who argue against implementation of minimum wage laws are engaging in fraudulent activity that has an immediate and measurable negative impact on an identifiable segment of the population. As such, there are credible legal claims to be made that they are violating several federal and state civil statutes, engaging in actionable fraud, violating fair labor laws and operating as an ongoing criminal organization thereby triggering, at the very least, civil RICO liability."

"What is the next step?" DeStefano inquired.

"Mr. Mayor, we believe you should make a speech at the same time the president is appearing in Westchester County," Ritzie responded. "Using data we can share with you and your staff, you can make the case for a national minimum wage." He looked at Rosen and winked at the mayor and the attorney general. "We can pretty much guarantee you that your arguments for a national minimum wage will make the front pages of several newspapers across the country."

There was a collective laugh among the assembled group.

"Jake, I would consider it an honor to lead the charge," a now grinning mayor said. "We can certainly arrange for one of our civic associations to sponsor my presentation. Perhaps we can tie this in with a fundraiser?"

"Look, Mr. Mayor," an immediately agitated Rosen said, "we view this as an opportunity for you to confront this president and highlight his shallowness and lack of concern for the working class. We do not see this, and neither should you, as a money-making opportunity."

"Sure, sure, Jake, I hear you," the mayor replied quickly. "It's just that my campaign people are always looking for new revenue streams for us. But I understand your point and I'll convey it to them."

Now smiling, Rosen turned to Schneiderputz. "And, General, I do not suppose you need any coaching on your role, do you?"

The attorney general laughed. "No, Jake, I already have a pretty good idea as to how we'll proceed. I'll reach out to some of the AGs I have worked with in the past on similar issues. We can count on at least fourteen states lining up behind us. We'll start out by sending document subpoenas to some of the companies and think tanks on your list. We'll make them disclose any information or studies they may have exchanged regarding the minimum wage. While we're at it, we'll get these experts to disclose the sources of their income or funding. Want to bet that several of those companies will have made payments to those think tanks?

"Depending on how much information we get, we can then file complaints against these companies, lobbyists, etc., seeking cease and desist orders, fines and other civil sanctions. We have a great many tools at our disposal."

"If we're lucky, some of those records will have the Koch Brothers in them," the mayor blurted.

For a moment, the four men gazed vacantly around the room, wistful looks in their eyes. *If the Koch Brothers could be implicated....*

"Well, yes, Mr. Mayor. Hope springs eternal, I suppose," Rosen said, as he regained his train of thought. "But if that is not the case, we will still be in a position to move against the administration on this issue. We will get information over to you shortly, so you can prepare."

"Where else are they going on their road shows, Jake? Will I get to follow them around the country?" the mayor asked.

"Mayor, it is foreseeable that you would make additional appearances, and we are certainly not discounting your prominence as the

Mayor of New York City. But we are trying to line up local talent, so to speak," Ritzie answered. "Our thinking is that we'll need local personalities to generate interest among the populace and the media who will be covering our undertaking."

"Yes, Mr. Mayor, when the White House finalizes the schedule," Rosen continued, "we will reach out to our contacts nationwide to make arrangements for opposing speeches. But to the extent we require your assistance, we will not hesitate to reach out to you."

"That's great, guys, I'll do whatever I can to help out. I don't mind leaving the city at all, so you can count me in wherever and whenever you need me."

"Jake, have you told the governor about these plans?" Schneiderputz asked warily.

"Actually, no, I have not yet told him about what we just discussed."

"Well, in that case, why don't you let me tell him?" the attorney general offered.

A hint of a smile crossed Rosen's face. "Sure, General, you can let the governor know about this whenever you feel the time is right." Rosen stood up and opened his office door to usher his guests into the newsroom.

As he approached the door, Schneiderputz turned to face Rosen. "Is Maura O'Reilly in town, Jake? We keep missing each other. I have some information on our climate change suit against the EPA she may find newsworthy."

Rosen looked at Ritzie. "I do not think so," as Ritzie shook his head "no." "But I will pass on your interest when I talk to her."

"Thanks, Jake. Please do."

After his guests left, Rosen returned to his office where Ritzie was waiting. "I thought that went well," Rosen said.

"So did I," Ritzie replied. "I guess the next step for us is to advise the Network that DeStefano and Schneiderputz are on board. I'll let them know about the plans for Westchester. When we get the final schedule from Washington, I'll notify the Network members in those areas that they will have to gear up for Whitcomb's appearance. I'll also get my Alpha team up to speed for Westchester. Since it is local, we have plenty of time. When do you anticipate getting specific information on Whitcomb's schedule, where he will be staying and so on?"

"I am not sure. I assume they will have to plot out their road shows several weeks ahead for security and logistical purposes," Rosen said. "That should give us enough time to set up our parallel campaign. I am sure it will. The Network can move quickly. It is a question of how soon the Italian gets the information from the DC source. So far it has been working smoothly."

The Network was a loosely organized, somewhat informal group of like-minded journalists, commentators, think tank members and academics who shared information of common interest among the group members. Ritzie was one of the founders and a presiding member of the group. The members agreed to keep the existence of the group a secret; they sought no official standing or formal recognition by any government or media organization. They simply wanted to ensure, through coordinated effort if necessary, that the progressive message on various issues made its way to the public.

"By the way, Jake, I thought you mentioned Whitcomb's road shows and our plans to the governor a week ago," Ritzie said with a quizzical look on his face.

Rosen laughed. "Yes, I did. But Schneiderputz did not need to the know that. And the governor will look surprised when Schneiderputz tells him. But I will wager you a bucket of pickles from Katz's that Schneiderputz does not tell him until after he calls a press conference announcing his investigation.

"Schneiderputz is a sneaky little shit," Rosen said, laughing again.

"One last thing, Jake. I'm just still a little leery of basing our campaign against the administration on the minimum wage," Ritzie said hesitantly. "I know it's an important issue to a large number of our readers, but at the end of the day, I don't think it is an issue that will arouse people like topics like immigration, climate change and criminal justice reform that people are more passionate about. I think many in the Network would agree with me."

"I understand your concern, Fran," Rosen replied patiently, "and that of some of the Network members. But as we have discussed, the issues we are raising are almost secondary to main purpose of our operation: to follow Whitcomb as he leaves Washington and away from the White House press corp. To see if he develops a false sense of security while on the road. To see if he decides, after a long day of speeches, handshakes with countless strangers and meetings with donors and local Republican schmucks, to unwind with a few drinks in his hotel room with an old friend, who coincidentally is in the same city, staying at the same hotel."

Chapter 6

Denis Lenihan convened a meeting of various White House staffers and Republican party operatives in the Roosevelt Room. In attendance were Lenihan's assistant, Fawn Liebowitz, the Chair of the Republican National Committee, H. Carlton "Carl" Winthrop and one of the RNC vice chairs, Muffy Vanderweghe. Don Mangini and his chief assistant, Sean Thornton, press secretary Joel Hirsch and Whitney Holloway of his staff rounded out the group.

Lenihan opened the meeting. "Thank you all for coming today. I want to get you all here so you could hear from me personally about our plans for the president's road shows, as we are calling them.

"We view this as an opportunity to get the president out of the White House and the bubble the Washington media put around him. We're going to expose him to people who can judge him by what he says, not what someone at the *Post* or on Twitter *says* he said. He will address their concerns, not the concerns of commentators on

MSNBC, CNN and that ilk. We'll get this administration's message unbiased and unfiltered by the media directly out to the voters.

"The first appearance is in three weeks in Westchester County, New York. We have decided on appearances in Pittsburgh, Phoenix, Orlando and Charlotte, in that order. You all received the schedule released last week. Depending on the results of the first two or three events, we may add a few more on the back end.

"Don, his people and the Travel Office are responsible for booking the venues and reserving hotels, transportation and related details. He will also coordinate with the Secret Service regarding the necessary security arrangements.

"Carl, we need your people to do most of the legwork for the scheduled fundraisers. You've identified several people who are willing to host the fundraisers, either at their homes, local theaters or halls. Right now we have Whitcomb to the Future Committee events scheduled in each city except Pittsburgh and RNC events set for Phoenix and Orlando."

Continuing to address Winthrop, Lenihan said, "Carl, you and your team will also be responsible for lining up the attendees at these events. You'll have to coordinate with Don and, again, make sure you give Jerry DeNigris enough time to check out the background of the attendees, at least those who will be in proximity to the president."

Lenihan continued. "And I cannot emphasize enough that I want to see diversity in pictures of the crowds attending the events. I am sick and tired of seeing pictures and screenshots of the wall of white faces standing behind the president during some of his speeches in the last campaign. You would think that the Huffington Post, CNN and the AP only have three-year-old pictures of the president in their files. Jeez, that really pisses me off. I don't care if you have to get dishwashers and valet parkers at these hotels to stand back there; just make sure it gets done."

Sean Thornton glanced at Don Mangini with a concerned look as if to say "Does he really mean that?" Mangini smiled and winked at his young assistant.

"I understand, Denis. We'll make sure the local people who are helping us make that happen," replied Winthrop. "But can't we add an RNC fundraiser at each city also? I've been asking the White House for months to have the president make some more appearances at RNC events. He's pretty popular out there, and when was the last time there was a popular Republican president? Many of us never considered President Trump a true Republican." Winthrop looked around the room, almost apologetically. "And we can really use the money for the congressional races that are coming up. There are several Democratic seats in play. I don't want to miss these opportunities."

"Look, Carl, I explained this to your predecessor, and I'll explain it to you. This president, for good or bad, is not comfortable asking strangers for money. He is an otherwise fairly good campaigner and, I think, is doing pretty well in office. He knows his campaign needs money to run smoothly and that the RNC needs money too. It is something we have dealt with since he first ran for office in New Jersey. He will make himself available for ad campaigns, and we will schedule some White House visits or lunches with the heavy hitters you identify. One of the purposes of this tour is to get him in front of people and let them see him up close. The popularity you referred to will also result in increased donations to the RNC. It has happened in the past, and I know it will happen again. I just can't commit right now to more RNC fundraisers.

"That's the way it is going to be, Carl. You'll have to live with that," Lenihan concluded.

"Well, Denis, I understand but nevertheless I would appreciate anything you can do to push the president to add some RNC fundraisers."

Lenihan did not respond.

The group spent the next thirty minutes going over logistics, discussing the venues and listing out whether friendly media types were accessible in any of the cities to be visited.

At this point, Lenihan's intercom buzzed, and his administrative assistant, Charlene, said, "Mr. DeNigris and his team are here for your 3:30."

"Thank you. I'll be right with them.

"We'll reconvene this group next week so we can update everyone on the progress of plans and any issues or concerns. You'll get an email notification of the next meeting in a day or two. Thank you all for coming." Lenihan stood as the attendees left the Roosevelt Room. After a few moments, Jerry DeNigris entered the room with his deputy, Diana Surlee, and Special Agent Jamal McDaniels.

Lenihan shook hands with the group as they entered the room. "It's nice to see you, Jerry, Diana. Agent McDaniels, I believe we've met."

"Yes, sir," McDaniels said. "We met in New York a few months ago at the Waldorf."

"Well, it's nice to see you again." Lenihan said, gesturing toward the table against the wall. "Please, help yourselves to water, soda, coffee, whatever, and we'll get started."

Lenihan grabbed a Diet Coke and sat down. He loosened his tie and unbuttoned his collar as the Secret Service agents joined him. "Jerry, I have to tell you, I almost always like being in a room with you and your people." He looked around the table. He knew that these agents and their coworkers would step in front of a bullet meant for his best friend without hesitation. Many in the White House and Washington took that for granted. Lenihan didn't.

Lenihan and Whitcomb had met when Lenihan was in law school. Whitcomb, a few years younger, had frequented Tierney's Tavern, a local landmark in Whitcomb's hometown of Montclair, New Jersey when he was home from Rutgers and where Lenihan tended bar during law school. When Whitcomb was leaving the Marines, Lenihan convinced him to go to law school. Whitcomb followed Lenihan's advice and joined Lenihan at his firm after graduation. Their friendship grew as they leaned on each other through their legal careers and, now, their careers in public service.

Whitcomb used his best friend as a sounding board and relied on his advice more and more as their public careers advanced. He slept well most nights knowing Lenihan always put Whitcomb's interests first. And Lenihan made sure the Whitcomb was protected, in every possible manner, from those who might try to harm him, which meant having a good relationship with the Secret Service.

"Sometimes, I think you folks are the only ones in this city that I know I will get the truth, the whole truth, and nothing but the truth from," Lenihan said as he took a large swig of soda and looked at DeNigris with a grin. "The only time I don't like meeting with you is when you have bad news for me. And the only time you ask to meet with me is when you have bad news for me."

"So tell me, Jerry, why did you ask for this meeting?" Lenihan said seriously.

DeNigris looked down at the floor for a moment, then raised his head, laughing at the chief of staff. Surlee and McDaniels looked at him and then at each other. They had never seen DeNigris react to a senior member of the White House staff in such a manner. DeNigris was a gruff, no-nonsense twenty-five-year veteran agent. He had risen through the ranks at the Secret Service and now had his dream job as head of the Presidential Protection Division. He was a fair boss but very demanding. No president was going to be attacked on DeNigris' watch. He rarely, if ever, showed his emotions while on the job. Surlee thought, *I've never seen him laugh like that in the three years I've worked for him.* But DeNigris truly loved serving this president. He treated the Secret Service agents as professionals, not as maids, chauffeurs, butlers or pimps. But, more than that, he was a compassionate man who knew how to treat people well. DeNigris' oldest son was a Marine and was killed in a training exercise a year earlier. POTUS flew from an important European conference to attend the funeral and then jumped back on Air Force One to return to the conference. Jerry and his wife never forgot that.

Lenihan was the most fair and straightforward senior White House staffer DeNigris had ever met. Unlike many in Washington, Lenihan understood that the Secret Service had a job to do and worked with them to make it as smooth as possible for all sides. When the head of the Secret Service had wanted to transfer DeNigris to another post after his son's death, Lenihan intervened. Lenihan and POTUS had fought to keep DeNigris as head of the protection detail, which DeNigris found out after the fact. DeNigris valued loyalty above all else. But loyalty was a two-way street, and DeNigris new that POTUS and Lenihan felt the same way.

"Forgive my reaction, Mr. Lenihan, but I didn't know if that was a compliment or criticism," DeNigris responded, still smiling. "And, yes, I did ask for this meeting. I don't have bad news for you, but we did want to alert you to some intelligence we recently received from our Phoenix office."

"You do know that Phoenix is one of the cities we'll be visiting on our road show?" Lenihan asked.

"Yes, Don Mangini has been keeping us in the loop. When we saw the list of cities POTUS intends to visit, as is our protocol, we alerted the local field offices and asked them to report back to us any items that we should be concerned with in light of an upcoming presidential visit.

"It appears there may be radical group in the Phoenix area that warrants some examination. Diana will fill you in."

"What group? Who is it? What's their name?" Lenihan was now very alert.

"DAFFIE," responded Surlee.

"DAFFIE?" Lenihan looked at the three agents. "Seriously? DAFFIE? Who or what the hell is DAFFIE?"

"Dykes for Animal Freedom, Feminist Independence and the Environment," Surlee said.

Lenihan rubbed his hands through his hair, which had thinned quite a bit since he came to Washington. He could feel the beginning of that dull ache at the base of his skull that appeared when he was stressed, which was happening all too frequently lately. "You have got to be kidding me."

"Unfortunately, no," Surlee responded in a very neutral, business-like tone. "They are a group of radical, vegan, lesbian ecoterrorists."

Lenihan looked at Surlee. If jaws could actually drop, his would have bounced off the floor. "Radical lesbian ecoterrorists?"

"They're vegan too, sir," Surlee said.

"Radical vegan, lesbian ecoterrorists. I guess I shouldn't be surprised by anything I hear in this job. Why haven't I heard of them before?" Lenihan asked.

"They started out small in California approximately two years ago and have apparently opened some cells in other western states," responded Surlee.

"Where else would they have started," Lenihan mumbled under his breath, then said, "Such as Arizona?"

"That is correct, sir.

"The concern here is that as they have grown, they have become bolder in their tactics," Surlee said as she continued her presentation. "At their inception, they would deface residential construction sites that were being built on the boundaries of deserts or national parks. Several times they entered small fracking wells and vandalized the equipment with sledge hammers, axes and such. They followed several oil tankers from refineries, and when the drivers stopped to use a restroom or get food, deflated the tires of the tankers.

"They made these incursions on relatively small sites, at night or early morning and left a few fliers identifying themselves. Otherwise, there were no public announcements, Internet postings, tweets or other typical social media output. Local law enforcement investigated these incidents as ordinary acts of vandalism. There was no sharing of intelligence among local agencies, even those in the same state. In fairness to them, however, there were no instances of injuries or significant property damage."

"And now this has changed?" Lenihan asked, hands rubbing his face as he looked at the ceiling.

"Yes, sir, we believe so."

"How so?"

Surlee cleared her throat. "Well, sir, in several ways. In the past six to eight months we have seen incidents of vandalism much greater in scale. For instance, six months ago they broke into a building that housed the control room of the sprinkler system for a 2,000-acre farm owned by Monsanto in Nebraska. Monsanto develops various types of genetically modified crops there. They detached the sprinkler pipes from water tanks and connected them to their own tanker that contained a potent herbicide. They turned the sprinklers on and destroyed more than fifty percent of the crops.

"They recently conducted two simultaneous attacks relating to the mink industry, also approximately six months ago. Early in the morning hours, a group of three or four, possibly more, invaded the home of a mink farmer in Idaho. They tied up the farmer, his wife and three teenaged children at gunpoint. They cut holes in various fences of the farm to make a path and laid bait down. They then released approximately 850 minks from their cages, letting them escape into the wild.

"On the same day, a truckload of mink coats being delivered to an upscale store in Denver was sabotaged."

"What?" Lenihan said.

"Yes, sir," Surlee continued. "About one hundred miles from Denver, the driver pulled into a truck stop for a meal. He met a young lady who coincidentally needed a ride to Denver because her car had just broken down. The trucker offered her a ride. When they went approximately twenty miles from the rest stop, the young lady pulled a gun from her purse and ordered the driver to exit the highway. A few miles away, he was ordered to pull off the road into a secluded area. Two cars waited there with another three DAFFIE members. They forced the trucker to open the back of the truck, took his cell phone and told him to walk back to the highway. They then threw a homemade grenade in the back of the truck that contained a purple dye. Upon explosion, the dye rendered the mink coats worthless.

"We know that these two attacks were coordinated. They left a note on the mink farmer's kitchen table with the location of the truck. They also gave the address of the mink farmer to the trucker so that someone could call the local PD and the family could be released. They proclaimed DAFFIE's participation in both incidents in various Internet postings."

Lenihan looked at Surlee with a furrowed brow as he rubbed the back of his neck. "Now, these last two episodes you just described sound vaguely familiar. Did they make the national press?" he asked Surlee while also looking at Jerry DeNigris.

"What you may be referring to is the aftermath of these two events," DeNigris responded. "The 850 or so minks that were released? Most, if not all, died in the next three to four weeks, either from starvation or predators."

"Really?" the chief of staff replied. "That's not good for the minks."

"Well, they had been raised in captivity for several generations," DeNigris said. "They didn't know how to survive in the wilderness. I guess the DAFFIE girls didn't take that into account when they set them loose. And the grenade containing the dye? It exploded prematurely. It still made the fur coats worthless but it also injured the DAFFIE girl who tossed it in the truck. She had two fingers blown off and lost sight in one eye."

"And she is…?" Lenihan asked, sensing there was more to the story.

"She has filed a personal injury suit against the manufacturers of the component parts of the grenade."

Lenihan looked at DeNigris. If jaws actually could drop, his once again hit the floor.

"Two of the defendants have settled. The case is in the pretrial stage as to the remaining defendants.

"That brings us to Phoenix," DeNigris said.

"Of course it does," Lenihan let out a noticeable sigh and looked at Surlee. "Go ahead, Diana."

"Yes, sir. Last month a busload of exotic dancers from a high-end gentlemen's club was commandeered at gunpoint outside of Phoenix. They were heading to a local golf course. The dancers were going to be pin girls and hostesses at a tournament sponsored by the club.

"The DAFFIE members took them to a secluded ranch they had rented for the month. Once there, the dancers were blindfolded, tied up and detained for six days. We know this was a DAFFIE cell because one of the captors identified the group to a dancer while she was, attempting to recruit the dancer to their cause. I can give you the details of the recruiting if you like."

Lenihan, with an alarmed look on his face, said, "No, that's not necessary. Were they tortured?"

"No, sir," Surlee replied. "At least, not what we would consider torture. They were not beaten or placed in stress positions. They were given sufficient food and water and adequate sleep. They were, however, subjected to significant behavior modification and aversion therapy sessions."

"Are they okay?"

"They were dropped off in the middle of the night at a women's shelter in Phoenix. However, they will only get undressed alone and in the dark. They also now have an inordinate fear of poles, dollar bills and any white, powdery substances resembling cocaine. Otherwise, they're fine."

Lenihan leaned forward, placed his chin in one of his hands and looked at the table for a few moments. He lifted his head. "This is all very interesting, but what about this group makes them of concern to us and the president's visit to Phoenix?"

DeNigris responded: "The Arizona State Police were able to locate the ranch. One of the dancers hid her cell phone on the bus that was later abandoned and located. They were able to retrace the route of the bus from her phone. The dancers confirmed the location from photos of the ranch the troopers showed them. The forensic investigation has only identified the dancers, so far. However, the troopers did examine the remnants of a bonfire the DAFFIE girls held one night. According to the dancers, this occurred on the last night of their captivity. The captors viewed it as a celebration of the strippers' transformation from 'oppressed victims of the compulsory heterosexual patriarchy to free womyn in nature,' whatever that means.

"In the ashes of the bonfire, a burned copy of POTUS's book about global warming was found. What was left of the book was heavily marked up with angry anti-Whitcomb markings and comments throughout.

"There were also several charred pieces of brochures from the Arizona Science Center," Surlee concluded.

"Where the fundraiser and the president's speech are scheduled?" interrupted a clearly alarmed Lenihan.

"One and the same," DeNigris said. "The Arizona State Police notified the Phoenix field office. The charred remains of the book and brochures are being studied by our forensic lab. Two agents from the Phoenix office also spent a few days at the Science Center reviewing security tapes. They observed that two women made three separate visits to the center in a two-week period. On each visit, they leisurely strolled through the center and left after a few hours."

"I'm sure a lot of people leisurely stroll through science centers and then leave, Jerry. What made these two stick out?"

"If you look at the videos long enough, you see that while they are meandering through the building, they stop at the entrances and exits. One of them seems to then walk slowly to the next entrance or exit, or stairwell to the next level, as if she is pacing the distance. When she gets there, the second one joins her and they talk. The second one then takes out a small notepad and jots something down. They went into auditorium where the fundraiser will be. Again, they seemed to be measuring distances by the way they walked around the space. But they almost never stop and look at the exhibits as they walked through the building. Once or twice they stopped in front of an exhibit for a few moments, but they were whispering to each other the whole time and not really examining the exhibit as you would expect visitors to do."

"Didn't this arouse any suspicion at the time they were in the center?" an incredulous Lenihan asked.

"No, it didn't. But don't forget, we viewed the tapes looking for suspicious activity," the senior Secret Service agent responded. "They also stopped in the gift shop to purchase items and went to the cafeteria and had a cup of coffee. They paid in cash. They wore nondescript flannel shirts, plain jeans, floppy hats and sunglasses. They blended in pretty well and didn't attract any undue attention while they were on site."

Diana Surlee continued the report. "The center also had cameras in the parking lot. On each visit, the two women came and went in three different cars, which we traced to three different rental agencies. We visited the rental agencies. The clerks didn't remember the persons who rented the cars. Two of the rental offices had cameras recording the rental transactions at front desks. In those videos, the women who actually rented the cars are different. Also, none of the renters appear to be the women who are on the videos at the Arizona Science Center.

"The names on the rental agreements are aliases and the addresses are vacant lots. The drivers' licenses used were from out of state and forgeries. They paid with credit cards in the names of people who had their identities stolen.

"We are continuing to investigate what we believe is the DAFFIE Phoenix cell, jointly with the Arizona State Police. They have been very cooperative and are easy to work with. However, we have no new information on DAFFIE other than what we have reported to you today. We have also alerted our field offices in the other locations at which DAFFIE has conducted operations so that they can look into those cells," Surlee said, concluding her report.

"What we have as of today, therefore, is a group of women acting in concert surreptitiously surveilling a building at which the president is scheduled to appear," DeNigris added. "They have taken several fairly sophisticated steps to, up to this point, successfully mask their identity. They are likely connected to a known domestic terrorist organization that is becoming increasingly daring and is now using weapons in its operations. Furthermore, this decentralized, dispersed and loosely organized group with no apparent leader or leaders now appears capable of coordinating its unlawful activities across state lines.

"POTUS is on record as questioning the legitimacy of the various claims and predictions relating to global warming, correct?" DeNigris asked Lenihan.

"They call it 'climate change' now, sir," Surlee interrupted.

DeNigris looked at Surlee, rolled his eyes, and continued to address Lenihan. "To the DAFFIE girls, climate change is their new religion. According to the road show schedule released to the public, POTUS is to speak about the environment at the Arizona Science Center."

"Yes, that is correct," a drained Lenihan replied.

"Well, sir, while our investigation is ongoing, I just wanted to alert you that we are close to recommending that you either cancel the Phoenix visit or at least reschedule it for a different time and location," DeNigris concluded.

Lenihan stood up and began to pace along the wall of the Roosevelt Room. He stopped under the portrait of FDR and stood there for a few moments, deep in thought. He then looked at DeNigris. "I appreciate your report. I see the link between these two women at the Science Center and DAFFIE. I also agree with you that the level and intensity of DAFFIE's wacko attacks, stunts, whatever you want to call them, have ratcheted up. I can just tell you folks, and you know this very well, Jerry, this president does not scare easily. I'm not discounting anything you have told me today, but from what I've heard so far, I seriously doubt that the president will agree to any changes to the Phoenix trip." *He will never cancel Phoenix* Lenihan thought, then he said, "I assume you have a written report for us?"

"Yes, it will be on your desk in an hour," DeNigris responded.

"Fine. I will make sure the president sees it. What's your plan going forward?"

"Agent McDaniels is going to Phoenix at the end of this week to personally supervise the inquiry into the girls of DAFFIE. He will be reporting back to me directly as to the status of that investigation. We have several weeks before POTUS's visit. I am cautiously optimistic we can clear this up before then." DeNigris answered as he closed his binder.

"Let's hope so."

The agents stood to leave. Lenihan shook hands with all three and thanked them for their visit and report.

"Jerry, one last thing."

"What's that, sir?"

"Please don't ever put 'DAFFIE girl' in a memo or email to me."

"Understood, sir."

Chapter 7

"So, PJ, when were you going to tell me about your girlfriend?" Krissy Whitcomb playfully asked the president's personal aide. "You didn't think I'd find out? I'm actually kind of jealous."

Krissy and PJ were in the White House Mess having coffee while she was staying at the White House for a few days. They had been friends for years, ever since the Whitcomb family began visiting the Howleys at their Hamptons house for one or two weekends most summers. Their friendship blossomed when PJ began working for then Governor Whitcomb in Trenton. Krissy was a few years younger than PJ, who was the oldest of the three Howley boys. At some point when they had been younger, Krissy had had a crush on PJ. After a few years, however, Krissy matured into a beautiful young woman, and PJ, who had a great personality, told good jokes and was always fun to be around, became a very good friend, more of a brother.

Laughing, PJ replied, "I didn't know that I had to check in with you about my love life. Let's just say I am having much more fun down here than I expected."

"How did you meet her? You have to tell me," Krissy demanded playfully.

Still laughing, PJ responded, "Well, it's nothing special or glamorous or anything like that. There is a nice little coffee shop around the corner from my apartment. I stop there most mornings to get coffee and a bagel, or sandwich, whatever, on my way here. After a few months, Cassie, which is short for Cassandra, started working behind the counter. She was really nice and, after a while, we got to be friendly. I finally built the nerve up to ask her out. We went to dinner at a nice Greek restaurant in the neighborhood, and what can I say? Things just seemed to click between us almost immediately."

"Can I see a photo?" asked Krissy. "You do have a picture of her, don't you?"

PJ pulled out his iPhone, scrolled through some photos, and handed Krissy the phone. "There are four or five, I think."

Krissy took the phone and began to look at the pictures. "Wow, she's beautiful. And Chinese?" she asked in a voice loud enough to make others in the Mess to turn to look at them.

"No, Korean," said PJ quietly, as his face began to redden. He quickly grabbed the phone from Krissy, realizing that all the other people in the Mess were now staring at them.

Just as quickly, Krissy grabbed the phone back. "I didn't see all the pictures," she said, trying not to laugh.

PJ, clearly annoyed, said to Krissy, "Would you please keep your voice down? I have to work with these people."

Krissy finished studying the pictures. "Wow. A beautiful Korean girl named Cassandra. How exotic, PJ. I'm so happy for you. And impressed. Good job!" Krissy said exuberantly as she reached across the table and slapped her old friend on the shoulder, again gaining the attention of most of the other people in the Mess.

PJ took the phone back and put it in his pocket. "I'm so glad I can meet the high standards that you set for me, Nightingale," PJ replied, his face still a deep red.

"So tell me about her. What's she like?" Krissy asked, excited to hear what she considered wonderful news for her good buddy.

"She's great. We get along great," said PJ, as he started to calm down. He could never stay mad at Krissy. "We can talk for hours. She is very quiet, almost shy. But she likes spending time with me. We both like the same foods, same movies, same TV shows. We like to have a few drinks, cook a nice meal and watch something on HBO or Netflix."

"Wait a minute," Krissy said in a tone indicating she just realized something. "Those pictures. They're all from inside your apartment?" she asked, laughing as she threw her head back. "Don't tell me this girl doesn't let you outside!"

"We get outside plenty," PJ responded curtly. Actually, as PJ thought it through, they really didn't. "Look, I don't have a 9:00 to 5:00 job. Depending on what is going on here, I may not get home until 8:00 or 9:00, sometimes later. She left the coffee shop shortly after we started dating and is working in her family's business. She has to work a lot of weekends when I am usually off. We get to see each other one or two nights during the week and at night on the weekends. We both work long hours, and it just seems like we get together and relax in my apartment."

"Spare me the gory details," Krissy said, putting her hands over her ears in an exaggerated motion.

"Do you want to hear our story or not?" PJ said, now glowering at Krissy again.

"Yes, yes, come on. I'm only teasing you. What's her family like?" Krissy asked, trying to get him talking again.

"Well, I haven't met any of her family yet."

"Oh, really? It seems like you have been going out with her for—"

"Almost six months. You see, she's the oldest of three, like me. She has two sisters. Her parents and both sets of grandparents are from Korea." PJ hesitated a moment as he collected his thoughts. "I'm the first white guy she has ever dated."

Krissy looked at PJ with her eyes wide open.

"I'm the first white guy any girl in her family has dated."

"So, is this a problem?" Krissy asked, studying PJ closely.

"It's not a problem for her. It certainly isn't a problem for me. But she feels that it might be a problem for her family. That is why we don't go out a lot. She's afraid we'll run into a relative or a family friend who will then go back to the parents. She definitely wants me to meet her family, but she wants to wait for the right time."

Krissy looked at PJ with her eyes open wide, her chin down, trying to hide the growing sense of disbelief she was feeling.

"I understand these cultural things," PJ continued. "I really do. Don't you remember that funny story my dad likes to tell how he walked into a family party in Bay Ridge with the Italian girl from Bensonhurst, and one of his uncles threw a can of beer at him?"

"You mean when the beer can missed your father and hit the girl in the face? That 'funny' story?" Krissy answered. "My mother and I never thought that story was funny."

"Look, my point is we're having a great time together. I'm not going to nag her to go out to restaurants or bars. I'm way past that anyway. I'm also not going to rush her to introduce me to her family and friends. I can wait until she thinks the time is right."

"Has she met your folks or your brothers? Are you taking her to the Hamptons this summer?" Krissy continued to poke.

"No, and I doubt it. My brother Tim was down for a weekend a while ago, but she had a bachelorette party in Nashville the same weekend. And now, she doesn't like to leave the DC area. One of her grandparents is pretty old and frail and could pass at any time."

"Is she living with you?"

"That's a no as well. After we started dating, she moved home to save money. She doesn't even sleep over. If she stayed over, she would have a lot of explaining to do for her folks, who are old school. She usually leaves at midnight or so."

This girl has an answer for everything, Krissy thought.

"I can only tell you that, unlike most of the girls I know from New York and the Hamptons, she is more interested in me than herself. Most of the girls I know only talk about themselves. And then ask you what you think of them," PJ said, the look on his face clearly expressing how lucky he felt. "Cassie, on the other hand, is now a Mets and Jets fan because of me," he continued. "The first thing she asks when she comes over is how they did the night before depending, you know, on what season it is. Then she loves to hear about my day and what I did. She wants to know who I met in the White House that day, who I'm going to meet in the White House later in the week and what I talked about with your father on any given day. She doesn't like to travel but she loves hearing about the road show plans we have, what hotel we're staying at, who your father is going to meet. She's amazed that I help prepare your father's daily schedule and the White House guest list."

"And how did she find that out?" Krissy asked with a raised eyebrow.

"I may have let that slip out over a few beers one night," PJ responded, grinning. He pushed his coffee cup to the side and looked at Krissy. "But it's not just that she's impressed with me because I work in the White House. She is saving money for grad school in poli-sci. She feels that hearing how government at this level works will only help her when she gets in a program."

"Where is she applying to?"

"She hasn't decided yet. She has to save some money first. I think she is looking a year, year and a half out."

"When do I get to meet her?"

"I would love to have you meet her. Maybe you can come over for dinner one night. It's just that she is a little shy, as I told you. They only spoke Korean in her house when she grew up, so she still has a slight accent, which, honestly, only makes her more attractive to this thick Irishman. She is a little reluctant to meet my friends. But I'll talk to her, and we'll set something up soon."

"Sounds like a plan." Krissy had to think about that one. "I can hardly wait. She sounds wonderful. I'm really happy for you, PJ. I hope it works out for you."

"Me too. I really hope so. And I really want her to meet you. We'll try to set something up when you're back in town. Maybe when we get back from Phoenix."

Chapter 8

"So, how will ND be this year? Do you think they will win March Madness?"

PJ Howley laughed as he got out of bed to put some clothes on. The pizza delivery guy would be at his apartment soon. He was getting hungry, but more importantly he was thirsty. He cleaned the white powder residue off the top of the kitchen table, grabbed a couple of beers out of the fridge and went back to his bedroom.

"You're so damn cute, Grasshopper, I don't know what I'd do without you," PJ said as he gave Cassie a kiss and handed her one of the beers.

Cassandra had come over after 2:00 PM, and they had enjoyed a very relaxing afternoon. Thank God Cassie liked sports. The Mets had a game tonight with playoff implications, and there was a pretty good west coast college football game on later that night (Notre Dame's first game was next week). After some wings and pizza from his favorite Italian restaurant, PJ was looking forward to a relaxing evening with his girl. "As I've told you before, Cassie, March Madness is the college basketball tournament. College football has a much smaller tournament. Only sixteen teams. And, yes, the Irish will have a good football team this year."

After the food was delivered, they moved into the kitchen. "So, PJ, what about the road shows. When is the next trip? Where is it going to be? Are you going?"

"The next one is a day trip to Pittsburgh. He will be making his speech at the University of Pittsburgh, then going to a small reception for some local Republican bigwigs, then back to DC that night. They told me I don't have to go on this one."

"But you're still going on the Phoenix trip, right?"

"Yeah, it looks like I am. He is staying overnight so he'll need my services."

"Wow, that is so exciting. I mean, you get to travel on that big jet he flies on?" Cassie said.

"That's right. Air Force One. It is actually pretty impressive."

"What is the president going to do out there?"

"First he is flying to a military base in Arizona. He'll give a speech to some soldiers and their families then have lunch with the troops. A nice photo op, as they say."

"Wow," Cassie said. "Then what?"

"Then we get back on the plane and head to Phoenix. There is a fundraiser dinner at some rich guy's house that will take up the rest of the evening."

"Do you get to go to that?"

"Yeah, probably. I mean, I don't do anything. Nobody there will want to talk to me. There will probably be a few other staffers there for me to hang out with. We'll stand in a corner, smile, and eat their food and drink their liquor. That's all."

"But, still, you're there."

"Yeah, I know. But, really, it is kind of getting old hat."

Cassandra looked at PJ, her head tilted. "You have to wear an old hat there?"

PJ laughed out loud. "No, baby, that's just an old American saying. It means it's no big deal. Been there, done that. You understand?"

"Sure, PJ, I get it. You're so clever. And so funny."

PJ laughed again and shook his head. *How lucky am I?*

"So what about the next day?" she asked.

"He's visiting a hospital in Phoenix in the early afternoon. He has a few hours off, then there's a speech and a fundraiser at a local museum."

"What about in the morning?" she asked. "Is he sleeping in? You've said before he likes to get up early."

PJ cleared his throat. "Well, it's not going to be announced publicly, but he apparently has an old friend in the area, and they're going hiking in a state park that's somewhere nearby."

"That's cool. Are you going with him?"

"No, no. I don't always go with him wherever he goes. He's just going to spend some time with an old friend. It'll be just them and his Secret Service detail."

"So, who is this friend?"

"Don't know. Don't care. All it means to me is that I get to sleep in," PJ said with a chuckle as he chugged his beer. "They're also having dinner together later that night. So I get the night off too."

"Dinner? They're having dinner together too? Where? Aren't you even curious, PJ?" Cassie pleaded. "I mean, what if it is somebody important, somebody like...oh, I don't know. Somebody like Lebron James? Or Katy Perry?" Cassie put her beer on the nightstand and slid across the bed to cuddle with PJ.

PJ let out a big laugh. "I doubt either of those people would be invited to go for an early morning hike with the Republican President of the United States. Honey, I really don't know who this person is other than a close friend. I do know it's no one famous or noteworthy, beyond being an old friend of POTUS, at least."

"Is it another politician? Somebody from New Jersey? Somebody he was in the Army with?"

Now PJ was starting to get annoyed with Cassie's questions. She had been doing this lately all too frequently. Question after question about POTUS, the road shows, where they were going, who they were seeing. Why so many damn questions?

PJ finished his beer, rolled away from Cassie, and got out of bed to get another drink. He looked down at his lovely little lady, who was now staring up at him with her almost childlike, inquisitive eyes, which could almost melt PJ. He had never been with a woman with such beautiful and sexy eyes. He kept staring at her. "Look, Grasshopper," he said, "I don't know who this friend is; I don't care who this friend is; I don't care if I ever know who this friend is. All I know is what it means for me. It means that I get a few hours to myself in a place I've never been to before."

PJ paused and crossed his arms, looking sternly at Cassie. "As matter of fact, if you came out with me, it means that you and I could have a few hours to hike in the desert ourselves. Or explore Phoenix. Or just hang by the pool." PJ casually surveyed Cassie's naked body from head to toe. "We could probably stay there an extra day or two after everyone comes back here. I'd finally get to see you in a bikini."

Cassandra jumped out of bed and ran to PJ, throwing her arms around him. "You know I'd really like to, PJ, but my halmeoni isn't doing well. I could never leave now. I'd never forgive myself if she passed, and I wasn't here. And neither would my parents."

PJ looked at Cassandra for a moment, then kissed her on her forehead. He'd heard this story before. He turned to go into the kitchen. As he reached the entrance, he turned to face Cassandra. "And one other thing," PJ said in a very serious tone, "when you finally get to meet the president, and I am taking you to meet the president, don't ever accuse him of being in the Army. He was, and is, a Marine. Those guys can get very touchy about that. You accuse a Marine of having been in the Army, you're likely to get your nose bit off."

Cassie looked at PJ. He'd never seen her eyes open so wide. He turned to go into the kitchen with a smile on his face.

Chapter 9

Bobby Manzi walked through the *Chronicle's* parking garage and entered Jake Rosen's car as the large chauffeur opened the door for him. Rosen was waiting for him. And Rosen didn't like to be kept waiting. Nevertheless, he forced a polite smile and greeted Manzi. "Good afternoon, Robert, and thank you for coming in," he said as he poured Manzi a drink. "What news do you have for me?"

"Good afternoon to you, boss, and thanks for the drink," Manzi said as he accepted the glass. "The trip to DC went fine. I met with our local contact. She knows her stuff."

"What is her name again?" Rosen inquired.

"Cory. Cory Chan. She's a cousin of Spanky Chan. Spanky sent her down to DC to open a BAGI operation there two years ago. There's always a demand for beautiful Asian girls in big cities, I'm told."

"And our source in DC? Did you meet with her?" Rosen asked as he smiled, thinking of Spanky's girls, as he liked to call them. He had, on occasion, availed himself of their services.

"Sure, I've met her. A few times," Manzi said. "We got nothing to worry about there. But, boss, the way this works is she gives the information we need to Cory. Cory gives me the information. Then I give you the information. Simple. See?"

Rosen hid his annoyance at being lectured by an underling. "I am just concerned that we are receiving this information second-hand," Rosen responded, as calmly as he could, as he swirled his drink and looked out the town car's window.

"Look, boss, we've been using Spanky for jobs for years. She taught Cory very well. I can tell you that they both run a tight ship. The girls who work for them are well trained and get away with nothing. And this girl knows what she is doing. Anyway, all the information they've given us from the beginning has been good, right? There's your proof that this thing of ours is working well."

"All right. What have you got for me?" Rosen said impatiently.

"It looks like they're pretty happy with their tour."

"Road shows," Rosen corrected Manzi.

"Yeah, sorry, their road shows. They thought that the first gig in Westchester went well. Apparently, they were surprised when DeStefano made a speech around the same time? But they had some laughs over that? You know what she was talking about?"

Rosen closed his eyes and laughed to himself as he shook his head. "Yes, we are aware of the reaction to DeStefano's speech. You need not be concerned with that. What about the upcoming trips to Pittsburgh, Phoenix, and Orlando? Do you have anything for us that we do not know already?"

"Pittsburgh is still going to be just a day trip. Nothing there for us," Manzi said. "As far as Orlando is concerned, also nothing new. He is making his speech in the Villages on the day he arrives and holding a fundraiser the next day. They rented out a few houses in the Villages for his group, security detail, you know what I mean. It seems they're just going to have a little party for the staff after the speech in one of the houses. They're inviting a few local politicians to the party but no one who sticks out. The next day he's going to visit a grammar school before the fundraiser. They're coming right back to DC after the fundraiser. That's about it. It doesn't seem that anything unusual is going to happen down there."

"What about Phoenix?"

"We may have a little digging to do there. He is going to Arizona in about six weeks on a Tuesday. He's leaving DC in the morning, spending a few hours at an Air Force base then flying down to Phoenix. There's a fundraiser at some rich guy's home. They're expecting eighty people plus at $25,000 a pop. The people going are businessmen and their wives, a few athletes, some lawyers and doctors. It's going to last until 10:00 or 11:00 that night. I don't see anything there for us.

"On Wednesday he'll be getting up early to go for a hike in some park around there. It's supposed to be just him and a friend who lives in the area and his security people. I don't know yet the name of that friend, but I do know that this hike is not going to be on his public schedule.

"He's visiting a local hospital in the early afternoon and meeting with the patients there. He then has a few hours at his hotel to do whatever presidents do in the middle of the day. He is giving a speech in a park to an invited crowd. That speech is scheduled to begin at five o'clock or so. After the speech he's meeting with some locals at a museum that's near the park. That's going to be another fundraiser. The rest of the night? I can't seem to pin down what is going to happen other than his friend from his morning hike is also going to have dinner with him after the fundraiser. He's spending the night in Phoenix and going back to DC the next morning."

"So, who is this mystery friend?" Rosen snapped at Manzi as he put his drink down. "Do you know a name? Where are they having dinner?" Rosen was now sitting up straight and leaning forward.

"Wait a minute, boss. Firstly, we're working on it. Secondly, we still have five, six weeks to sort this out. Fourthly, I just found this out. It will take me some time to get the details."

Fourthly? Can't this idiot count. Rosen picked up his glass and refilled it, taking time to think. He would have Alpha team immediately delve into Whitcomb's friends, contacts, etc., in the Phoenix area. He would have Ritzie contact the Network members in Phoenix to ascertain who in the area might be acquainted with the president from college, the military and so forth. Rosen would also have his people at the *Star Examiner* review their files to see what, if any, connection Whitcomb had to Arizona. "Well, Robert, what I think you need to do is to go back to Cory Chan and impress upon her the necessity of finding out who this friend is. I would not presume to tell you how to do your job," Jake said after he took a long sip of Scotch. "But this sounds like the type of information we were looking for when we set up these shadow road shows. If the target is currently unable to provide the information we are seeking, he will have to be encouraged to get that information. I agree with you; the girls of BAGI have been very useful in the past and can be very persuasive. With your guidance, I am sure Cory's girl can use her wiles to extract the information we require from the target."

There he goes again: "wiles?" Does he mean her tits? "Yes, boss, let's just try to be patient. I'll go back to Cory. Between Cory and her girl, they'll be able to find out some more information on this friend. We are getting a lot of information from this target, and we don't want to put too much pressure on either the girl or the target. Give me a few days, and we'll see where we stand."

"I am willing to give you a few days, Robert, that is not a problem. Just do not lose sight of the fact that this Phoenix trip appears to be shaping up as critically important to us. We cannot afford any slip-ups." Rosen motioned to the chauffeur to open Manzi's door.

"Okay, boss. Will do. I'll reach out to you in a few days to let you know where we stand. Have a good night."

Manzi put his glass in the console. Rosen nodded at him and smiled, patting Manzi on the shoulder as he stepped out. "You too."

After Manzi left, Jake lost his smile and pulled out his cell phone. He dialed Fran Ritzie. "Convene a meeting of the Council ASAP."

"Sure. I'll let you know when I have it set up. Any news?"

Rosen took his last sip of Scotch. "I think so. We may be close to getting the information we need. I think a Council meeting is warranted so we can marshal the Council's resources. I do not want to be premature, but this is something we should address immediately."

Rosen ended the call. He lowered a car window and called the chauffeur over. "Billy, we can head home."

"You got it, Mr. Rosen."

As the car pulled out of the garage, Rosen made some notations in his tablet. The next few weeks were going to be busy for him and the Council. He wanted to be prepared. He wanted the Council to be prepared. Rosen had spent many hours thinking his plan through. As in soccer, he reasoned, he would probably have very few opportunities to score. Rosen intended to do everything in his power to ensure that he and the Council were in perfect position to score the only goal that mattered to him now.

Chapter 10

Diana Surlee walked into Jerry DeNigris' office. "Good afternoon, Diana. Time for our call?"

"Yes, sir. Agent McDaniels should be in Agent Masters's office." Steve Masters was the Special Agent in Charge of the Secret Service Phoenix field office.

Jerry dialed Masters's office number. "Hello, this is Steve Masters."

"Good afternoon, Steve. This is Jerry and Diana."

"Good afternoon Jerry and Diana. Jamal is here with me."

"Hello, all," McDaniels said into the speaker phone.

"What have you got for me?" DeNigris asked.

"There has not been much progress since our call last week," McDaniels began. "The lab has not identified the DNA samples except for the dancers. There have been several other DNA samples retrieved from the ranch, but they don't match anyone in the system. Moreover, the lab believes most of these other samples predate DAFFIE's rental of the farm. The farm had been rented by a family up to two months before DAFFIE took over. Therefore, it's possible that the samples they have yet to identify are not those of the DAFFIE members.

"We interviewed the dancers again. Some are still pretty traumatized. They were blindfolded most of the time, and if their blindfolds were taken off, the DAFFIE members in the room wore masks. They believe there were up to five DAFFIE members present during their captivity, but only two spoke to the dancers. They're not going to be able to identify any of the others by voice if we do detain anyone."

"What about the rental cars those two women used to get to and from the science center?" Surlee asked.

"We checked them out," McDaniels responded. "However, each of those rental agencies cleans the interior and exterior of the cars after they are returned. Each car had been rented a few times after the women on the video rented them. No evidence was found.

"As to the identity of the renters, the videos from the two agencies were sent to our lab. They have attempted to enhance the videos, but it seems clear that the renters knew they were being videotaped. The cameras did not get clear pictures of their faces. At least, not clear enough to enable us to identify them. It's the same with the videos from the science center."

"Have you been able to locate *any* DAFFIE members of the Phoenix cell?" an exasperated DeNigris asked.

"Not yet. In the fifteen months prior to the kidnapping of the dancers, there had been several low-level incidents of property vandalism, similar to what we have seen in other parts of the country where DAFFIE cells are active. The local PDs were never able to identify the perpetrators or make an arrest," McDaniels said. "They did identify two persons of interest in Phoenix in the vandalism investigations. One was a women's studies professor at a local community college. The other owns a coffee shop here in Phoenix. There was not enough evidence to connect them to any of the incidents. One of Steve's agents and I are reviewing the local PD's files on these two. We are going to interview them again and look into their backgrounds and see where that leads us."

DeNigris' frustration was evident. "Look, I appreciate all the work that is being done by everyone but, quite frankly, we are not making much progress. POTUS's trip is coming up in just a few weeks now. We don't have anything to either recommend cancelling the trip or to tell the White House everything is clear. This isn't all on you. The other field offices investigating DAFFIE have so far come up empty handed too. I just want to emphasize how vital this inquiry is. We have to be on top of our game.

"Steve, I would like you to assign two more agents to assist Jamal. We are coming on crunch time, and I want us to devote as many resources as we can to this matter."

"Not a problem. I will have two additional agents assigned to Jamal by the end of today," Masters responded.

Masters then leaned into the speaker phone. "Have we considered infiltrating DAFFIE with an undercover? I know we haven't identified any DAFFIE cell members yet, so we can't flip one. But maybe we can get them to invite us in? There are several very active and vocal environmental groups in this area. There have been protests in the past several months, for instance, involving mining and the development of areas that local Native American groups claim as ancestral tribal lands. From the descriptions of DAFFIE I've read, they are likely to be at protests like that. Would we consider sending a few agents undercover to a couple of protests to see if they can meet a DAFFIE member?"

Back in Washington, DeNigris and Surlee looked at each other. DeNigris nodded to Surlee.

"Steve, we did consider that," Surlee said. "However, we haven't identified any current or former DAFFIE members, or even someone who knows of the group, in Phoenix. That means making the initial introduction would be tough if not impossible. Also, we need to identify the DAFFIE cell in Phoenix in the next few weeks. As you know, placing an undercover into a criminal enterprise can take months, sometimes many months. In this case, from what we have seen, they are a fairly sophisticated group and we don't believe we have the time to insert an undercover agent."

DeNigris then spoke. "That leaves us with the need to identify the DAFFIE cell in Phoenix as soon as possible and take whatever actions required to neutralize them. Jamal, if you need any additional resources from this end do not hesitate to contact Diana."

"Understood," McDaniels confirmed.

"Okay, thank you all and let's circle back in two days. Jamal or Steve, if anything pops up before then please let Diana or I know immediately."

Chapter 11

"Hello stranger," Paul Enrony said to Maura O'Reilly as she entered his office and plopped down in a chair. "How was the trip up?"

"Uneventful, and uneventful is always good. How goes it with you?"

"No complaints from me. Who would listen anyway?" he replied with a casual laugh. "What brings you up here?"

"I'm having dinner with an old college friend who is in town. Then I'm meeting a senator's aide for drinks later in the week for a story I'm working on. All the time avoiding calls from that asshole Schneiderputz."

"Is he still stalking you?"

"He's drunk dialed me twice in the last month. He leaves me messages about how he is the most powerful AG in the country, the things he could do for my career, the things we could do together," she said. "Annoying little shithead. But I don't mean to burden you with my problems," O'Reilly continued. "How is young Ms. Whitcomb's internship going? I haven't heard much about it."

"There's not much to hear. It's turning into a nonevent. She's worked in the sports and metro bureaus. They sent her to some fashion shows and a technology conference at the Javits Center. When she is in the building, she is watched. One of Ritzie's Alpha team guys cozied up to her a few times, trying to get information from her. She didn't bite. She apparently is actually a nice kid and pretty smart. I don't know what Jake thought he would accomplish by babysitting her for the summer."

O'Reilly shrugged and held up her hands. "Beats me. I don't understand the man all the time, either."

Enrony closed the folder of papers he was reviewing and pushed it to the side. "So, tell me what's new in the nation's capital."

O'Reilly stood up and closed the office door. She returned to her seat. "I have to say, it's starting to look like our fearless leader got this right. My White House source is telling me that Whitcomb has been energized by these road shows of theirs. He is particularly looking forward to the Phoenix trip. He does have a 'special' friend somewhere in the Phoenix area, and they're going to meet up sometime during the trip. I don't know when or even if I'll be able to get more details about this friend. He or she must be someone special, though. I've never seen such a tight lid kept on something that I would think is fairly routine information. I'm not sure whether my source is keeping something from me or whether the information is being kept from him."

Enrony cocked his head. "Or her," O'Reilly quickly said, grinning.

"Does Jake know you have a source in the White House?"

"Of course not. One of the first things Morty told me when he hired me was 'never share sources with anyone, including my son.'"

"That was very good advice," Enrony said, grimacing, as he looked down at the floor.

"As you well know."

"Yes, as I well know," Enrony sighed.

"I'm sure that between you and the Alpha team, we'll find out who this special friend in Phoenix is," Enrony continued after a moment of thought. "But to what end? What does Jake expect to accomplish that we can't by our usual methods? And at what risk to the *Chronicle*, and, quite frankly, to us personally? If Jake wants to take down this administration, he should do it the way we've done it in the past: line up a bunch of former high-level government types, well-known think tank senior members, an Ivy League professor or two, who we know will parrot our positions on immigration, the economy, race relations, whatever. Present them as 'experts.' Have them push our ideology as theirs, not ours. Splash their pictures and resumes on the front page, throw some video interviews up on the website, do a couple of feature stories in the Sunday magazine," he said, but O'Reilly didn't jump in, so he continued: "The Network will do the same thing at their papers and news stations. We can drown Rush Limbaugh and Sean Hannity and that scum in a sea of progressive thought and opinion. That's the way Morty and Abe did it. That's the way we've always done it. And it works! There's no magic here. It's not brain surgery."

Enrony was now energized, so he went on: "And what's with Jake and this Italian mobster? Are we freely associating with gangsters now? Is Jake going to start leaving horse heads in beds? What if that news gets out? What will that do to the *Chronicle's* standing in the media and, by the way, this country?"

"Well, you do have to agree that we never have labor problems with the deliverers' or pressmen's unions."

Enrony ignored O'Reilly's comment. "What Jake is proposing to do is reckless. The path he's taking us down is risky and unnecessary." Enrony slammed his hand on his desk.

O'Reilly, in an exaggerated fashion, recoiled from the imagined force emanating from the impact of Enrony's hand on the desk. "Whoa, down boy," she exclaimed, extending her index fingers in the form of a cross, as if to ward off evil spirits.

"This isn't funny, Maura," an exasperated Enrony said.

"I know it's not funny, Paul," with a grin that belied what she had just said. "But the difference between us is that I recognize this is not a fight with Jake you or I can win. As long as Ritzie is in Jake's corner, there is not much anyone can do or say to change his mind."

"I know, I know. That's what's so frustrating. When Ritzie agrees with him, Jake thinks he's infallible," Enrony complained as he rubbed his face with both hands.

"Like a Jewish Pope?" O'Reilly said with a straight face.

"Leave. Please leave. Please leave now."

O'Reilly stood up to go, still grinning. "One last thing. Have you ever heard of DAFFIE? Supposedly a domestic terrorist group? Of lesbians?"

"Isn't that the group out West that inadvertently killed a bunch of domesticated animals by releasing them into the wilderness?"

"Yes, them. My source tells me the Secret Services' collective panties are in a knot. The group is active in Phoenix, and they feel Whitcomb might be a target. But apparently the White House isn't considering any changes to the Phoenix trip."

"If I hear of anything, I will pass it on, even though I'm not very happy with you right now. See how mature and level headed I can be? You can really leave now," Enrony said, grabbing his pile of papers and looking at O'Reilly over the reading glasses perched on his nose. "I have to do some research on the minimum wage for the upcoming road shows."

"Oh, be still my heart," O'Reilly said, gently patting her chest as she walked out. "Who ever said economists don't lead exciting lives?"

Chapter 12

Melinda Katzenberg checked the French baguettes baking in the oven. She cleaned the flour and sugar residue off the long prep table and moved the trays of freshly baked rolls and croissants to the racks next to the retail area. She pushed the cart with the fifty-pound sacks of sugar and wheat and rye flour into the walk-in storage room and returned to make several trips to dump the day's used utensils, pans and mixing bowls into the big sink in the back for the night shift cleaning guys. She struggled to lift and drag several large garbage bags to the dumpster in the rear parking lot. She took a breather while washing her hands at the sink in the middle of the work area.

All this manual labor. Melinda had never had a job like this in her life. The work was more difficult than she thought it would be when she applied. Her anthropology courses at Berkeley routinely described the everyday labors of Australian aborigines, early Native Americans and slaves in the American South as "back breaking." Well, they should have studied the most popular bakery in Phoenix!

She had been working at Carolyn and Julie's Bread and Bake Shoppe, known as "CJ's" throughout the Phoenix area, for almost three weeks. The DAFFIE Phoenix cell learned that CJ's would be providing a dessert table at Whitcomb's upcoming fundraiser at the Arizona Science Center. Melinda had been selected by Elle, the Group leader, to obtain a job at CJ's. Having a person inside the store, Elle surmised, would present an excellent opportunity for DAFFIE to make its presence felt at the fundraiser.

Melinda began to work as a baker's apprentice. She was one of the few English-speaking workers in the back of the bakery, and work she did, almost nonstop from the early morning to the late afternoon. She ignored the males as much as possible, which was not difficult; most men never paid attention to her. She attempted to reach out to her Latina sisters but, besides the language barrier, she found relating to them difficult. They were primarily interested in talking about their children, their husbands, family parties and what the priest talked about in church on Sunday. *The poor womyn*; they had no idea that they were the living, breathing victims of Western institutionalized patriarchy. She just hoped that someday, maybe not too long from now, womyn like these would look back and thank DAFFIE and other forward looking womyn for freeing them from the shackles of patriarchal oppression.

"Kacey, get out here now. You need to bring the empty trays from the display cases to the back of the store," Domingo, the bakery's day manager said, sticking his head through the door into the back of the bakery and calling Melinda to the front. Kacey Hughes was the name on the forged driver's license she used when she applied for the job. Melinda walked to where Domingo was directing the removal of that morning's product and the placement of fresh breads, rolls and pastries for the evening rush. She grabbed all the empty trays she could carry and went to the back. She noticed the empty office off to the side where Domingo and the catering manager had their desks. After she got rid of the empty trays, she headed to the managers' office. A few days ago, she had overheard the catering manager finalizing the menu for the dessert table at Whitcomb's upcoming fundraiser. There would be copies of the menu on or near the catering manager's desk by now. As Elle had suggested, she grabbed her time card, so she could say she was checking her pay records in case anyone came into the office, and quickly located a science center folder on the desk. There were several copies of the work order detailing the menu in the file. She grabbed one, folded it, and put it in her pocket. She then quietly left the office and went unseen to the back of the bakery. Thirty minutes later she punched out her time card and left through the rear exit. Mission accomplished.

The Group would be pleased with Melinda. And why not? After all, she had spent many years in the trenches preparing for this moment. While at Berkeley, she participated in campus protests against racist, misogynist or otherwise offensive commencement speakers, statues and Halloween costumes. Once out of school, she joined all the right advocacy groups: antiwar (when Bush was in office), anti-fossil fuel, anti-GM foods, stop-the (insert name of animal here) hunt, Occupy Wall Street, Black Lives Matters and RESIST. Dedicating herself so wholly to these causes left no time for any formal employment. Luckily, the bank account Melinda's father, an executive at a Fortune 500 company, set up for her when she turned eighteen had a never-ending supply of funds. The only caveat was that Melinda was to never participate in a drum circle. For some reason, that's where her father drew the line.

Thanks to her insatiable desire for promoting equality, born from a crushing sense of white guilt and parents who displayed their love and affection through monetary gifts, Melinda had built a resume to rival any top political activist. But joining DAFFIE was the best move she had made to date. She became a vegan, embraced the fourth wave of feminism and vowed to save the environment. To be surrounded by such enlightened, provocative, like-minded feminists was exhilarating and uplifting. She had finally found her place in life.

She was glad to have the opportunity to redeem herself after her lapse of judgement during the womyn's land ranch reprogramming operation. She now recognized that her attempt to recruit one of the dancer-survivors, as DAFFIE called them, had been an error. She may have revealed more about DAFFIE than she intended during her conversations with Jasmine and jeopardized the security of the group. In Melinda's defense, she honestly thought Jasmine was a good candidate for the group. The DAFFIE members in Phoenix were all white womyn from upper-class backgrounds. Shouldn't they include womyn of color in their cause, Melinda wondered. That was all Melinda was trying to do that night when she entered Jasmine's room. And sat down next to a sleeping Jasmine. And stroked her hair. And caressed the silky smooth, ebony skin of her exposed shoulder. And gently rubbed her thigh. And began to unfasten Jasmine's pants. Melinda understood how unnerving it had been for the Group when, upon suddenly waking up, Jasmine had screamed "Get your hands off me, you fat, ugly white bitch! Aw hell no, you lost your damn mind? Get out of here before I cut you!" Her actions toward Jasmine had been misinterpreted. After the reprogramming operation was over, Melinda willingly submitted to an intervention, run by Elle, which, by all accounts, put Melinda back on the right path.

Elle showed her renewed confidence in Melinda by assigning her to infiltrate CJ's. Now, back in her apartment, Melinda brewed herself a cup of organic, caffeine-free, fair trade certified herbal tea and inhaled deeply the familiar earthy scent of dandelion mixed with skunky valerian root. She sat down, took out her cell phone and dialed the designated number. After three rings her call was answered.

"Yes."

"I have the menu for the party. There are a few cakes listed. Just as you expected."

"Perfect. Bring it over tomorrow night at eight o'clock, and we'll look it over."

"I just want to say how happy—"

Click.

Melinda was still getting used to the Group's communication protocols, but she understood that they were necessary to protect the security of the Group. She took the battery out of the cell phone she had purchased with cash from her meager paycheck at CJ's. After she finished her tea, she walked three blocks in one direction and dropped the battery down a storm drain into the sewer. She then walked three blocks in a different direction and dropped the phone in a dumpster and circled back to her apartment. When she returned, she was exhilarated. She was part of a team. She had an important role. If only those mean girls from junior high, the ones who had laughed at her when she was cut from the cheerleading squad, could see her now. Mentally patting herself on the back, she replayed her actions in the bakery that afternoon.

Then she noticed the CJ's bag on the kitchen counter she had brought home. When she joined DAFFIE, she adopted the vegan lifestyle enthusiastically. She had lost weight and felt physically better in the six months she had been with the Group. But working in CJ's placed so many temptations before Melinda. She opened the bag and reached inside. She glanced around her apartment, although she knew she was alone. She also knew she could not make it through the workday at CJ's without having something to look forward to. *No one in DAFFIE will know.* She took a big bite of the oversized red velvet cupcake with buttercream frosting, one of CJ's specialties.

Chapter 13

Denis Lenihan walked into a conference room in the White House for a meeting with Press Secretary Joel Hirsch, his assistant Whitney Holloway, Don Mangini and his assistant Sean Thornton. Lenihan's deputy, Fawn Liebowitz, accompanied him.

"Good afternoon, all, let's get started," Lenihan said to open the meeting as he sat down. "I called this meeting so we could review the Westchester appearance and also prepare for Pittsburgh. What is the consensus as to how Westchester went?"

Joel Hirsch responded first: "I think it went very well. Speaking on the economy was a good choice. The jobs report, the Federal Reserve interest rate move, and even the upswing in Britain's economy post-Brexit were all positive and tied in nicely with the president's speech. The informal feedback I got from friendly reporters was that the president's speech was well received." As press secretary Hirsch felt his main responsibility was to cultivate strong relationships with administration-friendly reporters, and he exceeded expectations in every way. He proved to be a dedicated and talented team member, but he was always haunted by his one tragic flaw: he was a touch awkward and aloof when interacting with reporters who had a more critical take on the administration's policies, to which pretty much anyone at the *Chronicle* could attest. During the past two years Joel had tried to work his way into the circles run by his more liberal-minded counterparts, but was never truly able to build those same relationships. As a result, he was limited in the damage control he could do when Jake Rosen played God with American popular opinion.

He was, however, developing a special relationship with one of the *Chronicle's* top people. He hadn't let anyone in the White House know because he felt it was too soon to tell if anything positive would come of it. He saw this as an opportunity to get the Whitcomb administration's policies, goals and point of view portrayed honestly and accurately in the liberal media. He wasn't sure if the president or his chief of staff would approve of his adventure. He would tell them when he had something important to let them know. A few get togethers in the dark corners of out-of-the-way bars or restaurants and one late night session in a bedroom had not led to anything worth sharing with his bosses yet.

Mangini spoke: "The focus group surveys we conducted immediately after the speech were also very positive. They commented favorably on the fact that even though oil prices have risen in the last six months, the adjustments to the flexible federal gasoline tax kept the price at the pump reasonable. People are really buying into that tax as necessary but very fair. All in all, I think it went very well. There were protesters, but they were confined to a small area in a parking lot off to the side of the arena. There were less than thirty-five of them."

"I saw on a report on MSNBC that there were over seventy protesters," Lenihan said.

Mangini replied. "Yeah, I saw that too. But that's not accurate. The group of protesters seemed so small that I sent a staffer over to take a headcount. She counted thirty-three about thirty minutes before the speech began. I'll take one of our staffers over Chris Matthews anytime. No protesters made it into the arena," Mangini continued. "And, Denis, you'll be happy to know that about twenty African Americans were in the crowd. We arranged for eight or nine of them to sit in camera range behind the president as he spoke. As I said, I think it was a good night."

"Good," Lenihan responded.

"Mayor DeStefano's press conference right after the president's speech was like a rebuttal speech," Holloway said.

"I read about it, but I didn't see it," Lenihan replied. "I didn't quite follow what he was saying. It wasn't clear to me from the article I read."

Hirsch piped up: "Oh, you really should see the video. DeStefano went on and on about the minimum wage, and how great it has worked in New York City and state..."

"Which is not true," interjected Thornton.

"And how it has improved the living standards for lower income New Yorkers," Hirsch continued. "Since the Republican Party opposes minimum wage laws, we are therefore against helping lower income folks. We've heard that before. But then he starts in on the president, and this administration, and how the president is a product of the military-industrial complex..."

"Jeez, people still talk about that?" Liebowitz asked.

"I guess they do in Gracie Mansion," Hirsch said. "Anyway, he goes on, saying that the president has existed and thrived in a system of white entitlement and systemic privilege . . ."

"I guess the president was privileged to have his helicopter shot up in Iraq," a visibly agitated Lenihan chimed in.

"Right, right," continued Hirsch. "But then he goes on to say that this administration projects 'an aura of toxic masculinity which permeates the entire federal government.'" Hirsch used air quotes for the last bit.

"Wow," was all Lenihan could say as he shook his head.

"It sounded like a speech written by a gender studies professor at Oberlin," Holloway chuckled.

Lenihan shrugged. "I guess that type of speech appeals to their base."

Hirsch laughed too. "I was told it was actually written by DeStefano's wife. She apparently writes most of his speeches. The camera showed her a couple of times. She was sitting in the front row, glancing side to side at the crowd as her husband spoke. Positively beaming. She looked like—"

"She was having an orgasm!" Holloway exclaimed.

The group erupted in laughter. Even Lenihan joined in. "All right, all right. Enough of this," he said. "One thing I noticed, and none of you have mentioned, is the extent of the national coverage the president's speech received, much of it negative, contrasted with the positive coverage DeStefano's got. Did that jump out at anyone else? Joel?"

"Yes, I noticed that too," replied Hirsch. "I would have expected coverage from the *Chronicle* and other New York metro papers and news stations. But not the papers in Chicago, LA, Atlanta and San Francisco. And they reported the same day as the *Chronicle*. You would expect some lag time for newspapers outside the Northeast to report on DeStefano's speech."

Hirsch and Lenihan looked at each other.

"Could the Network be resurrected?" Hirsch asked.

"I was never convinced it died," Lenihan responded.

"What's the Network?" Thornton asked.

Hirsch responded to Mangini's young assistant: "The Network was, or is, a loosely organized unofficial group of progressive media types—and by progressive, I mean liberals on steroids—who attempt to manipulate public opinion by coordinating their reporting on various issues deemed important to the group. They'll publish selected leaks of emails, internal memos, and so forth, of government agencies or political organizations, usually passed to them by sympathetic politicians, the deep state or congressional staffers. They typically ensure that their articles on Democratic politicians or candidates have the correct spin by providing articles prior to publication to the subjects of the articles for review and comment. In the case of a televised interview of a favorite politician, they'll give the politician or a staff member some or all of the questions they intend to ask ahead of the interview. Of course, neither the interviewer nor the interviewee acknowledges that before, during or after the interview.

"In instances of critical news appearing about a politician they like, they either play down that information or release new, negative information, or even recycle old negative news, about that politician's opponent. They can be pretty effective."

"I don't recall anyone mentioning the Network during our presidential campaign," a quizzical Thornton said.

Hirsch responded: "That's because they went into hibernation after President Trump won in 2016. Like most progressives, when Hillary lost, they went into shock and were comatose for some time. Some went into rehab, some into therapy. It was not pretty. It was like the Network didn't exist anymore."

"Apparently, until now," the chief of staff said.

Hirsch turned to Lenihan. "I'll look into it. If it is the Network, it'll be tough to point to any specific source or person. They're pretty tight knit and don't expose themselves to outsiders."

"Still, I would just like to know what we are dealing with," the chief of staff replied. "If it is the Network, we can respond accordingly. In any event, Westchester is over. Pittsburgh and Phoenix are up next. Do we do anything different in Pittsburgh based on what we saw in Westchester?"

Don Mangini spoke first: "Let's stay the course. We're working on his Pittsburgh speech now." Mangini opened a large briefing folder and began to thumb through some sections. "We're going to focus on the economy again for this speech. Pittsburgh is perfect for a speech on economic issues. The region's economy was formerly based on heavy manufacturing. Over time, it successfully transformed itself into a diversified economy focused on the service industry, banking, medicine and high technology. The president can speak to the new and better economy facing voters now and into his second term. As an aside, the new Pittsburgh Steelers' quarterback is a big fan of the president, and we're trying to line him up to introduce the president or at least appear on the stage with him."

Lenihan looked across the room. Everyone was nodding in agreement.

"In any event," he continued, "the local Republican committee has booked the arena on the campus of the University of Pittsburgh for the speech. It's a nice, cozy space. We'll easily fill it."

"The president is pretty popular in western Pennsylvania," Holloway interjected.

"Yes, he is," Mangini said. "So I think this will go well."

"Good," Lenihan replied. "But let's not let our guard down. The likely emergence of the Network concerns me. They really did some job on President Trump. They had all the late-night talk and comedy shows attacking him after he won the election. And collusion with the Russians? They never stopped beating that dead horse. We can't let that happen with this president."

Hirsch looked up from his notes. "This president is not Trump by any stretch of the imagination."

"No, he is not," Lenihan responded. "My concern is just that even though President Trump won, and we won, they may try it again with us the next election. Remember, they have still not fully recovered from either Clinton's loss or our win. They may strike out at us, at this president."

Those final comments left the group silent and somber.

"Let's just be prepared, that's all I'm saying. Okay, thank you all for coming," Lenihan said, signaling the end of the meeting. "Don, can you stay for a minute."

As everyone left the room, Mangini moved closer to Lenihan at the conference table and said, "We didn't get a chance to talk about your meeting with the good Reverend Hood last week. How did it go?"

Mangini paused to organize his thoughts. He then chuckled and sat back in his chair. "It was unique? Intriguing? Eye-opening? Words just don't do it justice."

Lenihan looked at his valued aide skeptically. "Was this a meeting with a minister or your dream girlfriend?"

"Well, the former, certainly," Mangini replied. "But when the meeting was over, I walked out of there patting myself down to make sure I still had my wallet, my phone and my dignity."

"Really? I've never met the man," Lenihan confessed. "I've seen excerpts of a few of his sermons on television. He doesn't seem to be one of those fire and brimstone, 'Jesus loves me and hates the Devil' stereotypical Southern preachers."

"Oh, no, that is not Reverend Theodore Hood. First off, to get to his campus you drive an hour from the Atlanta airport. You turn off a country road and go up a half-mile long driveway. To the left is the Church of Faith in God's Redemption of His People with a spire that dominates the farmland and pastures surrounding the property. This megachurch seats over 15,000 people. There's a daycare center, television and radio studios, several classrooms and a fully staffed kitchen and dining hall as part of the complex. Marble floors, top of the line light fixtures, mahogany paneling, plush furniture, you name it. I got a tour from his communications director before meeting with Hood. I've been to the Vatican twice, and believe me, the Vatican ain't got nothing on this rev. Up the driveway to the right is a thick grove of trees, about an acre. You drive through the grove and pull up to this huge mansion."

"As big as the guy's at the *Chronicle*?" Lenihan asked.

"I've only seen pictures of Tom Freeman's estate on the Internet, but I'm sure this was bigger. Definitely bigger. I had to walk through a portion of the mansion to get to his home office where we were having our meeting. Just like the church. Marble floors, tiled ceilings, sculptures and artwork in the hallway. It was like being in a museum. And I passed room after room after room. I lost my bearings by the time we got to his office."

"And the office?"

"Denis, unbelievable. You could fit two or three Oval Offices in it. The furniture looked like museum pieces. Eighteenth and nineteenth century fine antiques. I don't know if there were more religious portraits or those of Civil War generals.

"On the flight down I did some research on him," Mangini continued. "An article from a year ago says he is worth over $30 million. I believe it."

"I guess he has a very loyal and generous congregation," Lenihan opined.

"Yes, he does. And a publishing, recording and broadcasting subsidiary that generates millions of dollars in annual revenue for his Church of Faith, as it is known. Two best seller books, a weekly television show that is syndicated across most of the country and a weekly radio broadcast that is carried on 250 radio stations. The CDs of his sermons are also best sellers, and the sermon podcasts have a terrific subscription rate."

"Nice work if you can get it," Lenihan said. "Tell me about the meeting."

"I was ushered into his office," Mangini began, "and he was sitting behind this immense desk, which he came from behind to greet me. He's a huge guy, six-four, and I'd say two hundred seventy pounds, at least. He walked up to me, extended his hand, and said 'It is a pleasure to meet you Don—may I call you Don?' and proceeded to crush my hand. He invited me to sit in an overstuffed wing chair that was placed in front of his desk. He went back behind his desk. The communications director moved off to the side and stood there with his hands clasped in front of him; he didn't say a word the entire meeting."

Lenihan stared at Mangini intently; he was mesmerized by Mangini's account of meeting Hood.

Mangini smiled. "I immediately noticed that the chair I sat in was close to the floor, much closer than you would expect for that type of chair. The upshot was that I sat at a lower level than Hood and spent the meeting gazing up at him.

"Look, I'm five eight," Mangini continued. "I've dealt with taller men most of my life. And I can tell you that Hood is one of those guys who was usually the biggest person in the room. He played football in college and is a physical guy. I know guys like him, I'm sure you do too. Guys like him, they intimidate people physically as a matter of habit. Sometimes, they don't even do it consciously. So, at one point he walks around the desk and sits on the edge facing me. Now he is even higher up from me." Mangini started laughing again. "Did you ever see the pictures of LBJ leaning into people, using his size and sheer physicality to bully them?"

"Sure. I've seen them."

"Well, Hood took a page out of LBJ's book. He leans over toward me, still sitting at the edge of his desk, and starts in: 'Listen, y'all didn't need me the last election. After President Trump chased that Clinton woman out of Washington, the Democrats couldn't find their asses with both hands. My Lord, the Democratic National Committee had to lock all the windows above the fifth floor and keep a dozen grief counselors on retainer for a year. Bill and Hillary got divorced, the Clinton Foundation faded into oblivion and Huma opened a bunch of 7-Elevens. For the next three years the Democrats wandered around lost, like the biblical Jews in the desert after they fled Egypt. All the Democrats and their media friends did was talk about the Russians and Stormy Daniels. What good did it do them? Your boss could've won that election with half his brain tied behind his back.'"

Mangini started shaking his head as he looked at Lenihan, remembering his time in Hood's office. He couldn't help but laugh, although he didn't recall feeling that he was in a humorous or light-hearted situation at that time.

"Now, bear in mind, I'm sitting in this high back chair," Mangini continues. "He's leaning into me, and I can't lean back, away from him. There's just no place for me to go. He gets inches from my face. 'This next election, Donny'—now he is calling me 'Donny'—'is going to be a different story. I don't know who the Democrats are going to put out there, but this time around, all y'all are going to need the votes of the good and loyal Americans who attend *my* church, watch *my* television show and listen to *me* on the radio when they're driving to their hunting cabins, gun ranges and Friday night high school football games.'"

"I think he is right," Lenihan sighed. "I've been telling the president that for months. You agree?"

"Without a doubt. Not only that, I get the distinct feeling that *Hood* knows that we know we need him and his people."

"I'm sure he does. So, what does he want from us now?"

"Well, he is mighty pissed off, for a man of the cloth, that we pulled the Wainsworth nomination," Mangini began.

Lenihan started to rub the back of his neck and grimace.

"But, listen Denis, he is actually more upset with the Democrats and the whole situation, in general. He understands that we really didn't have much of a choice in the matter and had to withdraw the nomination. He's not unintelligent or politically naive."

"I guess that's good?" Lenihan asked.

"I think it is," Mangini continued. "In addition, he likes the president, for all the reasons that any conservative leaning person in this country does. What he's really concerned about is the Supreme Court and potential nominees. I think he needs some hand holding on that issue. He's convinced Justice Ginsburg can't last much longer, and we'll have the opportunity to get another conservative seat."

"You have any ideas?" Lenihan asked.

"Well, during our conversation he mentioned that a daughter and son-in-law live in Phoenix and recently opened a Church of Faith in the city. He told me he's following our road shows closely. I took the liberty of inviting him to the speech and fundraiser at the science center as a special guest of the White House. He was very pleased and said he would make every effort to be in Phoenix then."

"You invited him to Phoenix?" Lenihan asked, with raised eyebrows and in a somewhat concerned tone.

"Yes. Is that a problem?" Mangini asked, surprised with Lenihan's reaction to what he assumed would be good news.

Lenihan paused as he looked down at the floor. *I will just have to deal with that too.* "No, that's fine. Actually, that's good," Lenihan nodded at Mangini. "The president will be happy with that, I'm sure. I'm also sure he won't have any problem sharing our thoughts on potential SCOTUS nominees with Reverend Hood."

"Or reacting positively to the names Hood gives him? He may also want to know how we plan to prevent a fiasco like what occurred with Justice Kavanaugh's nomination. Those are distinct possibilities," Mangini said.

"We'll prepare the president for both of those eventualities. Not a bad trip for you, Don, would you say?"

"No, considering everything," Mangini said, "it went well. Sore hand and all."

Chapter 14

Truth be told, President Whitcomb did not relish the nuts and bolts of politics. He was a personable guy who genuinely enjoyed meeting and interacting with people. Whitcomb came from a middle-class family. His father was a fireman who was an electrician on the side, his mother a legal secretary. His two sisters are both married with families. Whitcomb had a great many friends growing up, excelled in sports, and was an above-average student. According to his political consultants, his upbringing and ability to connect with people from various walks of life, coupled with his military service, contributed significantly to his popularity and overall electability.

For Whitcomb, mingling with neighbors at a cocktail party or reminiscing with old teammates or military buddies was one thing, but going to political events and glad-handing strangers for the express purpose of having them write checks was another story entirely. Whitcomb did it because he had to; fundraising was the reality of modern American politics, but he didn't revel in it as some politicians did. Except, of course, for the Schwartz brothers annual summer party at their Livingston, New Jersey family compound.

Roger and Moshe Schwartz were long-time supporters of Whitcomb, going back to his first gubernatorial campaign. Their annual summer bash was, in reality, a fundraiser for Whitcomb. Both Schwartz brothers were more than happy to engage in some gentle and if needed, not so gentle, arm twisting to fill Whitcomb's campaign coffers.

The Schwartz brothers' fortune stemmed from a national chain of high-end retail hardware stores. The flagship store was in West Orange, a neighboring New Jersey town, which had originally been their father's store. After college, and their father's retirement, Roger Schwartz took over the store while Moshe went to live in Israel for several years. When Moshe returned, he convinced Roger that for them to run the store together, they needed to expand. Moshe's plan was to transform the neighborhood hardware store into a high-end hardware and men's fine lingerie boutique. Thanks to Moshe's foresight, a guy could now go to Schwartz Brothers to get a wrench set, a chainsaw, and leopard thongs, lace mini-shorts and crotchless panties. The popularity of the Main Street store eventually led to the opening of outlets in New York, Boston, Chicago and Miami. Home Depot, Lowe's, Ace Hardware couldn't keep up with the Schwartz Brothers. And Moshe was the driving force. He appeared as one of the main models in the catalog that the brothers eventually published to support the store's nascent online business. Indeed, Moshe was often seen in the flagship store, assisting customers while wearing some of the store's offerings, such as tool belts, safety goggles and erotic leather collars.

As they expanded their business, the Schwartz brothers became two of the wealthiest businessmen in the Northeast and prominent supporters of Whitcomb and the State of Israel. For Whitcomb, it was an easy fit. Whitcomb was always a strong supporter of Israel and was quick to condemn the sometimes subtle, sometimes outright, antisemitism that seemed pervasive in pockets of America, such as college campuses, the boycott, divest and sanction Israel movement, and, at times, the United Nations. However, what was not known by any of the Schwartz brothers' guests, and to only a very few people in the Pentagon and the Israeli government, was that Whitcomb and Moshe Schwartz had been friends for years, going back to Schwartz's time in Israel. Schwartz had enlisted in the Israel Defense Forces when he arrived in Israel, became a commando and served with distinction in the IDF. Indeed, some of his exploits with the IDF are still, to this day, kept secret by the Israeli government (Schwartz's multiple scars, visible when he modeled the men's lingerie offerings, only served to heighten his allure to female customers).

During the Persian Gulf War, Iraq fired multiple SCUD missiles into Israel in an effort to draw Israel into the war, hoping to fracture the coalition of forces the United States had formed to liberate Kuwait and attack Iraq. To placate the Israelis, Vice President Dick Cheney permitted Israel to secretly send several IDF commandos and intelligence officers to assist US forces that were searching for Iraq's mobile SCUD launchers. Schwartz had been deployed to the same base to which then Marine Captain James Whitcomb was assigned. They connected over their shared New Jersey roots and became fast friends.

On a mission to locate a SCUD launcher Whitcomb's helicopter was shot down. Back at the base, Schwartz had to be restrained by several burly Marines to stop him from jumping on one of the helicopters that were being sent to rescue Whitcomb and his crew. When Whitcomb decided to run for governor, the first person he told was Denis Lenihan. Moshe Schwartz was the second. Throughout Whitcomb's political career, the fortune of the Schwartz brothers was always behind him.

Whitcomb and Lenihan arrived at the Schwartz family compound in the middle of the afternoon. They exited their vehicles with their Secret Service detail. The presidential party walked around the Schwartz's mansion to the expansive backyard, where the guests were gathered. They were greeted by several of the guests, many of whom knew both Whitcomb and Lenihan from New Jersey connections and attendance at the affair in years past. Both Whitcomb and Lenihan were happy to be at the Schwartz brothers' estate and catch up with old friends, who had paid up to $20,000 per person for the opportunity to reminisce with the president. Roger Schwartz and his wife, Beth, made their way to Whitcomb and Lenihan.

"Mr. President, it is wonderful to see you. We're so glad you could make it," Roger said as hugs and kisses were exchanged. "Denis, it is wonderful to see you, too."

"It's great to see you two, also," a genuinely happy Lenihan responded.

"Roger, I don't think I have missed this party in the last five years. I really appreciate that you do this for us. Beth, how are Sam and Abbey?" Whitcomb asked, referring to their children.

"They are away at camp, Mr. President. I think the only time they wish they were home in the summer is when you're here."

Whitcomb laughed. "Tell them we'll make sure to have all of you down to the White House again when they get back."

Whitcomb, Lenihan and the two Schwartzs caught up on family stories, events in New Jersey and the like. As they conversed, Moshe Schwartz strolled over to the group with a stunningly beautiful woman draped on his arm. She was tall with the lithe body of a dancer or athlete and long, dark hair that fell over her shoulders. She wore a clinging, light-colored summer dress, which only served to highlight her almond-hued skin. She looked twenty years younger than Schwartz. Both held flutes of champagne.

"Mr. President, my friend, thank you for coming. You look wonderful. Denis, it is always a pleasure seeing you," Moshe said.

The old friends exchanged embraces and warm smiles as they greeted each other.

"Moshe, I told your brother, and I'll tell you: thank you so much for arranging this. It is certainly one of the highlights of my year; it's one of the few events I actually enjoy attending. And is this your lovely cousin from Israel Beth is always talking about?" Whitcomb said, turning to Moshe's companion and extending his hand,

Roger and Beth rolled their eyes and looked at the president, who acknowledged their glares with a wink as he felt the firm grip of Moshe's guest.

Moshe let out a loud belly laugh and slapped his thighs. "No, Mr. President, not my cousin. I am pleased to introduce you to my dear friend, Yael. Yael, this is the leader of the free world, the most powerful man on the planet and my good friend, President James Whitcomb, and his chief of staff, Denis Lenihan."

"Mr. President, it is a pleasure to meet you. I am a great admirer of you, as are many Israelis. I am honored to be in your presence," Yael said, while looking askance at Moshe. She then turned to Lenihan, extending her hand. "It is a pleasure to meet you also, Mr. Lenihan."

"Well, thank you, Yael. It's a pleasure meeting you too. And please call me Denis."

"Thank you, Denis."

Whitcomb met Yael's gaze and said, "Yael, it is a great pleasure to meet you." Having met several of Moshe's Israeli girlfriends previously, he knew not to ask her what she did for a living. Why make her lie to him in their first encounter? He felt the calluses on her right index finger and noticed the faint scars on her right forearm and across the top of her left shoulder. "Is this your first visit to New Jersey?"

"It is. I have relatives in New York City whom I have visited in the past. But this is my first visit here." She slipped her arm into the crook of one of Moshe's. "I have an uncle who served in the IDF with Moshe. He introduced us recently."

"And I'm sure Moshe's charm just swept you off your feet."

"Well, something like that," Yael said, and she and Whitcomb laughed, looking at Moshe. Roger and Beth shook their heads in unison, looking at the ground. Lenihan stood there with a grin as if he had seen this show before.

"So, tell me, Mr. President, if I may ask, how is your tour going? It has received a great deal of press coverage in Israel," Yael said.

"I think it has gone very well so far. My team has done a great job preparing us for the road shows, as we call them. We just visited Pittsburgh. I think it went well. Didn't you, Denis?"

"It went very well," the chief of staff replied.

Yael positioned herself a few steps closer to the President. "Do you intend to make a speech about Israel on one of your stops? For instance, Israel's request to purchase several of the new generation of fighter jets that will soon be available. Will you be discussing that issue?"

Whitcomb was taken aback by Yael's pointed question. Off to the side, Lenihan was no longer smiling. Whitcomb thought for a moment before responding. "Right now we are planning on a speech generally about the Middle East. Of course, to the extent we discuss Israel, we will reaffirm that Israel is our closest ally and the only democracy in that part of the world. A speech like this takes time to finalize. We will be working on it even as we prepare for our trip to Phoenix next month."

"Yes, but, given President Trump's withdrawal from the Iranian nuclear deal, don't you think Israel's position in the Middle East continues to be precarious, at best? After all, Mr. President," Yael said while Lenihan now stared blankly at her, "those jets would represent a significant first strike capability for Israel and certainly incent the more moderate Iranians to deter their government from attacking Israel."

At this point, Lenihan was about to step into the discussion to end it, but he was beaten by Roger Schwartz. "All right, all right, enough of this," Roger said as he moved between Yael and the president. "We're not here to solve the world's problems. We're here to collect some money and drink Moshe's stash of expensive champagne! Come on, Mr. President, there are several new people here who want to meet you. I told them to bring their checkbooks, so let's go hit them up!"

"Thank you, Roger, I appreciate it," the president said and then turned to Moshe. "Moshe, we'll get some quality time together later when the crowd dies down a bit." He looked at Yael and said, "Yael, it was a great pleasure meeting you. I look forward to continuing our conversation at some later time." With that, the president walked with Roger toward a group of guests standing by the pool.

Beth then sided up to the chief of staff. "Denis, there are a few of *my* friends who want to meet you. And they have checkbooks too."

"In that case, Beth, you lead, and I'll follow," Denis turned quickly to motion goodbye to Moshe and Yael and headed off with Beth in a different direction.

When they were alone, Moshe looked at Yael, smiling. "Tell me, my little gazelle, are you ever not working?"

Yael did not answer immediately. She was deep in thought. Finally, she said, "You know the answer to that, don't you?" She grabbed Moshe's arm and began to walk with him. "Come, let us fill our glasses." As they headed to one of the several bars situated throughout the yard, Yael leaned into Moshe and spoke softly. "I would like to be with you when you meet the president at the end of the party as he said." Moshe nodded his head. "That is not a problem."

"Thank you. I think I would also like to go to the next appearance on his tour, in Phoenix. Can you arrange that?"

"I don't see why not."

"I have never been to your American Southwest. Will I like it?" she asked coyishly.

Moshe gave a nonchalant shrug. "The desert is the desert. Here we have more hotels and resorts and less Palestinian goat herders.

"If I can arrange this," Moshe continued as he leaned into Yael and lowered his voice, "does it mean we'll have a midnight swim like last night?"

"Yes, chooki," Yael said as she patted his arm. "It means exactly that."

"Excellent. Then we are going to Phoenix next month."

Several hours later, President Whitcomb and Denis Lenihan reviewed the day's events while in the motorcade to Newark Airport for the return to Washington. "Well, Jim, we did pretty well today. I don't have a final headcount, but I do know that we collected an additional $150,000 or so from the Schwartz's new friends."

"Roger and Moshe are great guys. They have been so good to us over the years." Whitcomb then began to laugh. "That Moshe. He's amazing, isn't he? The older he gets, the younger his girlfriends are. What did you think of Yael?"

Lenihan leaned back and looked at Whitcomb. "She certainly passed the test."

"The test? Oh, you mean the 'would you have sex with her in front of your mother-in-law' test?"

"Yup. That's the one. And she passed with flying colors."

Both men doubled over in laughter.

"Moshe, is truly a great man," Whitcomb said as they stopped laughing. "He should start a line of calendars for their stores: 'The Girls of Mossad.'"

"That would be a bestseller, no doubt. She was pretty quiet during your sit down with Moshe at the end of the party. She seemed content to just listen."

"And not jump in my face like she did when we first met her?" The president said, shaking his head and thinking of his initial encounter with Yael. "You know, I love those Israelis, but sometimes they can be a little too, too—"

"Persistent?" Lenihan volunteered.

"Yes, persistent. That's a good description."

Lenihan said, "I had one of the Secret Service detail discreetly take photos of her. I'll give them to Jerry DeNigris to pass on to the CIA and the FBI. They can let Jerry know if she's on the list of Mossad agents operating in the country."

"Or add her to the list if she's not," Whitcomb replied.

Chapter 15

Jake Rosen and his wife Rachel stood in front of the mirrors in the dressing room off their bedroom as they got ready to go out. He was getting into his tuxedo; she was putting the finishing touches on her makeup. "Jake, let's not stay out too late tonight. I want to get up early tomorrow and go to my yoga class. I'll have Consuela wake the kids up, dress and feed them. When I get back, we're going to the beach house. Are you sure you don't want to see Jessie's new horse before I give the stable the check?" Rachel said.

"No, Rae, I just cannot get out of the city tomorrow. I would like to see the horse in person but the pictures will have to do. If you are good with it, so am I."

"Fine. You know Eli has two sessions with his soccer trainer this week? And next Saturday he has the tryout for that club team you want him on?"

"I would love to be there for the tryout. I will try to make it."

Rosen wasn't worried about Eli making the elite traveling team; he was a good player. Also, Rosen knew the parent who acted as the manager of the team. Rosen had recently helped him with a variance the parent was seeking for one of the properties he owned in the city. Mayor DeStefano was, at times, a useful tool. Eli would be making the team. Just then his cell phone rang. It was Fran Ritzie. "Hello, Fran. How are you?" Rosen asked as he inspected himself in the mirror.

"Hi, Jake. I'm fine. I have some news. I spoke to Tony Montanez today. Remember him? He is a Network member who is a columnist at the *Arizona Gazette*. He is helping us prepare for Whitcomb's Phoenix visit."

"Sure, I remember him. What does he have for us?"

"Well, I explained to him what we were doing to counter Whitcomb's road shows. I think he has something that we might be interested in."

"Such as?"

"There's a new federal highway spur being built south of Phoenix off Route 10. The proposed route encroaches on land that was once occupied by a local Native American tribe for hundreds of years. In the early 1900s a group of wealthy ranchers forced the tribe, with the help of the Bureau of Indian Affairs, to sell the land to the ranchers at dirt cheap prices, even by the standards at that time.

"The current tribal leaders contend that the land was stolen from their ancestors. They also say the construction project will disturb the local wildlife, interfere with the ecosystem, introduce excessive traffic and auto emissions into the formerly pristine area; you get the picture."

"Yes."

"Native American activists intend to pitch tents at the construction site and conduct demonstrations. They are even prepared to have children lie down in front of bulldozers in their native garb."

"Quite impressive."

"But there is a slight problem. According to Montanez, who is working behind the scenes with the activist leaders, they need cash. They were planning on holding some demonstrations over the next two or three months and soliciting contributions. They have to make signs, buy tents, camping equipment, food and cold weather clothing; apparently it can get pretty cold in the desert at night. Who knew? They're not going to be able to do all that before Whitcomb's appearance."

Rosen was puzzled. "But...they are Indians?? Do not Indians know how to live off the land?? In teepees?? That is what they do, correct??"

"Yes...well... but...you see, not all of them are full-blooded Native Americans...."

"Oh, right. We are supposed to call them Native Americans. Sorry," a contrite Rosen said.

"Not a problem. Quite frankly," Fran continued, "many of the protesters are not Native American at all. A good number of them are from San Francisco, Portland, Seattle. They're college students, unemployed recent college graduates, PhDs who can't find a job.

Since they're not from the area, they need transportation and provisions. They're going to need some financial support to pull this off on our timetable."

"What about local press coverage?" Rosen asked as he pondered this dilemma.

"Montanez says he can almost guarantee that several local newspapers will cover the protests. He is also confident that the local ABC and NBC affiliates will put the protests on the evening news almost every night. Montanez also tells me the local Democratic party has lined up a Democratic state representative, who will be running in the next senate election, to give a rebuttal speech after Whitcomb talks. He is a transgender former police officer who now operates a solar panel installation company. He opposes the NRA and has voted to ban nuclear power plants and NSA listening posts from Arizona. He went on a hunger strike for two months when Kavanagh was appointed to the Supreme Court. It would be fantastic if we could have the protest at the new highway site up and running at the same time."

"Sounds like a good choice," Rosen said absentmindedly. He was still trying to devise a solution for funding the protest.

"Jake, we have to leave soon," his wife said as she went to say goodnight to their children.

"I will be right there," he said then, suddenly, a light bulb exploded in Rosen's head. "Soros!" Rosen shouted into the phone. "Soros, Fran! George eats this stuff up. He would be more than happy to fund this group and their protests."

"Of course, I should have thought of that. This is right up his alley."

"Tell Montanez to have them to do some local fundraising, at least for a week or so. Make it look like they are raising money on their own. George would appreciate that. Soros will send them money from three or four dummy corporate accounts that will disappear once the funds are transferred. The money will be untraceable. At least, that is the way he has done it in similar circumstances in the past. Do you want me to reach out to him?"

"I don't think so. I got an email last week from his number two guy. He liked my column a few weeks ago encouraging the Florida AARP chapter to file that class action against the Florida Board of Elections over Bush v. Gore. I'm sure I can do this through him."

"Fine. Let me know," Rosen said. "By the way, Fran, that was an excellent column. I enjoyed reading it."

"Thanks, Jake. It's always good to get positive feedback from the boss. I also spoke to Montanez about Whitcomb's mystery companion in Phoenix," Ritzie continued. "He was not aware of any local who has a relationship with Whitcomb. He'll look into it and let us know if he discovers anything."

"Good."

"One last thing, Jake. The Council meeting you asked for will be next Wednesday. Sorry it took so long, but it was like herding cats, getting them all to agree to a date. I told Freeman he had to come up."

"That is fine."

"Where are you off to tonight?"

"We are going to the opening of a new opera at the Met. My wife refuses to miss it."

"Enjoy your evening. We'll talk on Monday."

"Thank you. You too." Rosen ended the call. He then called down to the building's garage and asked for his car to be brought to the entrance.

When he and Rachel arrived at the garage, his Jaguar was parked nearby. One attendant stood by the car, holding the keys. The other two attendants typically on duty on a Saturday night were nowhere to be seen. The attendant standing next to the car was looking down at the ground, clearly uncomfortable. Rosen held the door for his wife as she entered the passenger side of the car. He looked at the attendant again and began to walk around the car, slowly. He hadn't driven it since last weekend. When he got to the rear of the car, he saw it. A cracked tail light, scratches and a small dent on the rear bumper. "What is this?" Rosen demanded as he motioned the attendant over.

"I don't know, Mr. Rosen," the terrified attendant answered. "I didn't do it." When Rosen lost his temper, he spoke through clenched teeth, almost pushing the words out, slowly and deliberately. "I pay an extra $500 a month for a special parking space, so I can be assured something like this does not happen. So that means that one of *you people* hit something while you were moving the car?"

"I, I don't know, sir. I just know I didn't do anything," the now shaking attendant responded.

"Jake, come on, let's go, we're going to be late," Rachel yelled from inside the car.

Rosen could tell he was not going to get any satisfaction from the attendant. "Write up an incident report for your manager and send me a copy. Tonight! Do you understand?" He grabbed the keys from the attendant.

"Yes, sir, I do. I'll do it right now, sir."

Rosen looked disgustedly at the attendant as he moved to the driver's side and got in the car. He slammed the door closed.

"What's wrong?" Rachel asked. "What took you so long?"

Jake turned on the ignition, put the car in gear and lifted his foot off the brake.

"Schvartze," he muttered under his breath as he pulled out of the garage.

Chapter 16

Jake Rosen and Fran Ritzie walked into Jake's conference room with Kris Nickoff. Maura O'Reilly was in the room already, tapping away at her laptop. "Good afternoon, gents," she said without looking up. "I'm just finishing something up."

"Take your time, Maura," Fran replied. "Paul will be here in a minute."

Tom Freeman was also seated at the table, similarly engaged with his tablet, reviewing the architectural plans for the kitchen and sauna he was adding to his pool house. "Good afternoon, Jake, Kris. How are you, Fran?" Freeman asked as he looked up from his work.

"I can't speak for anyone else, but I'm fabulous," Ritzie said.

"Aren't you always," O'Reilly quipped, as she closed her laptop.

At this point Enrony entered the conference room. "Good afternoon, all," he said as he moved to the table, nodded to everyone and sat next to O'Reilly.

"Thank you all for coming. Let us get started," Rosen said as Ritzie shut the conference room door and closed the blinds along the windowed wall of the conference room.

"The purpose of our gathering is to update you on where we stand in our inquiry into the Whitcomb administration. Through the efforts of the Alpha team and other resources at our disposal, we have learned that Whitcomb will be meeting someone whose identity we do not yet know and whose identity the White House appears to be actively concealing when he visits Phoenix in the next—"

"You mean he has a friend in Phoenix?" Enrony said, cutting off Jake in a sarcastic voice. "That's what this meeting is about? To tell us Whitcomb has a friend in Phoenix?"

Rosen reflexively frowned in response to Enrony's interruption. He looked around the room, slowly, then turned to face Enrony. Ritzie sat back in his chair and otherwise did not react. Similarly, O'Reilly, Freeman and Nickoff were stone faced. Rosen looked at Enrony for a moment as Enrony leaned slightly forward with his elbows on the table. He stared back at Rosen with defiance etched on his face.

"Well, Paul, do you have something to say?" Rosen asked, his tone neutral.

At the same time, Maura O'Reilly struggled to keep a straight face. Based on her recent conversation with Enrony, she saw this coming. And she loved seeing men get in cat fights.

"Yes, Jake, I do. What are we attempting here? What exactly do you think we're going to accomplish? What's the long game, Jake?"

"The long game?" Rosen pondered Enrony's question for a moment. "My father was fond of saying that."

"Yeah, I know," Enrony shot back.

"The long game?" Rosen repeated. He inhaled and paused. "I would say that the long game, as you put it, Paul, is that we're seeking to set things right in this country. This country has lost its way: the repudiation of Hillary Clinton, the election of Trump, the election of the current president. We all agree on that. It is up to us to lead the country out of its malaise. The Democrats can't do it. My God, they still have Nancy Pelosi leading the House Democrats. She never read the Obamacare bill, didn't know enough about it to lead an effective opposition against its repeal, and is running for reelection from an assisted living facility. Schumer's strategy to retake the Senate? He held a press conference last Sunday to propose legislation forgiving loans for college students who were so traumatized by Trump's win that they never graduated. The Democrats still have not recovered from Trump's election. They are leaderless, rudderless and hopeless. The damn Russians do not even bother hacking their emails anymore."

"Fine. We agree on that," Enrony said in a calm voice. "We all want to take this president down. But why aren't we using the techniques that have served us so well in the past? We leaked that information about McCain and the female lobbyist when he was running against President Obama. And Obama won. What about Whitcomb and the stripper in Florida when he was in the military? You all remember that." Enrony looked at everyone in the room for support, which was not immediately forthcoming.

"Come on, Paul, we've gone through this before," Ritzie said, jumping into the fray. "Whitcomb was in a strip club with a few Marine buddies and they got in a fight with other customers. Whitcomb wound up taking the stripper who was at the center of the fight back to her apartment for a couple of hours. He wasn't married at the time; no arrests were made. It only made the papers because one of the Marines was the son of a general. The girl later told a local reporter that Whitcomb was a gentleman without divulging any details about their night together.

"I had one of our reporters track her down during Whitcomb's primary campaign. She is married now with children, and she will not say anything about the incident, or her life back then, other than Whitcomb will always get her vote. There's nothing there to help us."

"Okay, what about his divorce?" Enrony continued. "Have we seen all the papers filed in his divorce?"

"No, we have not," Fran said. "But, once again, Paul, what papers we have seen make it clear that the wife was the one who had the affair and wound up marrying that guy. They also make clear there were no alcohol or drug abuse issues or any domestic abuse issues on either side. They just didn't get along. Although, they seem to get along pretty well now. The daughter was here all summer, and no one heard her say anything bad about her father. And believe me, we gave her the opportunity. There's nothing there either."

Ritzie looked around the room. After a few moments to let everything he had said sink in, Ritzie continued, "Look, Paul, we gave it our best shot. In three of the four presidential debates during the last campaign, a Network member was the moderator. Most of the debate questions made their way to Senator Warren's campaign staff beforehand. Just like we did with Donna Brazile and Hillary. It didn't help either time. For most of the press conferences she conducted, any questions to be asked by Network members were made available to her staff beforehand. That didn't help either.

Enrony's defiance of Rosen was slowly fading away. The other Council members, while sympathetic to their colleague, showed no signs of joining in his uprising. They mostly stared into space as his harangue was rebutted by Ritzie.

"The profiles on Warren and her VP that we ran," Ritzie said, "and that other Network members wrote? We ran them by the campaign staffs before publication to make sure they were good with them."

Rosen spoke up. "We did what you are suggesting, Paul, we used the old tactics against both Trump and Whitcomb. They didn't work. Rather, I should say that they worked as far as college students and faculty, Silicon Valley, Hollywood and celebrity types in Los Angeles and New York. But those baskets of deplorables between Scranton, Pennsylvania and Henderson, Nevada—all those working-class whites who voted for Obama—they do not listen to us anymore. We have lost them. The Democrats have lost them. The strategies my father and grandfather taught everyone in this room have not worked the last two election cycles, and Democrats do not know what to do.

"We have to take the initiative. We need to be bold and follow the path Fran and I have set out for us. This plan is somewhat unorthodox, I admit. It is not without risk. But if we succeed, and

I am confident that we will, we will be able to drag America out of the abyss in which it now finds itself. And Paul, may I remind you, we are not 'taking the president down.' Our intent is that he stays in office. But, if we succeed, we will have the power to control him like a puppeteer controls his puppet. Whitcomb will do our bidding. He will have no choice."

The room remained silent until Freeman spoke: "Paul, they're right. Climate change, global economic integration, free health care for the masses, increased taxes on the wealthy—those issues have faded into the background with these last two administrations. If we are to save our country, save our planet, we have to act now. Extreme times call for extreme measures."

"Stupid white people," Nickoff blurted out. Ritzie nodded in agreement.

O'Reilly rolled her eyes at Nickoff's comment and looked over at Enrony. He seemed deflated. He looked around the room as if searching for a long-lost friend. He didn't see much support in the eyes of his fellow Council members.

But he wasn't finished. "What about this Italian guy? Jake, you seem to be relying on him more than the Alpha team. This isn't a question of keeping peace with the *Chronicle*'s unions. Are you expecting to need him to break somebody's legs with a baseball bat? And a hooker, Jake? A hooker? We're actually using a hooker as the main contact with a source? Do you all realize the impact on the *Chronicle* if that became public knowledge?"

Ritzie cleared his throat. "I wouldn't call her that, Paul."

O'Reilly bit her tongue to keep from laughing.

Enrony could no longer contain his frustration. He screamed at Ritzie, wagging his finger like a teacher lecturing a disruptive student. "Oh, Fran, she may charge $3,000 a night, drive a BMW and live in Georgetown but make no mistake about it, she's a goddamn hooker! And she works for us!" With that, Enrony stood up and stormed out of the conference room, slamming the door behind him.

Everyone looked at each other. Ritzie spoke first. "He'll come back."

O'Reilly added, with a noticeable grin, "He always does."

"I can appreciate Paul's concerns," Rosen said, "but this is something we have discussed at length and agreed upon. Correct?" He looked at each of the remaining members of the Council.

They looked at each other. "No complaints here," Freeman said. O'Reilly and Nickoff nodded in agreement.

"In that case, I will pick up where I was before Paul had his episode."

"I'll fill him in when he calms down," Ritzie said.

Chapter 17

Special Agent Jamal McDaniels and Denise Mercado, an agent from the Secret Service's Phoenix field office, parked across the street from Elle's Cafe, located in a formerly rundown, now up and coming neighborhood in Phoenix. The owner, Elizabeth Wentworth, was one of the women previously interviewed by the Phoenix Police Department relating to possible links to DAFFIE. The Secret Service Phoenix field office had compiled a file on Ms. Wentworth. She was from a wealthy Dallas family, graduated Yale, then traveled around Europe for two years volunteering on organic farms and vineyards. She settled in Phoenix with several female friends. She started a small coffee shop, with an infusion of cash from her father. Over time the coffee shop had developed a loyal following. Elle's Cafe brewed coffees made from organically grown beans from various countries. Elle's was open for breakfast and lunch and also served salads, soups, breads and rolls made from non-GMO, gluten free, locally sourced ingredients.

Her Phoenix Police Department file indicated that two years ago she had been arrested at a protest for trespassing at a housing development being built next to a bird sanctuary on the outskirts of Phoenix. She had thrown a bottle of cat urine at a construction worker. The agents entered Elle's and asked the young lady behind the counter for the owner. Elizabeth Wentworth appeared from the back of the shop. She was wearing an apron over work clothes and was lightly dusted in flour. Her hair was tucked inside a baker's cap. She wasn't overweight but certainly not a skinny waif. She had sinewy wrists and forearms and a healthy, tanned complexion indicating that she availed herself of the many year-round outdoor activities in the area. She approached the two agents as she wiped her hands on her apron, exuding the quiet confidence of a successful business owner and a leader.

"Good morning, I'm Elle. How may I help you?" she said in a pleasant voice with a warm smile.

McDaniels introduced himself and Agent Mercado as they displayed their government identification.

The smile on Wentorth's face disappeared. She folded her arms across her chest, narrowed her eyes and leaned away from the two agents ever so slightly. The tattoos on both sides of her neck seemed to float as she repeatedly clenched her jaws and eyed the two government agents.

"We're following up on your interview with the Phoenix detectives you spoke to several weeks ago," McDaniels said. "We're looking into some criminal activity that occurred recently regarding the kidnapping of several exotic dancers."

"I have nothing new to say. I told them I knew nothing about that other than what I read in the newspaper. You should talk to those detectives. One of them was taking notes. Now, if you don't mind, I'm trying to run a business as you can see if you bother to look around."

"We were hoping that, since the interview with the detectives, you might have remembered additional information that may pertain to our investigation," McDaniels said in a pleasant tone.

Wentworth glanced at McDaniels briefly but faced Mercado when she responded. "I have nothing else to say. Do I have to talk to you? Do I need a lawyer? Do you have a warrant?" She was firing questions at the agents, but they got the feeling she already knew the answers.

Mercado politely responded. "We're not here to arrest you. You're not a subject of an investigation. And no, we don't have a warrant. We're simply trying to collect information about this incident and are asking for your assistance."

"Well, I have nothing to add to what I told those detectives. Please go see them if you need information. I'm very busy now and don't have the time to chat. Please leave."

Wentworth's gaze lingered on Mercado momentarily before she turned on her heels and went to the rear of the cafe without looking back. McDaniels and Mercado looked at each other and exited the shop.

"I don't know who she hated more, me or you," Mercado said as they walked to their car. "Did you get a chance to look in the back of the shop?"

"Not really," McDaniels replied.

"The police report described her as 'tight lipped, surly, not cooperative.' They got that right," Mercado chuckled. "Do you think she's hiding something, or she just doesn't like straight men and women?"

"She's a lesbian?" an incredulous McDaniels asked.

"Oh, big time. Where's your gaydar?"

"If that's the case, she meets at least one of DAFFIE's job requirements," McDaniels said, shaking his head.

"Also, she had an edge about her. She was wary of us but not afraid. Every answer seemed to be calculated. She knew what she was going to say before we asked a question. And asking about a lawyer? If we had a warrant?"

"Well, she had practice with the Phoenix police," Mercado reminded McDaniels.

"Exactly," McDaniels said. "She was prepared in case law enforcement came back to follow up. It was like she rehearsed."

The two agents reflected on their conversation with Elle as they approached their car. "She thinks she is smarter than us," Mercado concluded.

"Maybe she is," McDaniels said. "But we can use that."

"Yes, we can. She'll underestimate us."

"I expect she will. What next?" Mercado asked as they reached their car.

"Well, we certainly don't have enough to get a warrant for her shop. Her computer maybe?" McDaniels said.

"Yeah, well, there's that little thing called the Fourth Amendment that gets in our way sometimes."

"I know, I know. I'm just trying to think outside the box here. DeNigris is getting on my ass."

"I hear you," Mercado said as the two stood outside the car for a few moments, thinking of their next move. McDaniels spoke first: "How about you and I give up a few nights of our exciting social lives and follow Ms. Wentworth around a bit. See who she visits, who visits her, where she goes to relax? Get the license plate numbers of anyone she comes into contact with and find out who they are. See who's apartments or homes she visits alone or with others. I think it is time for a little old-fashioned detective work."

"Sure, count me in. It's not as if I have any type of life outside of work or anything. And, gee, I can always use the overtime. It's not a presidential election year, you know?"

"I'm not keeping you from your man, am I?" McDaniels asked as they got in their car and, in almost synchronized movements, adjusted the holstered guns they carried on their hips as they sat down.

"There is no 'man' right now. The last 'man' had a nervous reaction whenever he saw my gun. It didn't last too long. The 'man' before that felt like he had to compete with me anytime we did anything athletic, you know, biking, running, hiking. He was an athlete in college and thought he was Dak Prescott, Stephen Curry and Mike Trout rolled into one. He wanted me to teach him to box, which I didn't want to do. We broke up after our first sparring session. I gave him a bloody nose. Accidentally. At least, I think it was an accident." Mercado winked at McDaniels.

"Yeah, I hear you. Most women I meet in DC work for the government, a lobbying firm or a law firm. If I tell them what I do, they want to know what happens in the White House, did I know Trump. Did you have to carry Hillary's luggage when she was FLOTUS? Did Obama really smoke in the White House? It's not conducive to starting a relationship if that's what you want."

They nodded at each other in agreement. McDaniels pulled out of the parking space to return to the field office. "The cafe closes at three o'clock this afternoon. Let's meet at the office at two and head back over here."

"That's fine," Mercado responded. "You bringing the snack bag?"

"Sure. You got the coffee?"

"You bet. Dunkin' Donuts good for you?"

"That's perfect," he said. "Then we're good to go."

A few hours later, McDaniels and Mercado were back at Elle's, parked halfway down the block from the cafe. It was Mercado's turn to drive. At 2:45 PM, they could see the woman who had been behind the counter that morning and another female bringing the tables on the sidewalk in front of the cafe inside. One of them put a "Closed" sign in a window promptly at 3:00 PM. As 3:30 PM approached, the two women and Elle left the cafe, with Wentworth locking the door. They chatted for a few minutes as McDaniels took several photos, getting clear face shots of the two employees. The three women exchanged hugs and motioned goodbye. The two employees then walked a few yards down the block and approached a car. The woman who had been behind the counter took out keys from her purse and both women entered the car. As they pulled away from the curb, McDaniels was able to get a clear picture of the car and its license plate.

Meanwhile, Wentworth got into a Prius parked across the street from the cafe. The agents recognized the car as the one the Phoenix police had previously identified as hers. She drove away from the agents' position and signaled to turn right as Mercado started up the car to follow. The agents followed at a discreet distance. "No need to get much closer," Mercado said after Wentworth made another turn. "She seems to be heading to her apartment." The agents knew everywhere she had lived in the past ten years; where she had worked before opening the cafe; what websites she visited and every cell phone number she had called or received calls from in the past three years. The NSA has amazing capabilities.

Wentworth drove to her house. She lived alone in a two-bedroom apartment on the first floor of a two-family house in a residential lower middle-income area. The neighborhood was mixed race with single persons, young married couples and a few small families. The police file indicated they had interviewed several neighbors. Most either didn't know Wentworth or had simply exchanged pleasantries with her on the street. She apparently left early in the morning to open the cafe and returned home in the afternoon while mothers were picking up kids from school but before residents with 9:00 to 5:00 jobs came home. No boisterous parties, conspicuous gatherings or loud music had been reported by her neighbors.

The landlord told the police that Wentworth paid her rent by check on time every month. A few neighbors commented to the police that small groups of women, never men, periodically visited her apartment on various nights of the month. They would come individually, stay a few hours, and leave individually. They always walked up to Wentworth's apartment. (There was a bus line a few blocks away). No visitor was ever seen driving up to her apartment. As is often the case with surveillance of suspects, the first night that the two agents followed Wentworth home was uneventful. Fortunately for the agents, there was a small strip mall three blocks away that had a pizzeria and convenience store. The agents could go there to get fresh coffee, use a bathroom, etc. That first night they stayed at Wentworth's house until all the lights went out in her apartment.

The next two days were similar. Wentworth stopped on the way home to purchase groceries once, but otherwise followed the same routine. On the fourth night Wentworth had visitors. The agents were parked on the corner of a cross street and could see her apartment down the block. At approximately 7:45 PM, a woman, coming from the east walked up to the apartment and rang her doorbell. Wentworth answered almost immediately and ushered the woman inside, but not before quickly glancing up the street in both directions. McDaniels snapped a few pictures of the woman before she entered the apartment but was unable to get a good picture.

"I couldn't get a good look at her," Agent Mercado spoke up.

"Me neither," McDaniels said. "I don't think the pictures will do us much good."

"I just noticed something," Mercado said. McDaniels looked at her, waiting. "The porch light above the entrance isn't on. Look at the other houses on the block. Their outdoor lights are on. I'm sure that porch light was on the last three nights." She paused for a few moments as both agents thought to themselves. "You're going to have to get a picture of her visitor when she comes out and is under that streetlight in front of the house."

"Copy that," McDaniels said.

In the next fifteen minutes, after two couples and a man with a dog walked by, another woman came down the street, this time from the west. She strolled down the street at a normal pace but did not acknowledge any passersby or seem to pay attention to the street-scape. McDaniels photographed the woman as she reached the front of Wentworth's house and was illuminated by the nearby streetlight. She turned sharply onto the walk leading to the apartment, went up the stairs to the porch and rang the doorbell. Again, Wentworth opened the door instantaneously, as if she had been waiting, and let the woman into the apartment.

In fifteen minutes, several teenagers, apparently coming from the nearby strip mall, came down the cross street on which the agents were parked toward their position. Behind them, the agents saw two people, about a block away, also walking on the cross street, arm in arm. As they got closer to the agents' position, they could tell that the couple was two women. Before they reached the intersection with Wentworth's street, they stopped to chat for a few minutes. They were laughing and talking, seeming to enjoy each other's company. They then kissed, very passionately, released their embrace and began to walk, turning on Wentworth's street but not arm in arm. When they reached Wentworth's house, they went up to the porch and were greeted by Wentworth, same as the two other visitors.

After forty-five minutes, and no other visitors, McDaniels put a call into Steve Masters of the Phoenix office. Masters and McDaniels had prepared for this eventuality. If this was a meeting of the Phoenix DAFFIE cell, additional agents were needed to follow the women now at Wentworth's house. Two teams of agents were dispatched to meet McDaniels at the nearby strip mall. Leaving Mercado to keep watch at the house, McDaniels walked to the mall to meet the other agents. He texted the photos of the four visitors to the agents, and they agreed on the positioning of the new teams around the neighborhood. Mercado and McDaniels would advise the two teams when the visitors began to leave Wentworth's apartment and in which direction they were heading so that the two support teams could tail the first two women to leave. Mercado and McDaniels would follow the last guest (or guests, assuming the two who came together would leave together).

Shortly after 10:00 PM, the door opened from Wentworth's apartment, and the two women who had arrived last left the house. They turned onto the street and headed back the same way they had come. In fifteen-minute intervals, the next two women also left the house in the same direction from where they had come.

McDaniels alerted the teams of agents as the women began to leave. McDaniels and Mercado watched as the last woman left. She walked down Wentworth's street, away from the agents' position. When she was a block away from the agents, McDaniels exited the car and began to follow the subject. Mercado turned on Elle's street, drove to the first cross street and turned right. She then turned left at the next street that was parallel with the subject's and McDaniels's current route. She drove three blocks and turned back up toward the street on which McDaniels and the woman were walking. She immediately parked the car, got out, took off the blue windbreaker she had been wearing, and threw it in the back seat. She left the door unlocked and the keys under the front seat and walked a half block toward the intersection. She stood off to the side in the shadows of nearby shrubbery and waited.

In a few minutes, Mercado saw the subject walk across the intersection, heading in the same direction. Mercado strolled up the street toward the intersection at a normal pace. As she reached the intersection and turned right to follow the suspect, she saw through her peripheral vision McDaniels approaching from the left and turning onto the street she had just left. The agents ignored each other as McDaniels walked toward their car. Once out of the subject's line of vision, McDaniels sprinted down the street, jumped in the car and pulled up to the intersection he had just passed. He looked to his right, saw both Mercado and the suspect continuing up the block. Mimicking his partner's driving, he proceeded across the intersection, made the first right, went three blocks, turned right again and parked. He exited the car and began to slip a lightweight jacket and a baseball cap on as Mercado spoke into his earpiece. "She just turned right, two blocks from where I picked her up."

McDaniels jumped back in the car and headed toward Mercado's position. "You better get over here," Mercado said moments later. "It looks like she has keys in her hand."

As McDaniels turned onto the street where the subject had headed, he saw Mercado standing in the street waiting for him. He pulled up, and she jumped in the front seat. "She just made a left. We'll see her as soon as you turn. She's driving a blue Toyota Corolla."

As they made the left turn, both agents could see the Corolla ahead, slowing down at a red light.

"So, why would she drive her car, park and then walk six, seven blocks to Wentworth's house?" McDaniels asked sarcastically.

Mercado was entering a description of the car and its license plate number on her tablet to transmit to the Secret Service data center for identification. "Maybe exercise? She looked like she could lose a few pounds."

"Seriously?" McDaniels said as he turned to his partner.

"No, Jamal, not seriously. But all we have as of right now is admittedly unusual, but not illegal, behavior. Let's follow her and see where she lives. I assume she's going straight home at this hour."

They followed the subject for another ten minutes when she turned into a large, well-maintained garden apartment complex. As they followed her into the complex, Mercado's tablet pinged with a response to her inquiry. The address of the car owner corresponded with the apartment complex they had just entered. The car was registered to one Melinda Katzenberg. The agents followed her until she parked her car. They watched as she entered her building, confirming the information Mercado had received. After thirty minutes, and no further sightings of their subject, the two agents drove back to the Secret Service Phoenix office, rendezvousing with the two other surveillance teams.

The subjects followed by the other teams had also walked several blocks to cars and driven to what the agents assumed were their homes. The agents had now identified several individuals associated with a suspected DAFFIE member. The Secret Service teams had work to do, investigating these individuals' backgrounds and ascertaining if, in fact, they were members of the DAFFIE Phoenix cell and what they might be planning for POTUS's upcoming visit.

The problem was that POTUS's visit to Phoenix was fast approaching. Detailed, thorough background investigations of multiple individuals would take time, which was one thing Jamal McDaniels and his fellow agents did not have.

Chapter 18

Denis Lenihan walked into the small conference room off his office. His road show planning staff of Fawn Liebowitz, Don Mangini, Sean Thornton, Joel Hirsch and Wendy Holloway were seated at the conference table. Carl Winthrop and Muffy Vanderweghe from the RNC were on speakerphone. Lenihan was a few minutes late for the meeting. He hated being late for meetings, especially for ones he called. But consoling a few big Republican donors in the medical products field who didn't get all the exemptions they were looking for in a recent tax bill had taken more time than he expected.

"Good morning, all," Lenihan said as he entered the room. "I apologize for my tardiness. Let's get started. Sean, what's the feedback from the Pittsburgh trip?"

Thornton opened a folder on his laptop to give his presentation. "In terms of the media, it went pretty much as expected. The *Chronicle*, the *Post*, CNN, MSNBC, liberal blogs, etc., panned the speech. The *Journal*, Fox, etc., liked it as usual. So the media was a wash. However, the president's speech was well received by both focus groups we set up. One was comprised entirely of Pittsburgh residents, some middle-aged professionals, some blue-collar workers, a few people under thirty, a few African Americans, a nice mixture. They had very positive reactions, for the most part, to a majority of the speech."

Don Mangini nodded in agreement as Thornton made his report. Holloway and Liebowitz took notes while Hirsch looked over at Lenihan, who anxiously waited for Thornton's report. These road shows were going to be important for the administration and the upcoming election. In more ways than the people in this room understood.

"The second group was made up of folks from outside of Pittsburgh in the McKeesport area. Several retired couples, some factory workers, small business owners," Thornton said.

"You mean a bunch of 'deplorables?'" a chuckling Winthrop piped in over the speakerphone.

Lenihan rolled his eyes and motioned to Thornton to continue. "Whatever you want to call them, they liked the speech too. Their comments after the speech were particularly positive about the part when the president introduced the Carnegie Mellon graduate student who is conducting research to reduce methane gas leakage during the hydraulic fracturing process."

"And the optics?" Lenihan asked hesitantly, looking first at Thornton and then Mangini.

Thornton looked at Lenihan, then at Mangini. Mangini mouthed the words "the crowd behind the president" to Thornton who, finally realizing what the chief of staff was asking about, looked at Lenihan. "The crowd behind the president was very diverse. Just the way you want it," Thornton answered.

"Sean, tell Denis how you saved the day," Mangini said as he winked at Lenihan.

"Um, yeah, well, as the crowd was being seated, before the press was let in, I was walking through the section behind the presidential podium. I noticed there was a white woman holding an 'African Americans for Whitcomb' sign. The local RNC chapter made up a bunch of different signs for the speech. I guess she just grabbed one without reading it. I took the sign from her and gave it to an actual black person. Crisis averted."

Lenihan looked down at the table, shaking his head. He then looked up with a wide grin. "Thank you, Sean."

"You're a good lad, Sean me boy," Mangini said in a woeful attempt at an Irish brogue.

Lenihan chuckled, which he didn't do much of late, and addressed the room: "What about the protesters? They received some press coverage. The CNN report I saw made it look like there was a fairly big crowd of protesters."

"From reading about the protests in the *Chronicle* and the *Post*, I think I was at two different events," Mangini said. "There were groups of protesters that got to the campus about ninety minutes before the president. Thank God the Pennsylvania State police and the Pittsburgh Police were in charge, not the campus police."

"Jerry DeNigris made sure of that," Leibowitz said, looking at Lenihan as he nodded in agreement.

"The Pittsburgh PD wouldn't let anybody on the campus wearing a mask or ski cap. If they wanted to get on the campus, they had to turn those over. If they had a backpack, they had to show a student ID to keep the backpack. That cut out a good number of protesters right there. The Pennsylvania State Police cordoned off the approaches to the Soldiers & Sailors Memorial Hall, where POTUS was making his speech. There was a parking lot nearby in which protesters who made it on the campus were permitted to congregate. The lot had been closed to cars from the day before, so there was plenty of space for several hundred protesters. There were less than a hundred. You practically had to stand in the parking lot itself to hear the 'ho, ho, ho, Whitcomb has got to go' chants."

Wendy Holloway interrupted. "Because the parking lot was so big, and there were no cars, the crowd looked small. But I swear on my Alpha Phi sorority pin that I saw a guy with an MSNBC windbreaker walking among the protesters about fifteen minutes before the president arrived. He seemed to be herding them toward the part of the parking lot where MSNBC, CNN and local camera crews were standing. None of them, and I mean none, turned on their cameras until the guy in the windbreaker had pushed the protesters against the police barricades and packed them in like an overflow crowd at a student protest against Milo Yiannopoulos."

"Unbelievable," Winthrop said over the phone. Hirsch looked across the room, shaking his head as if he was embarrassed to have been previously part of the media. Mangini mumbled a few curses loud enough for the room to hear him.

"So, yes," she concluded, "the media staged the protest scene to inflate the number of protesters."

Lenihan looked around the room. "I am no longer surprised at anything the mainstream media will do. Was the MSNBC guy handing out envelopes with cash to the protesters?" he said, shaking his head.

"Funny you should say that," Hirsch replied. "My sources tell me that, as we suspected, the Network has been reborn from the dustbin of the Clinton campaign. They are alive but just barely. I'm being told they are really gearing up for Phoenix. They want to stop our road shows in their tracks."

"Why Phoenix?" a skeptical Lenihan asked.

"Because of a confluence of events," Hirsch responded. "They haven't really hurt us yet in their counter-road shows. DeStefano was ineffective in Westchester, Bernie Sanders seemed distracted during the speech he gave in Pittsburgh, probably because he rushed there after visiting his wife in prison. Meanwhile, our polling is showing that voters, even a fair number who didn't vote for the president two years ago, are reacting favorably to his appearances."

"Thank God he never tweets," Winthrop commented.

"Yes, we can all be thankful for small favors," Lenihan said. "Go on, Joel."

"Lastly, the DNC is running on fumes. With Harvey Weinstein and Bill Clinton holding women empowerment in the workplace seminars instead of fundraising, they're in debt up to their glass ceiling and they can't seem to do anything about it. They also have lost one of their shining stars in the media. Have you heard the rumors about Anderson Cooper? He may be quitting CNN."

"He's leaving CNN?" Lenihan asked. "For personal reasons? That's a shocker, to say the least."

"Yeah, well, maybe it is, maybe it isn't," Hirsch said.

"Is it money? It usually is," Holloway said.

"No, it's not money." Hirsch looked around the room. "He is leaving the business."

"What! Why?" the group said, almost in unison.

"Well, as any good journalist, Anderson studied up on Stormy Daniels before he interviewed her during President Trump's term." Hirsch looked around the room. "And studied."

The group looked at Hirsch. "He spent hours reviewing Stormy's porn movies. Hours. And hours. And more hours."

The group continued to look at Hirsch. Hirsch looked down briefly then raised his head. "Anderson Cooper is no longer gay."

"What?" Lenihan said.

"It's true. Watching all that Stormy porn turned him straight."

"No way!" Holloway said.

"Way," Hirsch replied. "He is leaving CNN to open a whiskey distillery. He is also going to study Krav Maga."

Everyone in the room looked at Hirsch with eyes and mouths wide open, and Hirsch said, "Also, he is now the recording secretary of a local Hell's Angels chapter."

"I have something to top that!" Holloway said. "Have you heard the DNC's latest money raising schemes? Madonna, Chelsea Handler and Rosie O'Donnell are having a threesome, which the DNC will tape and stream on its website, available to donors who contribute $10,000 or more in the next sixty days. And," she continued over the howls of the group, "for more family orientated contributors, Alec Baldwin will scream at their unruly children over the phone for two minutes at $2,500 a call. Additional thirty-second rants are available at $1,250 a pop."

After the laughter died down, Hirsch continued. "They are desperate. And they think we are weak on the environment. Since the president is speaking on the environment at the Arizona Science Center, they believe we are vulnerable. Their counter speaker is a retired transgender police officer who is now a state representative. He will be speaking after the president. Apparently, most, if not all, of the local network affiliates, except for Fox, will be giving his speech air time.

"I'm also hearing something about a protest by a bunch of Native Americans. There have been a few small and intermittent protests, thirty to forty people at most, for some time now at a federal highway project near Phoenix. But they are planning on staging larger protests to coincide with the president's visit. They're anticipating a large influx of protesters who support their cause from up and down the West Coast."

"You can bet that CNN and MSNBC will be there too." Holloway said, as the group nodded in agreement.

"What is curious about this is that, up to two weeks ago," he continued, "the local protesters seemed to be operating on a shoestring budget. Now, however, huge tents with built-in heaters are being delivered to a campsite near the highway extension route. Pallets of food and water are stacked at the protest site. There are reports that buses are being chartered to transport people from San Diego, LA and Seattle to the protest site. There are enough supplies to support several hundred protesters for several days."

"Where did they get the money?" Lenihan asked.

"Don't know yet," Hirsch replied. "But I think it is something we should find out. I'm sure it's no coincidence that they're ramping up this protest to coincide with the president's visit."

"I agree," Lenihan said. "I want to know where the money is coming from. But we can't have the White House involved in this. Carl, you still with us?"

"I'm here," Winthrop said over the phone connection.

"Look, Carl, we need to know who is funding this group. It may come in handy down the road." Lenihan's tone turned very serious. He reacted very negatively to any plots that he perceived as meant to undermine the president. His visceral reaction was always to hit back twice as hard, which is how they handled things in Vailsburg. "Carl, I want the RNC to look into this. I'd like your security people to arrange for private investigators you trust to discreetly, and I mean very discreetly, track down who is funding this group. You have to emphasize to your security people that this cannot come back to the White House. That would not be a good thing."

"I understand, Denis. And I agree. The people our security staff use are pretty good at this. We'll handle it."

"Good. Anything else, Joel?" Lenihan said.

"I'm just stumped over the Network and their fixation on Phoenix. They seem very excited, agitated even. It is as if the Phoenix road show is somehow different from the others. As if there is something special about this trip. I just don't get it."

Lenihan remained silent as he stared across the room, as if in a trance. The assembled group waited for his reply, but none was forthcoming. Instead, he began to massage the back of his neck, as that dull ache arose. This Phoenix trip was becoming more and more of a headache. Most people in the room and on the call didn't know about DAFFIE. None knew about the visits the president was having with his friend. Lenihan had made sure of that.

Lenihan lifted his head, pulled back his shoulders and addressed the group. "Where do we stand on the president's speech?"

"It's coming along fine," Mangini responded. "We're going with the 'Energy for the Future' theme that our consultants recommended based on their polling data. The president will talk about the continued success and benefits of fracking and also highlight the SunPower tax credit program."

"I must say, I'm actually pretty impressed with that program," Hirsch said. "If you recall, we tossed that tax credit in our first budget as a bone to the Democratic leadership. But it is actually working pretty well."

"I agree," Mangini joined in. "With the recent tech advances solar power is becoming more efficient and reliable. The better they get at it, the smaller the tax subsidies will be. A win-win for everybody."

"That's all well and good," Winthrop immediately chirped in over the speakerphone. "But until solar power is one hundred percent self-sufficient, the RNC's position is that the government should not be supporting specific industries with tax policies that necessarily work to the detriment of other sectors of the economy."

"Okay, okay, let's stay on point people," Lenihan directed. "When will there be a draft for me to review?"

"We'll have it to you two days max," Mangini replied.

"And what about the fundraiser on the first night, Don?" Lenihan asked.

"Coming along nicely. Some heavy hitters will be there. The host is very excited to be having us at his house. We have a list of the attendees put together, ready for your review. Should bring in a nice pile of cash."

"That is fine," Lenihan responded. "Carl, how are we set for the RNC fundraiser after the speech in the park?"

"We're finalizing the guest list. I'll have it in your hands before the end of the week. We're looking at a sellout crowd. One hundred seventy-five people at $15,000 a head. I'll send the final list to the Secret Service when it goes to you."

"Good," Lenihan said.

"The caterers, the waitstaff, all that stuff, is all set up. We're having the presidential podium shipped out with the president for his speech to the donors. They'll be impressed, I'm sure," Carl said. "Then the president is going to mingle with donors, meet a few of them, correct?"

"Yes, Carl, that is the plan. I doubt he'll meet all the people there, but he's going to shake hands with quite a few."

"Well, I plan on being there, and I will make sure he meets the dozen or so that he has to meet."

"Great, Carl, that is great."

"Denis, while we're on the subject, I see that Moshe Schwartz and a lady friend are on the president's guest list."

Lenihan narrowed his eyes and cocked his head somewhat toward the speakerphone. "Yes, they are. And?"

"Well, I would like to send Mr. Schwartz a note thanking him for coming. I'd like to see if he would like to make a contribution to the RNC. I know he is a regular donor to the president's campaign fund, and I would like to see if we can expand his beneficence to include the RNC. If we could develop a relationship with him and his brother...."

"No, Carl, you cannot hit him up for a contribution to the RNC. He is a close personal friend of the president and has always been very generous to him. But as far as the RNC is concerned, I don't even know if he is a registered Republican."

"He isn't," Vanderweghe interjected.

"There you go, Carl. I've known Moshe for years, and he is as apolitical as they come. He is coming to Phoenix to support the president, and that is it."

"Okay, I understand. But what about Reverend Hood? He's on the guest list too. He has contributed to the party in the past, although not recently. Between him and a number of his congregants, there are some prospective donors we would like to reach out to."

Lenihan thought for a moment. He had learned over the years that while his instincts were usually right, he sometimes reacted too quickly and spoke abruptly in a given situation, resulting in bruised egos and impaired relations with coworkers. He now tried to take a long-term perspective and not view every confrontation as a personal battle to be won. Lenihan recalled Don Mangini's account of his meeting with Reverend Hood. Hood was a big boy and could take care of himself. He was a political realist and knew how the game worked. He was also looking to get a foot in the door of this administration. Lenihan leaned across the table toward the speakerphone. "Sure, Carl, feel free to reach out to Reverend Hood. Let me know how it goes."

Chapter 19

Bobby Manzi walked into his midtown office. His crew chiefs Tony Delmonica, Ray Siconolfi and Vito Paterno were in Manzi's office.

"So, how was the meeting with the Jew?" Paterno asked.

"Not for nothing, but this gentleman does have a name," Delmonica said.

"Okay, let me reparaphrase myself. How was the meeting with Jake the Jew?"

"Much better," Siconolfi commented.

"Fine, fine. You know this guy. He's the nervous type." Manzi laughed with his crew.

"Just like his father and grandfather, according to Uncle Rocky," Paterno said.

"Yeah, tell me about it," Manzi said.

"So, when are we going to wrap this thing up, boss?" Paterno asked as he thumbed through the the *Daily News* sports section. Siconolfi was finishing a meatball parmigiana sandwich and Delmonica was on the Internet, looking for presents for his wife (wedding anniversary) and girlfriend (birthday).

"Not soon enough," Manzi said. "It looks like I'm going out to Phoenix in a few weeks."

"Hey, boss, you ain't missing my daughter Daniella's first communion, are you?" Siconolfi asked.

"No, no, I'll make it. I'm sure I'll be back for that."

"Great, boss. You gotta be there. My wife would be really upset if you didn't make it. But, jeez, boss, Phoenix? That's Arizona, right? You really going out there?"

"Yeah, it looks like it."

"Hey, are you going to meet up with Big C out there?" Delmonica asked. Carmine "Big C" Santucci ran the mob in Phoenix. Manzi knew him pretty well but hadn't spoken to him in sometime. "Tony, this ain't a friggin' vacation. I'm only going to be out there a few days."

"So what does Jake the Jew having you do out there?" Delmonica asked.

"I'm going to be keeping an eye on our friend from DC. Trying to see who he is going to be stepping out with in Phoenix."

"What, does he have a girlfriend out there?" Siconolfi asked, jumping in the conversation.

"Something like that," Manzi said.

"He's probably got girlfriends all over the place. I mean, a good-looking guy like that, with all that power. And he's not married. Probably gets laid every night of the week," Siconolfi said.

"Yeah, just like you, Ray," Delmonica said.

"Hey, hey, I do okay. You guys know that," Siconolfi said, slightly squirming in his seat, as the group enjoyed another laugh.

"So, what's the Jew having you do out there?" Paterno asked.

"Well, Vito, he wants me out there with this special photographer he has. I have to hold the hand of the photographer, you know, make sure he gets the right kind of pictures."

"Pictures of what?" Siconolfi asked.

"Pictures. Photos of this friend nobody knows about. Who knows? Maybe some of the embarrassing kind. The kind that makes someone do whatever you want them to,"

Paterno joined in. "I don't get it. Pictures of him with some broad? What good is that going to do anyone? Unless she's a ten-year-old."

"Look, this is a special job. Special jobs need special pictures. Let's leave it at that."

"Okay, boss. Just asking," Siconolfi said as he bit into his sandwich.

"How the fuck are you going to do this? Isn't he surrounded by Secret Service guys all the time?" Delmonica asked.

"Sure, sure. But this photographer has those long-range lenses. He don't have to be in a room with him, just within a couple hundred feet. He's going to be going hiking with this friend in some park out there early in the morning. There's only one road in and out of this park, and it leads to the one parking lot. We'll get there first, and we'll be set up with a view of the parking lot for when they get out of their cars, walk around, that kind of thing. This photographer should be able to get some shots of the DC guy's friend, you know?"

"And, that's it? What are you going to do then?" Paterno asked.

"No, that's not it. According to Spanky's girl in DC, a couple of Secret Service mooks are picking up this friend and bringing the friend to the park. They're then going to drive the friend home. We're going to follow the friend home. We'll sit on the friend's house and maybe see where the friend goes to work that day. By lunch we should have a face, a home address, and, I don't know, maybe a business address. We'll have the license plate number of the car parked in the driveway. The photographer will pass on that info to the Jew's crew that's out there too. By the time I'm having my first beer at the hotel pool that afternoon, we should know who this special friend is."

Paterno closed the newspaper. Siconolfi had finished his sandwich and was brushing crumbs off his hands. Delmonica looked up from his phone. They looked at Manzi, all nodding their heads in agreement. "Sounds like a plan, boss," Siconolfi said.

"Meanwhile, they're having dinner that night after a fundraiser at some museum. Just the two of them. Me and the photographer will sit on the friend during the fundraiser and follow him to the dinner. The Jew has arranged for some local reporters to follow our DC guy from the museum too. Reporters do that all the time so the Secret Service won't get suspicious. Between us, we should be able to find out where they're having their dinner that night."

"And maybe some more pictures," Paterno chimed in.

"Bingo. You got that right," Manzi said.

"Once we know who the friend is, and we get a couple pictures, the Jew's crew can do some digging on him. My job is done and I can get back here."

"And make my daughter's first communion."

"Yeah, and make your daughter's first communion. And the Jew gets what he wants, and we get paid. Nice and easy."

"Okay, boss. Whatever you say. You're the boss."

"I know that, Tony. Just you remember that too."

Chapter 20

Fran Ritzie knocked on Jake Rosen's office door, which was slightly ajar.

"Come in."

"You wanted to see me, Jake?"

"Yes, Fran, thank you for coming by. Please close the door."

Ritzie closed the door and walked over to Rosen's desk, which happened to be the first desk his grandfather had ever bought for himself, about thirty years ago after the *Chronicle* had experienced three consecutive years of profits under his leadership, a story Abe had frequently told first-time visitors to his office.

"First off, why do I have four messages from DeStefano? Do you know what he wants? I really do not have time for him now."

Laughing, Ritzie moved to the plush sofa to Jake's left and sat down. "He called me three times. I spoke to him earlier today. He says he really, really wants to go to Phoenix to help us out."

"Oh."

"What he really wants to get out of the city. Have you seen the *Daily News* series on the favors his administration has secretly been lavishing on his donors?"

"I saw some headlines. I did not pay much attention to them."

"There's that. And there's his public advocate."

"What did she do now?"

"Apparently, the Korean Merchants Association has approached the city and offered to set up a mentoring program in a few school districts for minority teens to introduce them to small business operations, job interview techniques, after school study programs and so on."

"I was not aware of that. Sounds like a worthwhile endeavor."

"Yes, one would think so," Fran said. "But, apparently, not the public advocate."

"Oh, no?"

"No. She has announced her opposition to it. Quite vocally. The exact quote, I believe, is 'we don't need those people telling black folk what to do.'"

"I see."

"So, between the budding donor scandal and his public advocate, the mayor, let's say, would like a change of scenery. But don't worry, I told the mayor, again, that we didn't anticipate needing him for any appearances outside New York, and we definitely would not need him in Phoenix, but would let him know if that changes."

"Thank you."

"You're welcome."

Rosen moved some paperwork off to the side to give his Council member his full attention. "What I really asked you here for is to hear about Phoenix. Where do we stand?"

"Where we stand is that so far Montanez has not found any connections or leads linking anyone local to Whitcomb."

"How about our Jersey people?"

"They haven't found anything yet either."

Rosen leaned back in his chair, running his hands through his hair. "Look, Fran, I do not mind telling you that I am getting a little upset and nervous. We still do not know who Whitcomb's mystery friend is. The longer it takes to find out who that is, the longer it will take to implement our plan. The longer it takes to implement our plan, the more this country regresses."

"I know, I know, I hear you Jake. This is frustrating for me and the Alpha team as well. We're all working as hard as we can on this."

"I know you are. But one would think that somebody somewhere would know something, anything, about a friend of the president of the United States with whom he is planning on spending time with not once, but twice, while on the campaign trail."

"Yes, one would."

"That, in and of itself, makes me think there is a conspiracy ongoing in the White House to conceal this person's identity from the media and the public." Rosen paused as he considered his options. "I would like you to send a few Alpha team members to Phoenix. We need some topsiders on the ground out there. We have been pushing Montanez for some time, but we are not seeing any results."

"I was thinking the same thing, Jake. I'll let Montanez know, so we can coordinate with him and his people. I'm sure he'll welcome the help. Are you still sending the Italian out there?"

"Yes. With Shooter O'Neill," Rosen said, looking at Ritzie sideways with an arched eyebrow. "Shooter is not drinking anymore, is he?"

"No, no, he's been sober for years now. Ever since Trump won."

"I suppose there was one good thing about that election. Shooter is the best there is when he is sober," Rosen said. "Then again, I can say that about many of the Irish I know."

"Agreed, on all counts."

"Since we know where and when Whitcomb is meeting his friend, at least for that early morning excursion in the desert, they should be able to get close enough to get some good photos of the friend."

"We find out where this person lives," Frans said, "we can most likely put a name to the face."

"I certainly hope so. But I am still exasperated that it is taking so long to do this."

"Look, Jake, we'll keep digging in Jersey and Phoenix. One way or another, we'll find out who this friend is."

"Yes, I know we will," Rosen said. "I just wish it was sooner. How are the plans for the Native American protests coming?"

"Exceedingly well. The Soros money has been received and split among multiple groups of protesters. Much of it has been distributed in cash, so it will not be traceable. If we wanted, the protesters could get almost daily press coverage, but we're holding back on that. We're still a few weeks away from Whitcomb's visit, so we don't want to peak too early."

"I agree. That is what Man U did last season. I saw it coming," Rosen said.

"Yes, right, of course," Fran agreed. "Anyway, the protests have been peaceful to date. But when Whitcomb arrives, we expect some Antifa elements will show up to liven things up a bit."

"Good. You have to admire those young people in the Antifa movement. I do not agree with all their methods, but they certainly are a committed group. Were we that committed when we were young?"

Ritzie laughed. "Sure we were, Jake. Well, not so much with throwing rocks and bottles filled with urine at the police, setting cars on fire or smashing office building windows, but, hell yes, we were just as committed."

"I think so too." Rosen smiled as he nodded at Ritzie.

Rosen leaned forward, resting his chin on his clasped hands, looking directly at his confederate. "This Phoenix trip, this hiking outing, this mystery friend, this is what we have been waiting for, Fran, ever since Hillary lost, ever since Whitcomb won. This is our chance to get things back to the way they were. I can sense it. We cannot waste this opportunity. We have to make the best of it. We may not get another chance."

"You're preaching to the choir, Jake. We will prevail. I'm confident of that. And confident in you."

"Thanks, Fran," Rosen said. "So am I."

Chapter 21

Joel Hirsch was seated in the back of the restaurant, in a corner booth. Tuesday nights were quiet for most restaurants and this one was no exception. The restaurant was due east of Washington, in a hamlet between DC and the Chesapeake Bay. The restaurant was known for excellent seafood and was popular with the locals, but not well known outside the immediate area. In other words, a good place for two people from the nation's capital, who didn't want to be seen together, to meet.

Joel arrived at the restaurant twenty minutes early. He wasn't much of a drinker, but he ordered a martini to calm his nerves before she arrived. A martini got him where he wanted to go quickly. He reserved the same table each time; she liked to have her back to the wall in the rear of the dining room with a view of the entrance so she could see who was coming and going.

Looking back over the last few months, he still wasn't sure how that first night happened. After a press conference, he wound up at a local DC haunt for journalists, which he once was, and did some background interviews with the reporters he routinely dealt with. Maura O'Reilly showed up, and after an hour or so, they were the last two. He always got along well with her; compared to others in the liberal media, she was not as strident, not as hectoring, not as angry at life since the Trump victory. They could have a discussion on policy or issues and disagree, without wanting to tear each other's throat out.

He didn't know if it was the alcohol (she had quite a few; he only had two and switched to sparkling water), but they wound up at his apartment. He may have shared some White House inside information with her that he would not ordinarily pass on to a reporter to get her to agree to go home with him. But the tipping off had been a two-way street; she let it slip that the Network was "getting the band back together." They had a wonderful evening, at least he had. She was gone when he woke up the next morning. He called her several times over the next few weeks, but the calls went directly to voicemail. The next time he saw her, at a cocktail party at the Swedish embassy, she winked at him from across the room. They eventually met at the in the middle of the reception. She was very pleasant but hadn't mentioned their recent evening together, or in any way intimate that it was, or wasn't, going to happen again. But Joel was nothing if not persistent. After all, it wasn't as if Joel had any girlfriends in the DC area.

Thereafter, Joel would get a return call from her if he left a voicemail referencing an upcoming White House announcement on some topic in the then current news cycle or a morsel of White House inside information he knew she would find interesting. Their last three assignations, if you could call them that, had been at this restaurant. She always insisted that it be early in the week, that they take separate cars and that they pay in cash. Joel could not help but notice that the owner of the restaurant always stopped by the table to say hello. He paid scant attention to Joel when he came over, calling Maura "Mary" with a big wink as he bent down to lightly kiss her cheek.

He would nod politely at Joel but otherwise ignore him. Joel got the distinct impression that he was viewed as one of Maura's many accessories. Try as he might, Joel could not convince Maura to go back to his apartment after these dinners. Or go to hers—come to think of it, Joel didn't even know where she lived. She always had a reason not to go home with him and would end the night with a simple "we'll see next time."

The last dinner had touched on, among other things, the White House road shows and the upcoming Phoenix trip. Maura had not written any columns yet on the road shows. Joel suspected they would be the topic of conversation for most of the dinner.

He would be correct.

As Joel was finishing his martini, Maura walked in the restaurant and immediately went to the table, avoiding any eye contact with the few patrons in the dining room. She slid into her seat, directly across from Joel. "How are you, my friend," she asked in a cheerful but not playful tone, while at the same time waving to the waiter, making a drinking motion. She spoke loud enough for Joel to hear, but if any customers or staff were listening, they would only be able to make out bits and pieces of the conversation.

"I'm great, just great, Maura. How was the ride out?"

"It was fine, once I got out of the District. My driver had never been here before, and he got a little lost. No biggie."

After a short conversation on Joel's last press briefing, Maura got down to business. "So, tell me, how are the road show plans coming along?"

"They're coming. The attendees for the fundraisers are being finalized, his speech on the environment is taking shape. Everything is going fine."

"Is there going to be anyone at these fundraisers I might find interesting?"

"Actually, no. No one of any national import. Certainly no one you would waste ink on in one of your columns. You can trust me on that."

"I will." Maura stopped to acknowledge the waiter as he brought her a glass of cabernet. He also bent down to kiss her on the cheek and exchanged greetings. He didn't bother to glance at Joel until he took his order. Maura ordered her usual salad and an appetizer as a main course. She took a sip of wine, placed her glass down, and looked at Joel. "And what about this lesbian terrorist group?"

"The Secret Service is still investigating them. They may have leads on some local activists. Nothing definite yet. The protection detail is getting antsy. But they're pretty good at their job. The president isn't worried. Unless something significant comes up, they're not changing the trip."

"And, Joel, how about the president's special friend? Don't keep telling me you don't know who that is. That's something I won't trust you on," she said with a grin as she reached for her wine.

Joel leaned back and held his hands out, palms facing the ceiling. "What can I say, Maura? It's no big deal. He has a friend out there who he's going to meet. It won't be on his schedule to be released to the public, but so what? It's not an advisor or someone involved with the government at any level. Did you know every friend that visited the Obamas when they were in the White House? Did they announce who they were spending every weekend with? Did you know everybody the Bushes invited to Camp David? You've asked me about this a few times. I swear to you I didn't even know about this until you told me." Joel leaned into the table. "You're the only one asking me about this. Very few people in the White House know about it because it's no big deal. No one is really interested in it."

O'Reilly reached for her glass, leaned back and took a sip of wine, all the while locking her eyes on Hirsch's. He could not help but notice her look of disbelief.

Joel looked at Maura, exasperated. "Why is this so important to you? He's just meeting a friend."

"You know I am the curious type of girl, Joel. And, I'm not so sure that this person is 'just' a friend."

The waiter arrived with their salads. After he left the table, Joel shrugged and looked at Maura. "What more do you want from me? I really think you are making too much of this. There is an old friend who lives in the area where the president is making a campaign stop. They're going to spend some time together. Come on, Maura, presidents have always done stuff like this. They're entitled to a private life, at least for part of their time in office."

Maura took a forkful of salad as she looked at Joel, studying his face as he talked. Over the years, she had become proficient at judging if a source was lying to her or withholding information. And Joel was pretty easy to read. Poor Joel. He was a needy guy. Just like many of her Jewish girlfriends described their husbands (or, more likely, ex-husbands). She was not ashamed or embarrassed about the one-night stand she had with Joel a few months ago. She was long past that type of female guilt, and the tryst had resulted in information she would not have obtained otherwise. Morty Rosen would have been proud that she "took one for the team," as he was fond of saying. Besides, she'd been stepped over by men early in her career more times than she cared to remember; she didn't mind taking advantage of one every now and then as simple payback.

She was trying to let Hirsch down gently tonight without destroying their relationship. He was a source that she could use for the rest of this administration. But she needed to know more about the president's friend. If Rosen was right about the friend, this could be a game changer for the *Chronicle* and O'Reilly. She had to tread carefully. If it meant leading Joel on a bit, so be it.

"Look Joel, let's just say we can agree to disagree, but I still think there is a story out there, whoever this friend turns out to be. If you can see your way to letting me know who this person is, if and when you find out, I would be very appreciative."

Well, Hirsch thought as his martini kicked in, *it can't hurt to try.* "And exactly how appreciative would you be?" he asked as subtlety as he could, all the while sounding like a drunk fraternity boy.

O'Reilly sat back in her chair and tried to not laugh in his face. "Look, Joel, I'm enjoying our relationship, sharing information that helps us both out. But there will be no side benefits tonight."

At this point, the waiter brought over their dinners. O'Reilly removed the napkin from her lap, smoothed it out and placed it back on her lap, all the time giving Hirsch a "don't fuck with me" look.

Hirsch looked at O'Reilly for a few moments after the waiter left, waiting for her to say something, anything. Then finally, Hirsch picked up his fork. "If I hear anything, and it's not sensitive, I'll think about it. But for the last time, I don't think you get it. This friend is no big deal."

With that, Hirsch looked down at his plate and focused on his food. They engaged in small talk thereafter, both intent on their meals and getting out of the restaurant. After they finished eating, the waiter cleared the table and brought the check. As Hirsch reached into his jacket for his wallet, O'Reilly threw a one-hundred-dollar bill on the table. "My turn, sweetie," she said. "You got the last one."

"Thanks, Maura," a very subdued Hirsch said. "I appreciate it."

They walked out of the restaurant toward O'Reilly's waiting car.

"Let's have dinner here before Phoenix. Okay? You can fill me in on the final agenda, guest list, whatever."

"Sure, Maura, sure. We can do that."

"I'll text you a few days before to confirm."

"Okay, Maura. Thanks for dinner and have a safe ride home. Do you want me to follow you?"

As Hirsch leaned in to kiss O 'Reilly, she quickly gave him a cheek. "No, Joel, that's not necessary. I might not be going directly home, anyway."

"Yeah, well, I guess the night is still young." It was eight o'clock.

The driver opened the door for O'Reilly to get in the back seat. She turned toward her dinner companion. "Joel, it was a pleasure." She gave his shoulder a gentle squeeze. "You're a good guy."

"Yeah. That's what my grandmother tells me."

O'Reilly got in the car, and the driver closed the door. As they pulled out of the parking lot, she told the driver to head back to the District. She looked out the back window and saw Hirsch standing in the middle of the parking lot, hands in his pockets, watching her drive away. *Poor Joel*, she thought. *I hope he doesn't get burned if Jake's plan works out the way he wants.*

Chapter 22

Jamal McDaniels stood up from his desk. He had been looking at the computer screen since 6:00 AM. He needed to stretch, walk around the office, get a fresh cup of coffee. He did no one any good if he misread another agent's report or missed a piece of information that was linked to something he read yesterday, last week or last month. Every criminal investigator learned in training that you had to stay fresh, stay focused, stay on point. It was just hard to remember that in the middle of a sensitive investigation like this one.

The meeting of the DAFFIE Phoenix Task Force was scheduled for 10:00 AM. The Task Force was formed at Jerry DeNigris' insistence once the existence of a DAFFIE cell in Phoenix was confirmed. The agents on the task force would compare notes, critique each other's theories on the case and discuss tactics going forward. After that meeting, McDaniels and Steve Masters would call Jerry DeNigris and Diana Surlee to bring them up to speed. At almost 9:00 AM, McDaniels walked to the kitchen at the other end of the floor, made himself a coffee and took the long way back to his desk. He reviewed his case file on Melinda Katzenberg. He was at a dead end. She definitely worked at CJ's bakery. McDaniels and his partner followed her there for three consecutive mornings. They observed her walk in the employees' entrance at the back of the shop, dressed in a baker's shirt, pants and clogs, similar to the dozen or so other workers who arrived at the same time.

However, the Social Security Administration had no record of any "Melinda Katzenberg" being on the payroll of CJ's. The SSA records did list four women with anglicized names on the payroll. They gave those names to their state police liaison who matched the names and personal information the Arizona driver's license database. The license photo for one "Kacey Hughes" matched Melinda Katzenberg.

She was their girl.

Now the Phoenix DAFFIE Task Force believed a suspected cell member was working under an alias in a bakery? DAFFIE infiltrated a bakery? Was DAFFIE planning to weaponize dinner rolls? Were they ensuring that CJ's line of gluten free breads and pastries was, in fact, gluten free? Were they preparing a retaliatory attack should CJ's refuse to bake a cake for a gay wedding?

The possibilities were endless.

The task force agents had done deep background investigations of the other suspected DAFFIE Phoenix cell members. A grade school teacher, a salesperson at organic food stores and a social worker, in addition to Wentworth and Katzenberg/Hughes. They all seemed to also work part time at Elle's. Nothing too out of the ordinary, nothing that stood out. They were all Caucasian, college educated, from upper-middle-class to wealthy backgrounds, who worked in mostly all female environments. The task force teams had the suspected cell members under surveillance for the past several weeks. They were never observed meeting as a single group, although they were seen together in smaller groups of two or three. But because of staffing shortages and the upcoming presidential visit, not enough manpower was available to place the cell members under surveillance twenty-four hours a day, seven days a week.

One team took videos of two of the suspects who lived together going to work, shopping and doing other daily activities. They posted those videos side by side with the Arizona Science Center videos for review by the task force. The faces of the two women at the science center were obscured. But the body shapes, gait and general mannerisms of the two DAFFIE suspects seemed similar, if not identical, to the women on the security tape of the science center. So, the task force was confident they had identified most of the DAFFIE cell members in Phoenix.

Now what?

Since the exotic dancer incident, the task force had not identified any terrorist or criminal acts attributable to DAFFIE. Indeed, no incidents tied to DAFFIE anywhere in the country had occurred in the past two months. McDaniels pointed this out at the last task force meeting and raised the question: was this the calm before the storm? But the task force could not answer that question. They could have Kacey Hughes/Melinda Katzenberg arrested on state charges with the fake driver's license, but what good would that do? Would the DAFFIE cell just go underground? How would they know if they had successfully disrupted DAFFIE's plans when they didn't know what the plans were?

No, McDaniels was resigned to the fact that the task force had not yet gathered enough evidence to form a plan of action against DAFFIE. That was what he was going to tell DeNigris in this morning's call. He did not anticipate the phone call being a pleasant one.

Chapter 23

Elle Wentworth placed a fresh pot of chamomile tea with lemongrass on the kitchen counter along with a plate of organically grown fruit. The group would be arriving soon. This was to be the first meeting since Wentworth returned from her "vacation." Wentworth had met her counterparts from the other DAFFIE cells. The cell leaders met periodically to share intelligence, evaluate prospective members and discuss proposed activities of the individual cells. While each cell operated independent of the others, the leaders reviewed and approved all undertakings of the individual cells to ensure that they comported with DAFFIE's goals.

DAFFIE cells also existed in Los Angeles, Portland and San Francisco. Members of the individual cells did not know the locations or leaders of the other cells. They only knew that sister cells were out there sharing their aspirations for a radical reordering of the male dominated society and willing to take direct action to see those dreams realized. The DAFFIE leaders always conducted their meetings at the same bed and breakfast outside of San Francisco. They rented out the entire house and had the place to themselves once the owners finished cleaning up after breakfast and left. It was a B&B that catered to lesbians and had an entirely vegan menu. For all the owners knew, these were a group of college friends who got together every few months to reminisce.

DAFFIE actually had its genesis at this B&B. Over the years a group of like-minded womyn from the West Coast met here, bonded and became determined to make a difference. Out of a shared sense of victimhood, stemming from a callous and unjust patriarchal power structure, hatred of climate change deniers and the love of cats, DAFFIE was born. DAFFIE had grown from a group of six womyn, united in their contempt for old white men and aged red meat, and was now prepared to strike a blow for woke womyn across the country, nay, the world.

Wentworth, of course, was the first to realize that Whitcomb's visit to Phoenix presented DAFFIE with an opportunity for the movement to make a real difference in society. The Phoenix cell had only two months to plan its operation but Wentworth, a resourceful and dynamic leader, was up to the task. The DAFFIE cell leaders agreed with her suggestion at the outset that the cells should go into a deep sleep mode so as to not attract the attention of law enforcement agencies as the Phoenix cell completed its preparations. She had presented the DAFFIE leaders with an operational plan at their meeting. Wentworth's confederates examined the plan in great detail, forcing her to defend every aspect of the plot. She had anticipated most of the questions and many of the objections posed by the other cell leaders. She had answered all their concerns.

By the end of the third day, as they sat in the hot tub with their chilled drinks, the DAFFIE leadership agreed with Wentworth's plan. Operation Layer Cake was a go.

Now Wentworth had to go over the final plan with the Phoenix cell again. And again. And again. Nothing could be left to chance. Wentworth trusted the members of the Group. Even Melinda Katzenberg had turned a corner and was no longer viewed as a weak link. They would continue to review and rehearse until Wentworth was satisfied. And Wentworth was never satisfied, which was one of the reasons she was a great leader.

As the Group began to arrive, in fifteen-minute intervals, Wentworth felt confident. They were moving forward according to plan. The only thing Wentworth worried about were the unknown unknowns. She had heard or read that term once, the idea that we do not know what we do not know, and the idea had stuck with her. She had forgotten where she had first heard this idea, but it made a great deal of sense to her at the time. It must have been a wise person. She would have to deal with these unknowns if and when they arose. And she would. This was going to be the chance for DAFFIE to make a difference for oppressed womyn, soon to be unyoked from the tyranny of the modern Western patriarchy. She wasn't going to let anything get in the way now.

Chapter 24

President Whitcomb took off his jacket and tie, loosened his collar and rolled up his sleeves. He was in the family quarters at the White House. He had just finished a dinner meeting with Denis Lenihan, Fawn Liebowitz, the vice president, the Secretary of Housing and Urban Development and three Republican governors. They were finalizing the proposals for middle-income and lower-income housing projects in each governor's largest city. Lenihan wanted the housing projects to break ground prior to the coming primary campaign seasons for the president and the three governors. Although the primary campaigns were more than a year away, the selection of housing sites, soliciting bids from contractors, awarding contracts, and myriad of other essential details for government projects of this size, was a lengthy and intensive undertaking.

President Trump had done a good job in reducing the morass of government red tape during his term. Nevertheless, Whitcomb and his allies still had to deal with the remnants of the deep state as well as ordinary government bureaucracies. Lenihan wanted to make sure visible progress on all three housing projects had been realized by the time primary season rolled around.

The president had dismissed his valet for the evening and was alone. He lit a cigar and poured himself two fingers of Jameson. The White House was probably the only government building in the District in which the omnipresent "No Smoking" prohibition was routinely disregarded, and no one cared. He moved to his favorite chair and kicked off his shoes as he sat down. After a few deep breaths and a sip of whiskey, he reached into his pocket to retrieve a small key chain. He unlocked the door to the side table next to his chair. He took out the cell phone with the strip of green tape from the basket containing three cell phones in the table. He dialed a number and waited.

"It's me," the president said, suddenly rejuvenated after another grueling day. "So, looks like we're going to get to spend some time together in a few weeks."

The president smiled and nodded. "Me too. It's been too long. I am really, really looking forward to this. Just so you know, as soon as my team decided to set up this road show extravaganza, I insisted that Phoenix be one of our stops."

The president sipped his drink and listened. "I hope you are ready for a workout. I know I'll need one. Squaw Peak has some good trails, right?"

"We'll see who keeps up with who. And no, the Secret Service doesn't help me up the steep parts."

"I'll keep up with you, don't worry. Besides, my guys will have the drinks and towels. You won't want to get too far from us."

"Dinner? Well, I think we should just have you meet me back at the hotel after the fundraiser. We can relax in my room. Yes, in private. We're bringing out the White House chef. I've already told him to make your favorite. Dry-aged New York strip, medium rare, with peppercorn sauce. That's still your favorite, right?"

"Yes, yes, butter and sour cream with the baked potatoes. I'll share my Lipitor with you that night. My daughter? She's doing fine. She has turned into a great kid. My ex-wife and I are very happy. And your son? That's good to hear. I'd love to see him sometime. It's all about them, right?"

"Okay. It was great hearing your voice. I'm really, really looking forward to this. What? Yes, I know I said that already. But I meant it."

The president laughed. "Unless the world ends between now and then, I'll see you in Phoenix. We'll have some fun. Talk to you soon."

Chapter 25

Krissy Whitcomb was staying at the White House for the weekend. She was in between boyfriends and had some time to spend with her father. She had visited her mother and stepfather a few weeks ago. Graduate school was starting in a few weeks, and she wasn't sure how often she would be getting to DC once classes started. The Phoenix road show was coming up soon, and Krissy loved the desert. She also heard from PJ that Uncle Moshe and a new girlfriend were going to make the trip. And she had got to thinking.

She and her father were having an early dinner in the Family Residence before he went out to a ceremony at the Kennedy Center. "So, Dad, how about I go to Phoenix with you? It's right before school starts. I'd get to see you in action!"

The president looked at his daughter, squinting his eyes as he finished his dinner and pushed his plate away. He wasn't expecting this. "Well, honey, I don't think so. Not this trip."

He could see a slight but genuine look of disappointment in her face. He was going to have to scramble now. "Look, you know I always enjoy your company. And I'm told by the campaign team having you make appearances with me always bumps up my favorables. But this trip, it's not such a good idea."

"No?" Krissy looked down as she pushed the food around her plate, not eating. Whitcomb recognized this as a sign of her disappointment; she had done that when she got upset since she was ten.

"No. You see, I have a fundraiser the first night at someone's house. It is a small one, which means there'll be heavy hitters there that I'll have to pay attention to. The next day I have to visit a hospital and meet with some of the patients and staff. But before and after that, I will be holed up at the hotel with my people. We have several issues, several significant issues, swirling around that aren't going to go away because I hopped on a plane out West. We're going to be working for a good part of the trip. I don't think this is a good one for you to tag along."

"But I can hang out with PJ. And I love meeting Uncle Moshe's girlfriends. They're always so beautiful and glamorous."

"Well, not to burst your bubble, but PJ is going to be working while he's out there. He's not going to have a lot of free time to keep you occupied. And Moshe, he and his lady friend are coming out, but I'm not sure when," Whitcomb said, lying. "He may not even get there until the fundraiser the second night." The president looked at his daughter with what passed as a stern face. "I don't think it's a good trip for you. Not this time. It's just not going to work out."

Krissy looked at her father. "Is there something you're not telling me, why you don't want me on this trip?"

Krissy was not coming to Phoenix. Whitcomb had complete confidence in Jerry DeNigris and his protection detail. He was personally unconcerned (well, maybe a little) with the specter of DAFFIE's Phoenix cell looming over the road show; he had already experienced and survived combat. But he was not going to place his daughter in a potentially hostile situation, especially since the Secret Service, according to his chief of staff, had not yet uncovered what DAFFIE was plotting. Krissy didn't need to know that.

Besides, he already had a hiking and dinner companion lined up. And nothing was going to interfere with that hike or dinner. Krissy didn't need to know that either. "No, honey, I'm not holding anything back. It's just not doable this time."

Krissy looked at her father. She knew from his tone this was a lost cause. She wasn't mad at him, just disappointed. Disappointed enough to exact some revenge.

The president stood up from the table. "We okay?"

"Yes. I'll get over it eventually."

"Good. I have to get going. What are you doing tonight?"

"Two friends from college are in town. They're coming over." Krissy stood up to leave. She said over her shoulder, "We're going to get drunk, smoke some weed and have rough sex in the Lincoln Bedroom. Enjoy the show, Dad."

That felt good, Krissy thought as she walked out.

Chapter 26

"Time for the call?" Jake Rosen asked as Fran Ritzie walked into his office.

"Yes, I'll get Tony on the phone," Ritzie said and went to Rosen's conference table, opened the contacts page of his phone, and dialed Tony Montanez's number on the speakerphone. Rosen moved over to the table as Ritzie hit the speaker button.

"Hello, Tony here."

"Hello Tony, it's Fran and Jake Rosen."

"Hello Tony, it is nice to speak to you again," Rosen chimed in.

"Hello Fran, hello Jake, good to talk to you both. And thanks very much for all your help on this, by the way."

"We are happy to be of assistance in any way we can," Rosen replied.

"Well, let me tell you, it is going better than I thought. With that influx of cash, we've been able to stockpile plenty of food, clothing and other supplies. Some people arrived here with only the shirts on their backs, literally," Montanez chuckled. "Actually, some of them, I think, have never lived outside of a city or suburb before. We've been holding remedial camping tutorials for some of these folks. But it's all good. We have plenty of tents. We've even put up a couple of teepees; there are some pretty good Youtube videos on how to erect them."

"Tony, I just wanted to say I saw a great photo earlier today," Ritzie interrupted. "The one I sent you, Jake, on the protests. The one with the children blocking the construction vehicle."

"Yes, Tony, what a fantastic shot," Rosen spoke up. "It reminded me of that fellow standing in front of the tanks at Tiananmen Square. Talk about great optics. Tell me, Tony, did the construction worker get out of the truck to yell at the children? Did the police come and drag the children away? Did any of those alt-right goons attack the children?"

Montanez cleared his throat to speak. "No, not really. That picture was taken after the construction workers had left. We were in a staging area, I guess you could call it. There wasn't any construction activity going on at the time. We had one of our guys put a hard hat on and get in the truck and then had the kids stand in front of the truck. And then we took the pictures."

Ritzie and Rosen looked at each other. Ritzie shrugged. "Works for me."

"Yes, me too," Rosen joined in.

"Tony, this is Fran. I'll get some of the Network people to publish it in the next few days."

"Excellent. Also, the camp is about half full. More people are going to be coming from the West Coast. They should be arriving over the next two weeks. By the time Whitcomb gets here, we'll have a full contingent. We've named it 'Camp Restless Spirit,' by the way."

"Very appropriate," Rosen said. "Has a nice ring to it."

Fran nodded in agreement. "What about the Antifa people," Ritzie asked.

"Oh, they'll be here. Our contacts tell us they'll be coming in gradually, mixing in with the protest supporters from Seattle and San Francisco. They intend to keep a low profile, at least initially. But we expect a fair number of counter protesters from the alt-right to show up. When they do, the Antifa people will swing into action. And we'll be there to get it all on video."

"Sounds like a plan," Ritzie responded.

"We also have our rebuttal to Whitcomb's speech set up. I've known this guy-I mean gal-for years. Since he-uh, excuse me, she-was a patrol officer. You'll be impressed. He carries himself-uh, dammit, she carries herself well. We have the draft of his-I mean her-prepared remarks. I gave it to one of your guys, Fran."

"Yes, he emailed it to me. I'll look it over in a day or two and get back to you."

"Ok, thanks."

Rosen leaned toward the speaker phone. "Tony, tell me where we stand on Whitcomb's friend. Any progress on that front?"

"We're still looking at that, Jake. Whitcomb was in this area twice in college during spring baseball trips. Colleges from all over the

East and Midwest came out here for one or two weeks. There's no mention of him in the local press, other than his name appearing in box scores. Of course, back then, the Internet and social media didn't exist like today. There haven't been any references to friends of his living in this area since he became president. No reports anywhere about anyone from here visiting him at the White House."

Looking at Rosen, Ritzie said, "You mentioned in an email a few days ago about his campaign stop in Phoenix a few years ago. Can you elaborate on that?"

"Sure. He made one visit to Phoenix during his campaign, about two months before the election. I reviewed all the news reports about that. I also spoke to two of the local reporters who covered his appearance. By the way Fran, both of them would like to join the Network."

"Great, Tony. Send me some information on their background, where they are now, and I'll get back to you."

"Sure thing. Anyway, in speaking with these reporters, it turns out that there was a three hour or more gap between campaign functions in the late afternoon of the day he visited."

Rosen spoke up: "That is somewhat unusual for a campaign stop. They always have the candidate's appearances scripted to the minute. And they go from early in the morning until late at night nonstop. Do you agree, Fran?"

"Certainly. Any idea what he was up to, Tony?" Ritzie asked.

"No, gents, we've tried to pin that down. But, although it seems like a big deal now, apparently at the time no one thought much about it. From what I gather, Whitcomb and the press who were traveling with him got in Phoenix after midnight the night before. And as you said, Jake, his first function was an early breakfast meeting with local Republican officials. People assumed his staff just cleared a few hours in his schedule for some down time in the afternoon. Quite frankly, most of the press following him back then were happy to catch up on some sleep that afternoon too."

Jake paused to consider Montanez's report. "What about the Alpha team members we sent to you?"

"Hey, I'm happy to have the help. I've paired each of them with a local reporter. They're out here as we speak, turning over every stone. But we haven't found anything yet, sorry to say."

Rosen and Ritzie looked at each other. Ritzie was prepared for Rosen to erupt in frustration at the apparent lack of progress. But Rosen looked more perplexed than angry. Rosen leaned back in his chair, deep in thought.

"You guys still there?" Tony asked.

"Yes, Tony, we're still here," Ritzie replied.

"Jake, I understand you are sending some other folks out here to help us out. A photographer and some other guy?"

"Yes, Tony. They will be arriving a day or two before Whitcomb."

"Well, I'm happy to help them out anyway I can."

"We will certainly let you know. But they are prepared to operate on their own. They have a specific objective, and they will know what to do."

"If you're telling us to stay out of their way, we can do that too."

"I am not saying that exactly, but I think you get the point. Anything else, Fran?"

"No, I think everything is moving according to plan. Tony, thanks again for all your help. I'll talk to you in a few days."

"Ok, gentlemen. Look forward to it."

Rosen looked down at the floor, his chin resting on his clasped hands with interwoven fingers. After a few moments, he addressed Ritzie. "It appears we will have to rely on Shooter and the Italian to identify Whitcomb's mystery friend."

"Well, if so, we're still in a good position with Shooter, you know that. Either way, Jake, we'll learn who the friend is. And we'll have photos of them together, to top it off. We're still in good shape."

"Yes, I hope so. I certainly hope so."

Chapter 27

PJ and Cassie were in his apartment, watching a game, drinking beer and eating in front of the television. He had spoiled himself a few weeks earlier and bought a sixty-inch ultra-smart television. The thing did everything except heat the pizza. They had a fight during Cassie's last visit. Her endless questions about the Phoenix road show. Never ending, annoying questions. He had finally yelled at her: "God dammit, if you're so interested in who the president's friend is, come out to Phoenix with me and I'll introduce you."

To top it off, he blew up when she suggested he ask one of the Secret Service agents who would be traveling with the president about the mystery friend. "You seriously want me to ask a member of the Secret Service about the private plans of the President of the United States?" he had said incredulously. "Do you want me to wind up in the basement of the White House, tied to a chair, with a bunch of pissed off guys with guns and rubber hoses asking me why I'm so goddamn nosy?"

That had not gone over well, so to shut her up, PJ told her he would try to find out with whom the president was meeting in Phoenix. He did check with the valets, a couple of buddies in the travel office and on Denis Lenihan's staff. A few people knew that a few open hours in POTUS's schedule had been slotted, but no one knew with whom the president was spending that time. In fact, some professed to be vaguely aware of the plans for the morning hike but unaware of the dinner plans for after the fundraiser at the Arizona Science Center. No one knew the identity of the president's companion. PJ couldn't decide if no one knew the identity POTUS's friend because it was being kept secret or it was no big deal to anyone on the presidential staff. And he didn't care.

"Look, grasshopper," PJ said as he opened his beer, "I asked around the White House about the president's friend."

"Who, PJ? Who did you ask?"

"I asked friends, friends I know who might know about this visit. No one knows who this person might be. Unless they're lying to me, no one knows who he is hiking with or having dinner with later that night. And no, I did not ask any Secret Service agents about this. Don't go there." Finished with it in his mind, PJ grabbed the remote to change the channel to another game. He then turned to face Cassie. "I'm tapped out, honey. I'll keep my ears open, but as far as I can tell, no one knows who he is meeting out there. And POTUS ain't talking about it." PJ turned toward the television to watch the game.

Cassie began to rub the back of PJ's neck. "You're so good to me, PJ, I love you. You're so smart. You keep asking around, PJ, you'll find out who POTUS's friend is. You will make me very happy. And I will make you very happy, too, PJ darling."

"Yeah, sure thing. We'll both be very happy, grasshopper." He put his beer down and pulled his lady friend closer. "It's almost halftime of this game. What say we retire to the bedroom to wake up some old echoes of Notre Dame?"

Chapter 28

Denis Lenihan took a sip of diet soda and pushed his dinner plate to the side. Another late night at the White House. Most of the staff had left an hour ago. He initialed the last action memo and put it in the approved folder. How many of these did he see each day? Ten? Fifteen? More? Agency heads, cabinet officials, military commanders, Congressional party leaders, all convinced that their particular budget request, pork barrel project, legislative initiative or proposed regulation would be the most important item on the president's agenda that day. Every day in the White House was a juggling act. Constantly trying to keep airborne the hopes, schemes, plans and dreams of senators, governors, donors, party hacks and sometimes ordinary citizens who somehow got the attention of the national media or a publicity seeking politician and demanded action from the White House TODAY! NOW! IMMEDIATELY! TO SAVE THE CHILDREN!

Lenihan would always remember the thrill of winning the Republican primary, the sheer ecstasy of victory in the general election, assembling a top-flight staff to hit the ground running once they assumed office, the joy and majesty of the inauguration. The confidence that the Whitcomb administration was going to do great things so that people across the globe would be happy and cheer for them. And, he asked himself, how did he feel now? Now that the administration was past its honeymoon phase, what never ceased to amaze the chief of staff was that the White House seemed to constantly perform damage control. A hurricane or tsunami hits a coastal area, a supposed ally backs out of a treaty or a trade deal, a judicial or executive branch nominee reveals a nanny problem, terrorists in some God forsaken part of the world or a major Western city attack tourists. Whatever was on POTUS's schedule for the day gets tossed out the window of the Oval Office, and everyone goes into crisis mode.

Having been a partner in a large Manhattan law firm, supervising teams of bright, energetic, enthusiastic young attorneys, negotiating with equally experienced and talented adversaries on multi-million-dollar deals, had done absolutely nothing to prepare Lenihan for the demands of working in the White House. His experience as chief of staff for a Republican governor of a blue state, having to deal with a Democratic legislative majority in thrall to public employee unions and identity politics, had certainly helped, but only to a small degree. He knew that former presidents uniformly said when they left office that nothing in their life prepared them for the responsibilities of the presidency. Well, if they ever asked that question of former chiefs of staff, Lenihan was sure the response would be the same.

And now, Phoenix, which a few months ago had been only one of several road show stops, was evolving into something much more. Reverend Hood would be joining them, looking to get his holy ass kissed and bringing a list of good ol' boys he'd like to see in those fancy Supreme Court robes. Moshe Schwartz was showing up with an intelligence agent from a foreign country. A protest by Native Americans, reports of which were sure to be spread across the country by the resurrected Network, seemed to be growing by the day. And a group of eco-terrorists was planning some sort of disruption for publicity purposes or worse.

Phoenix was becoming a problem for the chief of staff because he liked to be in control. Control was important to him. Many aspects of this job were controllable: the timing of the release of announcements, those with bad news as well as the ones with good news; the selection of candidates for political appointments; and doling out favors to allies or administering punishment to enemies. All of these could be done on his schedule, at a point in time of his choosing, to the greater benefit of the Whitcomb administration. The situations that Lenihan couldn't control gave him sleepless nights. And he couldn't control his best friend, the president, who was determined to spend some quality time with an old friend. This was not going to change no matter what Lenihan said or did.

Therefore, Lenihan had to ensure that news of the president's meeting did not slip out, for several reasons. Lenihan only had to look back at the track record of some of Whitcomb's Democratic predecessors in Trenton for cautionary tales of politicians who weren't in control. One of those predecessors was a career politician who described the governor's job as his dream. And it did turn into a dream of sorts, a nightmare, actually. Political observers in New Jersey still shake their heads in amazement. The governor's trip to Atlantic City. The muffled screams coming from his hotel room. The state trooper bodyguards who broke down the door only to see the naked governor tied spread eagle to the bed shouting, "Armageddon, Armageddon." A man in a thong and a Darth Vader mask straddling him, holding a double-bladed battle axe over his head, poised to strike. The first trooper through the door shot the masked intruder who, the bodyguards learned once they got the mask off, was the state's homeland security director. The axe turned out to be plastic. Fortunately for the director, it was not a fatal shot. Unfortunately for the director, and the governor, a few members of the hotel staff witnessed the incident and photos of the naked, bound governor shortly made their way to the Internet.

Another predecessor was a Goldman Sachs alumnus who, notwithstanding his huge personal fortune, never failed to profess his devotion to and affinity for the working class (as all millionaire bankers seem to do when they depart Wall Street to run for public office). He was so enamored of the labor force that he chose to divorce his wife and take up with an official of a large construction workers' union. He showered her with cars, clothes, jewelry and a house at the Jersey shore. Alas, when the relationship ended, a palimony suit ensued. The details in the woman's complaint proved to be very damaging to the governor, resulting in one term in office. Her claims that he made her wear overalls and steel-toed work boots to bed and used WD-40 oil as a lubricant raised eyebrows throughout the state. Her comment at the press conference announcing the palimony suit that "you wouldn't believe the things he made me do with a plumber's wrench" sealed the governor's political fate.

Of course, the sexual escapades of these two Democratic governors had no small impact on Whitcomb's victorious gubernatorial race. Whitcomb's divorce early in his first term in Trenton had a minimal negative impact on his favorability ratings. The fact that neither he nor his ex-wife chose a scorched earth approach during their divorce worked both to his and Kathleen's advantage. Since the divorce, Whitcomb's social life had not generated any significant reports in the press or social media. Occasionally, Whitcomb and Lenihan, himself divorced five years before Whitcomb, were seen in restaurants or at functions with women but not much was made of it.

Once Whitcomb assumed the presidency, periodic stories appeared describing friends from New Jersey or the military who spent weekends at the White House or Camp David. Always two or three couples, sometimes with an unattached woman, presumably Whitcomb's companion for the weekend. But never the same one. And none of them chose to grant interviews, post on Instagram or tweet about their time with the president. The public didn't seem to care about Whitcomb's divorce or his personal life. But Lenihan knew this lack of attention was because nothing salacious, crude or otherwise controversial was being publicized about Whitcomb's personal life.

Lenihan also knew that what Hollywood celebrities and New York sophisticates viewed as indecent or prurient behavior was a world apart from what a conservative evangelical minister, with a national following clustered in flyover country whose support in the next election was crucial, would find unacceptable in a political candidate. The president's insistence on including Phoenix as a road show stop didn't surprise Lenihan. And he knew not to waste his time trying to dissuade him from making that visit. Attempts to dissuade hadn't worked during his campaign a few years ago and wouldn't work now.

Lenihan had not attended any of the previous road shows. He preferred to stay in the background, as would any good chief of staff. Mangini and his crew were quite capable of handling any emergency that arose, with Lenihan at the White House to oversee responses from there. However, given everything that was going on in Phoenix, Lenihan decided that he would make the trip. They would get a few adjoining rooms and have the White House Communications Agency set up a miniature situation room in the hotel. He and Mangini would manage the road show from there.

The Secret Service would disperse a fleet of drones over Phoenix, monitoring the Native American protests and the fundraisers. From the situation room, they would be able to observe POTUS as he moved about Phoenix. The protection detail would create a movable barrier surrounding him. At least, that was the plan.

What was Lenihan's biggest worry? Lesbian eco-terrorists? Native American protesters with a taste of Antifa? A powerful clergyman from the heartland waiting to be coddled in return for political support? An Israeli spy consorting with one of POTUS's largest supporters?

And the president determined to meet up with an anonymous friend, no matter the what repercussions if the media got hold of that. What could go wrong?

Lenihan stood up from his desk and stretched. He wanted to get home, get out of his suit, have a drink. He grabbed his jacket and stuffed some folders in his briefcase. He still had an hour or so of reading ahead of him. As he left his office, he realized he would just have to tough it out and make sure Phoenix did not blow up. For himself. For his best friend. And for the good of the country. But mostly for his best friend.

Chapter 29

The Phoenix cell of DAFFIE was meeting in the back of Elle Wentworth's shop. Wentworth stood in the center of the room, the cell members arrayed before her in a semicircle. She began by congratulating the Group on how far they had progressed in the last few months. "We are acting, not so much as a machine, or a single unit, but as an integrated being comprised of different but complementary parts, working together toward the same objective. I want to emphasize to each of you, as we move closer to the day, we have to remain focused. I want you all to be confident in yourselves, your sisters in this room, and our plan, which we have practiced again and again."

As Wentworth spoke, she looked at each cell member, locking eyes momentarily but intensely. "You know your roles. And as I have told you repeatedly, each role, no matter how small, is important. You all have to succeed individually, or the Group will fail."

The DAFFIE members turned and looked at one another, nodding, acknowledging their leader's inspiring words.

"Thanks to Melissa, we have the dessert menu for the fundraiser reception at the science center," Wentworth continued, nodding toward the clearly thrilled-to-be-mentioned-in-the-pep talk member. "We will be making a special cake and, again, thanks to Melissa, switching it with CJ's. We will have a not so pleasant surprise for that Nazi, racist, fascist, hyper-masculine, misogynistic, planet destroying, animal killing leader and his mindless supporters of the corrupt and illegal Republican regime that has ruled this country for too long."

After Wentworth stopped speaking, one of the members raised her hand and slowly stood. She spoke in a halting tone. "Elle, I know we have talked about this before, but some of us," she paused as she glanced around the room, "some of us are still uncomfortable with part of the plan. Can't we please substitute one of our cakes, prepared our way, for the cake on CJ's menu? I'm sure we can duplicate CJ's cake using our recipes, which we all know are for the best for humankind, without raising any suspicions." She sat down, looking as if she were trying to melt into her chair.

Wentworth acknowledged the question with a nod. She was not surprised. This concern had been raised before, and she had abruptly dismissed it. In hindsight, she realized, dismissing it had been a mistake. She should have let the Group discuss the issue. They could have taken time to weigh the pros and cons. Everyone could have had the opportunity to voice their opinions and had their full say, and then Wentworth could have said "no."

Wentworth looked at the floor and paced back and forth, her hands clasped behind her back. She raised her head to look at the

Group. Her steely gaze met the face of each womyn before she spoke. "We have worked long and hard on this operation. We all have. And we have never before undertaken an operation like this, one in which the potential rewards are so great, matched only by the risks to DAFFIE and our cause. Because of that, we cannot jeopardize the success of this operation just to please ourselves. I'm not happy with some of the things our plan calls for, but I see no other way.

"No detail is too small to ignore. This cake has to be made precisely the way CJ's makes theirs. We can't take the chance that someone who is familiar with CJ's products detects a difference. Remember, our cake is going to be side by side with other baked goods from CJ's. What if someone notices a difference and raises an alarm? We can't risk the operation that way."

By now, the DAFFIE members were looking at Elle as if they were grade school children who were being firmly lectured by their teacher as to why they couldn't have a promised class picnic that afternoon because of their misbehavior.

Wentworth radiated authority as she continued. "The cake has to be made exactly the way CJ's does," she repeated, raising her voice. "We have to use unbleached all-purpose flour, sugar, cream, artificial coloring and . . ."

"Don't say it," one Group member called out, her voice quivering. Another started whimpering, her face in her hands. "Please don't say it."

Wentworth stared straight ahead, not a scintilla of doubt in her voice. "We have to kill an egg. As a matter of fact, we have to kill several eggs. It has to be done. For the integrity of Operation Layer Cake. For the good of our cause."

By now, the DAFFIE girls were sobbing, holding on to one another, tears cascading.

Wentworth softened her tone, trying to hide her annoyance. "Look, I know this is important to some of you, many of you. I understand your pain. But all I can say is that, as your leader, I have made this decision. And it is the correct one. It is for the good of Operation Layer Cake and the good of this Group. I believe, in time, you all will come to understand that. In fact, I know you will."

Wentworth gave the Group a few moments to digest what she had said then moved to the table off to the side, sat down and opened her laptop. As her laptop powered up, she looked at the Group and smiled. "Okay, let's go over the plan one more time, from the beginning."

Chapter 30

President Whitcomb and Denis Lenihan walked into the Oval Office, joining the staff members already present: Don Mangini, Sean Thornton and Fawn Liebowitz. They stood as the president entered the office. The group was meeting to brief him on the details of the upcoming Phoenix road show.

"Good afternoon, folks. How is everyone today?" the president asked then moved behind his desk as a flurry of responses was issued. He took off his suit jacket, draping it over his chair. He grabbed a pen and his road show folder off his desk and joined the group on the couches and chairs in the center of the room.

"Okay, let's get started," Lenihan said while Thornton handed the president a printed agenda. "Don, please take us through the schedule as it now stands."

"Sure. Mr. President, you leave Joint Base Andrews next Tuesday at 7:00 AM. You'll arrive at Luke Air Force Base at approximately 9:00 AM local time. Your briefing book will have the names of the base commander and his senior staff who will be greeting you on arrival. There will be a squad of helicopter pilots there for you to meet in a nearby hangar. You are then going to be taken up in the Air Force's newest helicopter with a team of pararescuers. They will be simulating a search and rescue mission with you observing. Not that you need an introduction to that."

The aides laughed at Mangini's comment, which drew a wry smile from POTUS. "Cool. That's cool. Those guys are good. I met a few of them in Iraq. I was always glad they were on my side."

Mangini continued the briefing: "When you get back from the demonstration, you'll meet with the base commander again. They'll be making a presentation to you on the base's missions, various functions and general capabilities. We'll have a few questions prepared for you to ask the base commander."

The president looked at Mangini with raised eyebrows. "Really, Don? You're going to feed me questions? That's not necessary. I've been on enough military bases in my time. If I see anything interesting, I'll ask the commander. I know the second-in-command there from a course we took together at the Naval War College. I'll have plenty to talk about with those folks."

"Okay, sir," Mangini said. "After your meeting with the commander, you'll be going to the cafeteria for lunch. There will be an NCO acting as your guide. You'll line up with the soldiers and get your lunch. The NCO will direct you to a table with ten enlisted troops and NCOs. He'll introduce you to them. Per your requests in the past, there won't be any officers at the table while you are dining.

There will be the pool press and photographers in the room during your lunch."

"Very good," the president said as he looked at his aides. "Believe me, it makes for more comfortable conversations with enlisted troops if there are no officers around."

"After lunch we're going to run you over to the base recreation center. There will be several dozen troops there with their families. You'll walk through the crowd in the gym. We'll give you plenty of time to stop and talk to the troops and their family members."

"Good. Excellent, actually."

"A group of grade school children are going to present you with a collage of family activities occurring on the base the last few months. Then you will give a brief speech on the new team heading the VA and the programs they're going to implement there. That will be a twenty-minute speech. You'll be on a stage, and there will be twenty troops seated behind you. You'll be able to mingle with them for a few minutes after your speech. When you leave, you walk out the back of the rec center, and your motorcade will take you to Air Force One. You are scheduled to be wheels up at 2:30 PM. It's a sixty-minute flight to Phoenix."

The president nodded as Mangini moved through the agenda. Lenihan was standing off to the side, gazing out a window, rubbing the back of his neck. He hadn't told anyone, but he was not looking forward to this trip.

"When you land in Phoenix, you'll go to your hotel to relax, change clothes, whatever," Mangini continued. "You'll be there for ninety minutes. The remote situation room will be up and running two days before you get there. We can swing by there in case you need to make secure calls or get on a video conference call."

The president nodded in agreement.

"I'll be there then," Lenihan said. "Don and I are going out the day before to make sure everything is in place."

"Good," the president replied.

"The Whitcomb to the Future fundraiser that night is at the home of David Schmidt. He's a former attorney who gave up law and made a fortune in real estate. Republican bigwig out there. Always attracted to women his own age, no Roy Moore problems there."

"Have I met him?" the president inquired.

"I don't think so," Mangini said, looking at Lenihan, who was shaking his head. "He was only active in local politics until President Trump was elected. He saw the unhinged tantrums, screeds, and Brian Ross-like fake news coming from Hollywood and the media and got involved with the RNC nationally. He started a 'Jews For The Republic' PAC that supported President Trump. He recently made a sizable contribution to your campaign with the understanding that he would be hosting the fundraiser. He's very excited to meet you and wants to bend your ear on a few issues."

"I'm a good listener. How many people will be there?"

"The headcount right now is sixty-seven," Mangini answered. "He can comfortably have up to eighty, so we may squeeze a few more in. You'll be arriving at 6:00 PM or so. The dinner, which is actually more like a cocktail party, is scheduled for three hours. I don't know if you'll get to meet everyone, but you'll get to shake hands with a good number of people."

"That's fine."

"Governor Rappaport will be attending the fundraiser, as you know," Mangini continued. "When you leave the fundraiser, the governor will ride with you back to your hotel. He'll be joining you with his chief of staff and one other aide for drinks. We'll set up a hospitality suite in one of our rooms. Maybe you can give him a quick tour of the situation room."

"Sure. He's a good man. I can have a drink with him."

"Yeah, we thought so. He'll want to discuss some things with you, some revenue sharing issues, Medicaid funding and probably our response to the Native American protests going on outside Phoenix."

"Okay. And that response will be what?"

"It would be that it is a federally funded project sought by the state and federal elected representatives of the people of Arizona for a number of years," Mangini replied. "The project meets regional transportation needs and is being completed in accordance with all local and federal environmental regulations."

The president nodded, making notes.

Denis Lenihan spoke up: "I'm still waiting to hear from the RNC about any information their security people were able to dig up." Lenihan turned to his assistant and said, "Fawn, please call Carl when we're done here and find out where we stand on that and let me know."

"I spoke to Jerry DeNigris yesterday," Lenihan continued. "The Arizona State Police are keeping an eye on the protests. Because of our road show, the Secret Service has met with the state police several times. There are noises about some extreme right wing, white nationalist groups mounting counter protests. Of course, if those knuckleheads show up, they anticipate that Antifa groups will make an appearance."

"Why miss an opportunity to get on CNN?" Liebowitz chirped.

"That's for sure," Mangini said. "What does it mean for our road show?"

"It means that the state and local police have to contain the protests to the construction sites," Lenihan said. "We're not going near there; so long as they stay there, we'll be okay."

"Okay, let's move on," the president said. He wasn't worried about the protests; he knew Lenihan and DeNigris would worry for him.

Mangini continued with his presentation: "We'll make sure to kick the good governor out of the hotel before 11:00 PM. The next day, Wednesday, you are free until noon," Mangini said and looked around the room.

Whitcomb stared at Mangini. Lenihan looked at the floor. The others focused on the printed agenda in their hands. The room was silent. Mangini continued: "You'll be visiting the Phoenix Children's Hospital and greeted by the president of the hospital and her senior staff. They will give you a tour of the hospital, and you'll wind up in the pediatric cancer wing. There will be several patients and their families there to meet you. We'll get some pictures of you with the families."

The president lowered his head, in effect, looking up at Mangini, a scowl on his face.

Lenihan saw his friend's reaction. "A photo opportunity with sick children? I assure you, Mr. President, we won't overdo it. It will be tasteful. But we're not going to miss it either. Go on, Don."

"After the visit to the cancer ward, you'll go to the hospital auditorium. You'll be giving a fifteen-minute speech on the proposed amendments to the health care reform bill that is pending in the Senate. After the speech, it's back to your hotel to return calls and respond to emails. There will be a brief staff meeting, then you'll have some time to review the speech for that night."

Mangini's presentation was going well, he felt. The president was paying attention and following the details. But, thought Mangini, *what is Lenihan pissed off about?* Lenihan didn't seem himself the past two weeks whenever the Phoenix road show came up. *Is he mad at me?*

"We head to the Arizona Science Center at 4:00 PM. You'll give your speech to the invited crowd in the adjacent park. The speech is thirty minutes or so. The state Republican organization has distributed tickets to about fifteen hundred people. It should be a friendly crowd. The most recent draft of the speech is in your binder. You'll finish the speech and meet a few local Republicans who will escort you to the science center. There will be about one hundred seventy-five at the fundraiser. The cocktail party will run from 5:00 PM to 8:00 PM. Your fifteen-minute speech is scheduled for 7:00 PM."

Lenihan looked around the room. He had done a good job assembling this staff. They worked hard, were loyal to the president and did whatever was asked of them. They were good people. As an attorney, he knew that the act of omitting material information was the same as affirmatively making material misrepresentations, or, in layman's terms, lying. At times, he felt bad withholding material information from them.

But not very often. And not today.

"We'll be dragging you out of the fundraiser at 7:45 PM. We'll head directly to the hotel. You're having dinner at the hotel. The chef will be serving dinner at 9:00 PM. A little late—"

The president cut him off. "Not a problem."

"We leave Phoenix at 7:30 AM local time the next morning. Back to DC."

The president looked at the agenda as Mangini finished up.

Lenihan stared straight ahead, looking at nothing in particular.

"That's the schedule, Mr. President. Any questions?"

"Nope, I'm good. Anybody have any questions?"

There was a collective shaking of heads.

"Okay, we're done here. Thanks for coming," Lenihan said and stood led the group to the door of the Oval Office.

As the group exited, the president sat in his chair, reviewing the Phoenix agenda. When everyone was gone, the president put the agenda to the side. "Looks like a plan, Denis."

Lenihan looked at the president, his face expressionless.

"You don't look too happy, buddy," Whitcomb said.

Lenihan headed toward the door leading out of the Oval Office. As he reached the door, he turned to face the president. "It doesn't matter if I'm happy. It only matters if you're happy. Are you happy?"

"Yes, I'm happy. And getting happier by the day. Phoenix will be fine. Everything will be fine, Denis. Have faith in the process."

"Sometimes I wish I had your confidence"

"Sometimes you have to fake it."

Chapter 31

Bobby Manzi and Shooter O'Neill arrived in Phoenix the day before Whitcomb was scheduled to land. They arranged to meet for the first time at a small Mexican restaurant near Phoenix Sky Harbor Airport. They had taken separate flights, rented their own cars and were staying at different hotels. O'Neill was in the parking lot, standing by his car, when Manzi arrived. Manzi recognized him from Jake Rosen's description. They introduced themselves and went into the restaurant. Their waitress took their lunch order. Manzi also ordered a frozen margarita; Shooter ordered water.

"You know, Mr. Shooter—that's what you want me to call you, right?—it would be easier if we stayed at the same hotel and rented one car."

"Listen, lad, Jake doesn't want that. And he's right. In case this goes south, we want as little to connect us as possible," he said and then laughed. "And Mr. Shooter is fine. I like the sound of that."

As Manzi sipped his drink he realized that Rosen was probably right this time.

After they finished lunch and left the restaurant, O'Neill said "Okay, let's swing by this park. What's the name again?"

"Squaw Peak."

"Squaw Peak. What the fuck kind of name is that? Indian, I guess," O'Neill said, answering his own question. "I guess there are a lot of them out here. We'll take your car."

The trip to Squaw Peak took twenty-five minutes. O'Neill hummed to himself the whole ride. "You want the radio on?" Manzi asked at one point. "No, lad, I'm fine," O'Neill replied as he continued humming. Manzi didn't recognize the songs he was humming, but he was reminded of the shitty Irish music he heard in New York around St. Patrick's Day. They arrived at Squaw Peak but had to park about a half-mile from the entrance. As they trudged to the entrance, they saw the steady stream of hikers entering and leaving the park and the congested lower paths of the park.

"Is it always this crowded?" O'Neill asked.

"Yeah, well, probably," Manzi said, "it's the middle of the day. They're going to be here early in the morning. According to our source, there aren't as many people around then. The Secret Service is going to block off a section of the park so they can hike on a trail by themselves. Part of the parking lot will be closed off too. We're going to have to get here early in the morning to get in here."

"Do you know which trail they'll be using?" O'Neill asked as he scanned the parking lot and lower trails.

"Nah. They'll get here before the park opens and pick one."

They entered the park and walked through the packed parking lot. O'Neill grabbed two maps from a kiosk and handed one to Manzi. They spent the next hour leisurely strolling through the parking lot and adjacent property, familiarizing themselves with the various trails and rest areas. As they walked around the park, O'Neill lit up a cigarette. Manzi tapped O'Neill on the shoulder and pointed to one of the "No smoking in the state park" signs that were displayed throughout the area. O'Neill looked at the sign, said "fuck it," and continued puffing.

O'Neill pointed to a nearby picnic area that sat on a rise, looking over the lot and the various trails. "Let's take a look."

When they got to the picnic area, Manzi sat down while O'Neill walked around the immediate area, surveying the park.

"We'll be fine," O'Neill said. "It's good that there will be other people here. It will be easier to blend in. And we do have to blend in. It probably gets more crowded later in the morning."

"Makes sense."

"I'm going to come here tomorrow when the park opens to see what it's like. You don't have to come. Actually, it's better that you don't."

"Okay."

After inspecting the park for a few more minutes, O'Neill sat down with Manzi. "I can cover most of the parking lot and lower part of the mountain from here," O'Neill said, throwing his cigarette stub to the ground. "I'll take photos of the mountain, those big cactus things over there, some of the other plants. The cops will think I'm just another photographer in love with desert scenery."

"What do you want me to do?"

"See those restrooms over there?" O'Neill pointed to an area seventy yards away. "The map shows trails behind the restrooms. You hang around there in case they use one of those trails. Between us, we'll see the entrances to all the trails. When he goes up, we'll know where he is coming down. I'll wander over and wait for them to come down and get some pictures. In the meantime, you can head to your car and wait outside the park. When this secret friend gets in a car to leave, I'll text you a description and license plate number. You can follow the car. That's the plan, right?"

"Right. I'll follow them to where they drop the friend off and we'll have an address."

O'Neill looked at Manzi in his imported Italian loafers, designer jeans and a dress shirt with several of the top buttons undone, his St. Francis medal on display. "You know we have to blend in, right? You're not wearing that outfit when we come here the next time, are you?"

"Nah, nah, I hear you, don't worry about it. I picked up some Lebron James sneakers and a desert camouflage Adidas tracksuit before I came out. I'll blend in."

"I'm sure you will."

*   *   *   *   *

Denis Lenihan and Don Mangini flew to Phoenix together on Monday, the day before POTUS was to arrive. They checked into the hotel, unpacked and met at the situation room. They were greeted by the ranking member of the technical staff, Navy Chief Petty Officer Katherine Chiocca. Both Lenihan and Mangini knew Chief Chiocca well and thought very highly of her.

She gave them a tour of the situation room, which was a conference room now guarded by a contingent of marines. The room was filled with two long rows of tables with multiple computer terminals, manned by technicians from the White House Communications Agency. The computers sat humming, whirling and pinging as the technicians monitored videos received from Arizona State Police and Secret Service drones, Phoenix Police Department and local traffic webcams and a satellite image of the greater Phoenix area. The screens displayed the hotel where the president was staying, the Arizona Science Center and adjacent park, and the highway construction site with the Native American protestors cordoned off in a designated area near their camp.

"We'll have a nice view of the festivities," Mangini chuckled.

Lenihan usually appreciated Mangini's easy going nature, but was not in a very good mood given all that was on his mind. His disposition did not improve when his cell phone buzzed, and he saw a text from his assistant in Washington marked "urgent." Excusing himself, he moved to the side. The venerable ambassador from Ireland, the Honorable Michael John Connelly Teehan, a fixture in the nation's capital for more than a decade, was requesting an immediate meeting with Lenihan. Informed that the chief of staff was in

Phoenix, he asked that a secure video conference call be scheduled as soon as possible, emphasizing the critical nature of the information he had for Lenihan.

Ambassador Teehan had been one of the first foreign diplomats Lenihan met once President Whitcomb assumed office. A devout Catholic, he had been a key intermediary between the Northern Irish Catholics, their Protestant counterparts and the British that resulted in the 1998 Good Friday Agreement that brought peace to Northern Ireland. Lenihan always found time to stop at his St. Patrick's Day reception at the Irish Embassy. Ambassador Teehan's warm personality was matched by his unique insights into Western European political and economic trends, which he freely shared with American government officials. He was a wise man.

Lenihan walked over to Mangini and Chief Chiocca. "Chief, could you arrange a secure video conference call in the next few hours?"

"Certainly. I can put you in the room next door. Who is the call with if I may ask?"

"The Irish Embassy in DC."

"That's fine. I'm sure their communications system is compatible with ours."

"I'll have my secretary send you the time and contact details."

"Aye aye, sir. Once I get that I can have you set up in fifteen minutes."

"Thank you, Chief."

Lenihan texted his secretary to schedule the call in the next two to three hours then confirm with Chief Chiocca and himself.

"What's going on?" Mangini asked as they left the situation room.

"Ambassador Teehan needs to speak to me urgently."

"Really? Why hasn't he gone through State?"

"Good question. I guess I'll find out in a few hours."

"Do you want me there?"

Lenihan looked at Mangini for a moment. "No, I'll handle this myself."

"Okay."

Lenihan rubbed the back of his neck as they walked to their temporary office.

*   *   *   *   *

Elle Wentworth, Melinda Katzenberg and one other cell member stood around the large table in the back of Elle's Cafe. The cafe was closed as usual on Monday. They had just taken several cakes out of the oven and were waiting for them to cool. Wentworth decided to do this in a small group. She knew that the other two cell members were still upset over her decision on the baking ingredients for Operation Layer Cake. They'd get over it.

"Let's make two cakes with our special ingredient. Let's layer them and ice them the way CJ's does," Elle said. "We want them to look just like CJ's."

Photographs of cakes from CJ's were laid out on the table. Katzenberg had taken the photos last weekend when CJ's staff was preparing for another event. There was also a cake from CJ's on the table. One of the DAFFIE members had picked it up on her way to Elle's earlier that day. Wentworth watched Katzenberg and her comrade layer the cakes and put the icing on, carefully concealing the cavity that had been baked into the cakes. DAFFIE's additional ingredient, made with the latest 3D print technology, consisted of a lightweight plastic compound and fit inside the cake perfectly.

When the cakes were finished, Wentworth picked up each one, inspecting the cakes with a practiced eye and comparing them to the photos. She then held each cake, one at a time, in one hand while she picked up the cake from CJ's in her other, comparing the appearance and weight of the group's cakes with that of CJ's. Wentworth was satisfied. She was confident that no one would notice anything out of order once DAFFIE's cake was switched for CJ's. Whitcomb's appearance at the Arizona Science Center was scheduled in two days. They would bake their own cake, with fresh butter cream icing, on the morning of his speech to replace CJ's cake. Operation Layer Cake was proceeding according to plan.

* * * * *

Chief Chiocca connected Lenihan with the Irish Embassy. Ambassador Teehan's assistant appeared on the screen. Lenihan thanked Chief Chiocca, who left the room, closing the door behind her as she returned the salute of the marine stationed outside.

Ambassador Teehan appeared on the screen, moving behind his desk. "Thank you, Siobhan," he said to his assistant. "Please close the door as you leave."

Lenihan could hear the door close. "Good afternoon, Denis," Ambassador Teehan said.

"Good afternoon, Mr. Ambassador."

"I am truly sorry, Denis, to impose upon you at this time. I'm sure you are, as you Americans like to say, juggling many balls with your trip to Arizona."

"Mr. Ambassador, it's always a pleasure to speak with you. I apologize for not setting this up sooner. I know it's later in the day for you, almost evening. What can I do for you?"

"No apology is necessary. Denis, the purpose of my call, the urgency about which I communicated to your assistant, is to relay sensitive information we have come upon. I believe you should be aware of this information and, actually, would want to be made aware of it."

"If that is the case, then I'm very grateful you called, Mr. Ambassador. I'm all ears."

"Another quaint American saying of which I am fond. Yes, well, Denis, I will try to put this as delicately as I can." The ambassador seemed hesitant to speak; Lenihan did not recall the normally gregarious diplomat this reticent.

"We are speaking today because of the indiscretions of one of our young embassy officers posted to Washington. This young man, let's call him Seamus, and that's not his real name, worked in our economic and trade section. An Irish company, working with the embassy to establish a presence in the United States, complained to us that confidential proprietary information, which had been provided to embassy personnel, including Seamus, somehow made its way into the hands of an unscrupulous competitor. As you can imagine, they were quite upset. Since the CEO of this company is a frequent golf partner of the prime minister, it caused quite a stir in Dublin."

"Economic espionage," Lenihan said.

"Exactly, Denis. Our security lads commenced an investigation. This investigation revealed that young Seamus had an American girlfriend of Korean descent. Our people determined that this young lady worked for a very high-end escort service in Washington named BAGI. Have you ever heard of that operation?"

"I have not."

"I didn't think you would. Neither did I until this matter. When Seamus was confronted with this, he, of course, expressed dismay that his girlfriend, who told him she was a prospective graduate business school student, would be involved in any nefarious activity. He finally admitted that on occasion he would describe aspects of his job to impress the young lady. Suffice it to say that he eventually realized that he had been played and that he had indeed shared more information with this woman than was prudent on his part. Her name, by the way, is Cassandra Park, although that is not the name she used with our Seamus."

"Did you contact the FBI?"

"We did not. Denis, this was an Irish problem. It didn't involve any US companies or people, other than the young lady. And, quite frankly, Seamus is from a prominent Cork family. We wanted to keep this as quiet as possible. I'm sure you understand."

"Yes, Ambassador, I do. You won't have any problems from the White House."

"Thank you. Our lads now tried to learn to whom she was passing this information and put her under surveillance."

At this point, even on the laptop, Lenihan could see that Ambassador Teehan again exhibiting signs of discomfort.

"It appears this young lady had more than one boyfriend. Our lads observed her with several over the course of a few months. They were able to photograph her other companions. One of our lads recognized, I'm sorry to say, one of your staff."

At this point, Lenihan was the one who became uncomfortable. "Who? Who is it?" Lenihan asked, grinding his teeth.

"Young Patrick Howley," Teehan said. The ambassador had met Howley on more than one occasion at the White House. Howley had repeatedly told the ambassador about his grandparents' relatives who live in Ireland. He knew of Howley's familial relationship with the president and seemed to be as pained to share this news with Lenihan as Lenihan was to receive it.

"What?" Lenihan said incredulously. "PJ? Our PJ Howley is involved with a hooker?" Lenihan was stunned. PJ was in a relationship or dating or just screwing a call girl. PJ from Bay Ridge, Brooklyn was hanging out with an Asian escort.

"There's more, Denis."

More? What more could there possibly be? Lenihan felt almost catatonic.

"On two occasions Ms. Park was observed leaving Patrick's apartment and immediately meeting a man in a nearby parked car. They sat in his car for some time and then she left, getting in her own car and driving to her apartment in Georgetown. We took photos of that man. With the assistance of our friends in the Metropolitan Police Department, who, I believe, consulted with the New York City Police Department, we were able to identify the man in the car."

Lenihan looked at the ambassador, waiting for the other shoe to drop.

The ambassador took a deep breath. "According to the police, his name is Robert Manzi. He is a known member of an Italian organized crime family in New York."

What could Lenihan say? He sat at the desk, staring into the laptop.

"You don't have to say anything, Denis. I'll wait."

Lenihan sat, digesting the news he had just received while, at the same time, trying to manage the combined feelings of anger, shock and fear.

In a soothing tone, Ambassador Teehan said, "I think you appreciate now why I wanted to speak to you privately."

"Yes, Mr. Ambassador. Yes, I understand. And I thank you for your discretion."

"Of course, Denis. I'll send you our files on Ms. Park and Mr. Manzi as soon as we get off this call."

Lenihan, still stunned, did not budge, trying to plan his next move.

"Will there be anything else, Denis?"

"No, no, Mr. Ambassador. Thank you for the information. I have to work on this."

"Yes, you do, Denis. If I can be of any assistance, please don't hesitate to contact me."

"Thank you, Mr. Ambassador. I will do that."

"Goodbye, Denis. And good luck."

Lenihan remained in the room, attempting to regain his composure. He had to devise a plan of action. First, he had to call Jerry DeNigris. Then he had to bring Don Mangini in the loop. He couldn't handle this by himself. The president would be arriving in a few hours. He had to be ready to brief him then. And PJ. He had to see PJ. But not alone. He might kill him.

Chapter 32

Bobby Manzi and Shooter O'Neill met at a small steakhouse near downtown Phoenix for lunch. Bobby ordered a martini; Shooter ordered a seltzer water. After the waiter took their lunch order, Manzi asked O'Neill, "So, Mr. Shooter, how did your visit to the park go today?"

"Pretty much as I expected. When the park opened at six o'clock people started showing up. There'll be plenty there for us to mix in with."

"Super."

"Two big SUVs with tinted windows showed up. Six huge guys in suits got out. They spent a good two hours walking around the parking lot, surveying the area like we did. They walked to the beginning of each trail, looking up the mountain, going over some maps. Two of them put on hiking boots and walked up three of the trails, a good way up each one. When the two guys came down, the six of them met at the bottom of one trail, looking up the trail, studying their maps. I bet that's the trail Whitcomb is going to use."

"Good, good."

"We'll still stick to our plan with you watching the trails behind those restrooms in case I'm wrong or they change their plans. We're still covering the whole park that way."

Manzi nodded.

They agreed to meet at a Dunkin' Donuts about a mile and a half from the park. They would leave Manzi's car on one of the side streets off the park entrance and drive into the park in O'Neill's car. The waiter came with their bill. Manzi took out a thick wad of cash and paid the bill, leaving a generous tip.

*   *   *   *   *

Agents McDaniels and Mercado were sitting in their car down the block and across the street from Elle's Cafe. The status of their investigation remained unchanged. They had followed Melinda Katzenberg for three consecutive days last week. One thing they confirmed was that she did not have much of a life. She left her apartment in the morning to go to CJ's and came home, dragging herself back into her apartment. She stayed there all night, never venturing forth. They did notice that one night she took what appeared to be several flat cake boxes into her apartment. But nothing otherwise suspicious or out of the ordinary.

The agents following the other suspected DAFFIE cell members had similar reports.

McDaniels's cell phone buzzed. Steve Master's administrative assistant was on the phone. McDaniels and Mercado were to report to the hotel were POTUS was staying. They were to meet Masters on the seventh floor west wing. Immediately.

"Understood." McDaniels relayed the order to Mercado, who was driving. "Let's go."

Mercado started the car and pulled away. When they were three blocks from the cafe, she activated the emergency lights and siren and sped to the hotel. They arrived at the hotel and went to the seventh floor. They were directed by a marine guard to a room serving as Denis Lenihan's temporary office. In the office was the chief of staff, Steve Masters and Don Mangini. They were on a conference call with Jerry DeNigris and Diana Surlee. Masters motioned the two agents to move closer to the speaker phone.

"Jerry, Agents McDaniels and Mercado just entered the room."

"Good," DeNigris responded. "For their benefit, and for all of us on this call, Diana please sum up where we stand on this new information."

"Yes, sir. We have learned that POTUS's longtime personal assistant, Patrick Howley, has been in a relationship for over six months with a woman named Cassandra Park. She is a Korean-American born and raised in Ft. Lee, New Jersey. She is employed by a very high-end escort service, BAGI, Ltd. This service operates in New York City and Washington, DC. Park lives in Georgetown. BAGI employs Asian-Pacific women who, well, do what high-end escorts do. An unrelated intelligence investigation by a Western European ally uncovered the relationship between Howley and Park. That same investigation also revealed some type of relationship between Park and Robert Manzi, a known member of a New York City Italian organized crime family. She appears to have met with Manzi at least twice immediately after leaving Mr. Howley's apartment."

McDaniels and Mercado glanced at each other, both with shocked expressions.

"In doing a background investigation of Manzi, we discovered that two weeks ago he purchased airline tickets on his credit card. He apparently flew from Newark Airport to Phoenix Sky Harbor two days ago."

"Where is he staying?" McDaniels asked.

"We don't know. There are no hotel reservation or car rental charges on his credit cards. At least none that we are aware of. We only found out about Manzi and Park yesterday afternoon."

Masters interrupted: "There are plenty of small motels and auto dealers out here who are happy to do business in cash."

"Yes, we assume that," Surlee said. "He is scheduled to fly back to Newark in two days. We believe, therefore, he is in the Phoenix area at present."

"What does Pat Howley have to say about this?" McDaniels asked. He had met Howley, very briefly, on a few of POTUS's trips but did not know him well. Still, someone so close to the president involved with a high-class hooker who, in turn, was involved with a mob guy? This meeting was making him forget about DAFFIE.

"We're about to find out," Masters answered. "He is being held down the hall."

All this time Lenihan stayed motionless, head bent, arms resting on his knees, staring at the floor.

Jerry DeNigris spoke over the speaker. "Steve will conduct the interview. Diana and I will remain on the line, but we'll put our phone on mute. Okay, Mr. Lenihan?"

"Yes."

Masters moved a chair in front of his desk. Lenihan and Mangini were on a couch off to the side. DeNigris said, "Mr. Lenihan, I'm sure you're chomping at the bit to ask Howley some questions, and maybe smack him around, but I would ask that you let Steve handle the questioning. I think it's good you're in the room, but you should not participate in the questioning. Understood?"

Lenihan again answered "yes," not lifting his head. He knew DeNigris was right. Lenihan wanted to kick PJ's ass, but he would defer to the law-enforcement professionals and keep his mouth shut. If he could.

McDaniels spoke up. "Does Howley have any idea about what's going on, what we know about him and Park?"

"Not to our knowledge," Masters responded. He dialed a number on his cell phone. "Please bring him over."

In a minute, there was a knock on the door. Howley was led into the room by two agents.

"Pat, please have a seat," McMasters said, gesturing toward the chair in front of his desk as the two agents left the room. "I am Steve Masters, special agent in charge of the Secret Service Phoenix office. I believe you know some of the other people in this room." Howley looked at Mangini and Lenihan, who was still looking at the floor. He recognized McDaniels and nodded to him. As he sat down, Masters looked at Mercado and McDaniels. They moved toward Howley, standing slightly behind and to the side. Howley quickly glanced at the two agents and asked Masters, "What's going on?"

"We have some questions for you." Masters opened a folder on the desk and took out an eight-by-ten photo and handed it to Howley. "Do you know this woman?"

Howley took the photo, immediately recognizing Cassie. "Yes, of course. That's my girlfriend. Why do you have a picture of her?"

Masters raised his hand. "Let me finish asking you some questions. Okay?"

"Okay."

"What is your girlfriend's name?"

"Cassie. Cassandra. Cassandra Kim."

"Where does she live?"

"She lives in Annandale in Fairfax County."

"With whom?"

"Her family. Parents, two younger sisters."

"Do you know where she was born?"

"In Annandale."

"Have you met her family?"

"No, no, I haven't. Why all these questions about her, her family?"

Again, Masters raised his hand and spoke to Howley in a voice that was calm but more authoritative: "Pat, we're going to get through my questions first. Where does Cassie work?"

"She works in the family business. An export business in Fairfax County."

"How did you meet her?"

"She was working in this little luncheonette near my apartment that I stop in almost every day. We got friendly and started going out."

"When was this?"

"Six and a half months ago."

"Did you tell her where you worked?"

"Yeah, well, eventually, of course. We would talk about it. She's going to study political science. She found it interesting."

"What would you tell her about your job?"

"Whatever. What I did during the day. Some of the people I met. That kind of stuff."

"Would you tell her about your interactions with POTUS?"

"Sure, sometimes."

"Did you tell her who POTUS met with on any given day?"

"Yeah. Sometimes. Yes."

Lenihan was struggling to remain still. He couldn't believe what he was hearing.

"Pat, what did you tell her about this trip?"

"Well, you know, the uh, the trip to Luke Air Force base, I was going to the, um, fundraiser tonight. I have off tomorrow morning because POTUS is going hiking with his friend."

"What?" Lenihan exploded "You told her about the hike? You fucking idiot!" With Howley's reference to the visit to Squaw Peak, Lenihan could no longer restrain himself. Everyone in the room, and DeNigris and Surlee on the phone, were taken back by Lenihan's outburst. Lenihan stood up and stepped toward Howley. "What is wrong with you? You told her about the hike? Why the fuck did you do that?"

"Mr. Lenihan, please sit down," Masters asked. DeNigris unmuted his phone and also asked him to sit down. The room remained silent as Lenihan stared at Howley, his reddened face contorted with rage. After a few moments, he sat down, muttering to himself.

Masters took another eight-by-ten photo out of the folder. He handed Howley a picture of Manzi. "Do you recognize this man?"

"No, no I don't. Who is he?"

Masters disregarded Howley's question. He continued interrogating Howley for another hour. When he was finished, he turned off his recorder and made a brief phone call. "You are going back to your room now. There will be two agents outside your room the entire time. Do you understand?"

"Yes."

There was a knock on the door. The two field agents entered the room and moved behind Howley as Mercado and McDaniels stepped back.

"Please give Agent McDaniels your cell phone." Howley did as he was told. "By the way, the phone in your room has been disconnected."

"What's going to happen to me?"

Masters paused, his face blank. "That remains to be determined. For now you are confined to your room. Do you understand?"

Howley mumbled an acknowledgment, head bowed. He was the most dumbfounded person in the room. Agent Masters, at the end of his questioning, briefly told him who Cassie's real employer was, where she lived, what her real name was and why he was being interrogated. He couldn't believe what was happening, how stupid he had been, how she had duped him. He really thought she loved him. Lenihan was right. He was a fucking idiot.

What have I done?

After Howley left the room, Lenihan remained silent. He was too numb to react. Mangini stood up, ran his hands through his hair and walked a tight circle. "Holy shit! Holy shit! What just happened?"

Masters sat at the desk, jotting down notes. He almost felt sorry for young Mr. Howley.

DeNigris spoke: "Okay, we now know there was a leak from the White House. To a third party with connections to a member of organized crime in New York City."

"Where do we go from here?" Mangini asked.

Lenihan's initial feelings upon hearing Howley's revelations were those of betrayal and anger. But Mangini's question was right. As he forced himself to calm down, his mood turned from anger to determination. This was a major crisis confronting the administration. He had to devise a resolution to that crisis. First and foremost, he had to protect POTUS.

"Don, we have to sit down and think this through. Jerry, can we reconvene in a few hours."

"Yes, of course. We'll continue looking into Park and Manzi."

"Good. Agent Masters, will you folks stay in the building?"

"Of course."

"Fine. Okay, we all have some work to do before POTUS gets here. Let's get to it."

* * * * *

"No, Denis, we are not canceling the hike."

The president had arrived in Phoenix uneventfully. He took his motorcade from the airport to the hotel and met the hotel manager and some of the staff at the rear entrance. He then went up to the seventh floor where several rooms had been blocked off for the presidential party. He had just gotten out of the shower when Lenihan came to his room. Somewhat unbefitting for the most powerful government executive in the world, he was sitting in a chair in a Marine Corp tee shirt and boxers, sipping an iced tea. He was reviewing the brief speech he was to give at the fundraiser that evening.

"You haven't given me enough of a reason to do that. PJ's gotten mixed up with a high-class call girl? Lucky guy. She was seen with a mob guy from New York? Yeah, that's out there, but since when has a president been the target of the Italian mob? Not since JFK, and that's if you believe those conspiracy theories. Which, by the way, I don't."

Lenihan hid his exasperation with his best friend. He had to look at this with a worst case scenario view. It was obvious to him that Whitcomb would not be doing the same.

Whitcomb started to grin. "Denis, come on, the last time I had a problem with an Italian was when you and I, my friend, you and I kicked the shit out of those North Newark guys outside the Belmont Tavern. You remember that, don't you?"

Lenihan didn't appreciate the president's humor or his trip down memory lane. "Look, Jim, why take the risk? PJ has been blabbing to this girl for months. Who knows what he told her about your routines, the people you've met with, you, Jim. Who knows what he told her about you?" But Lenihan could see from the president's expression that his rationale wasn't working.

"PJ is a kid. I know what I told him, what he may have seen, and I don't have anything to worry about. He doesn't know anything about me that can hurt or embarrass me. This is just a hike. The Secret Service has picked the trail. The trails on either side will be closed while we're on it. It's early in the morning. There won't be that many people there. I'll be fine Denis. We'll be fine."

Lenihan didn't reply. He knew he was not going to talk Whitcomb out of this hike. Now he had to make sure that nothing came back to bite them in the ass. Lenihan turned on his heels to leave the room.

"I'm getting dressed now to go to fundraiser. Are you coming?"

Lenihan faced the president as he reached the door. "No. I'm going to spend the night making sure your commune with nature tomorrow goes splendidly for you." He then left the room.

The president let Lenihan's sarcastic tone pass. He knew his chief of staff's only concern was his well-being and the success of the administration. But he was not canceling the hike.

When Lenihan got to his office, he called Mangini and asked him to join him with Agents McDaniels and Masters. There was now another threat to the president. He didn't know the nature of this threat, any more than he knew what DAFFIE was planning. He was going to protect POTUS. With or without POTUS's help.

Later that night, after the fundraiser, after having a few drinks with Governor Rappaport at the hotel, the president walked into the situation room. He found Lenihan, Mangini, Agents McDaniels and Masters, Chief Chiocca and a few of her technicians seated at a table in front of several computers. After acknowledging the group, Whitcomb moved to a corner of the room with Lenihan.

"How did the fundraiser go?" Lenihan asked.

"Fine. I actually enjoyed myself. The host was a pretty interesting guy. We raised a good chunk of change."

"Good."

"So, how was your evening?" Whitcomb asked, looking back at the group huddled around the table.

"We're about done. We're going to deploy additional Secret Service people at the park. We'll have two drones over the area, beginning one hour before your scheduled arrival. We're also going to set up an unmarked van at the park entrance with a camera that will link to the agency's facial recognition database. We'll get a picture of everyone in that park while you're there. We should be able to ID everyone. We'll monitor that from here."

"Good."

"We're going to have a DEA helicopter positioned nearby if, for any reason, we have to get you out of there immediately."

"Okay. Sounds like you have everything buttoned up tight."

Lenihan did not respond.

"Well, I'm going to bed now," the president said.

Lenihan walked with him back to the group. The president thanked them all for their help and diligence and expressed his confidence that everything would work out fine tomorrow. Lenihan and Whitcomb moved toward the door. "You going to bed too, Denis? You look beat."

"Yes. Shortly. As soon as we're done."

"Great. I'll see you sometime tomorrow afternoon, right?"

"Yes, you will."

"All right," the president turned to leave. Two Secret Service agents waiting to escort him to his room, prepared to swing instep behind him. "Thanks, Denis. Thanks for handling all this," he said, gesturing toward Chief Chiocca, Agent McDaniels and the others. "I appreciate it. I really do."

"You're welcome," Lenihan responded. *I know you do.* Lenihan patted the president on the back. "Get a good night's sleep. You have a long day ahead of you."

"Yes, I do. And I will," the president said, winking at Lenihan as he left the situation room.

At least one of them would have a good night's sleep, Lenihan thought to himself as he went back to the group.

Chapter 33

The next morning, at 6:15 AM, Shooter O'Neill approached the park entrance, cursing at the beat-up van with tinted windows jutting into the roadway, forcing him to slow down as he passed by it. He and Manzi entered the park and saw a number of SUVs with several men, all wearing sunglasses and earpieces, standing near the trail he assumed the president would be using. A few were dressed in casual or athletic attire; most wore suits. The area immediately surrounding the trail entrance was cordoned off. O'Neill parked as far as possible from the SUVs. A dozen cars were already parked in the lot, and hikers were standing around, surveying the park. He and Manzi got out of the car. O'Neill opened his trunk to take out his equipment while Manzi strolled toward the restrooms across the lot.

O'Neill set up a tripod and secured a camera to the stand. Keeping his back to the agents, he began taking photos of the scenic vista. He then focused on the desert flora in the vicinity, walking in different directions. He even got on his belly a few times to get closeups of ground hugging plants. If he was later questioned and his camera examined, they were going to have to review dozens of desert scenery pictures before they got to the photos of the presidential party.

As he was taking photos, a single SUV entered the park and drove to same area as the other SUVs. Two agents in the front seats exited the car. A passenger got out of the back as an agent opened the door. The passenger was wearing shorts, loose fitting, layered shirts, big sunglasses and a wide brimmed floppy hat. The new arrival shook hands with several of the agents and spoke with the two agents with whom the passenger had arrived, leaning against one of the SUVs, pointing to the different peaks within their view. In a few minutes, O'Neill saw a caravan of SUVs, followed by two vans, pull into the park. O'Neill took a few photos of the newcomer while most agents were focused on the incoming SUVs. The photos were not very good; between the sunglasses and the hat, his subject's face was obscured and probably would not do them much good.

But O'Neill was nothing if not an optimistic Irishman; the day was young, and he believed he would get his shot sooner or later.

As the cars carrying what O'Neill assumed was the president moved toward the assembled group, O'Neill meandered in their direction. Some of the people in the park, noticing the large gathering of men in suits and blocked trails, stopped to gawk at something that seemed to be worth gawking at. The president got out of his car and moved toward his friend. O'Neill stood next to a dozen park visitors surrounding an information kiosk. They were examining maps, discussing the views, gazing around the park. He said in a loud voice,

"Is that the president over there?" Everyone in the group stopped what they were doing to look at the two companions in shorts and boots ringed by a legion of men in sunglasses, dark suits and darker cars. Momentarily, someone proclaimed, "That is the president! I read in the newspaper this morning he's in town!" Those with cameras took them out; everyone else got their cell phones ready.

And now O'Neill was one of a multitude looking to capture a picture to post on Instagram.

The president approached his friend. They shook hands and embraced, giving each other sustained hugs. They seemed oblivious to the desert heat, the large, stern looking Secret Service chaperones and the gathering crowd. They engaged in animated conversation, looking at each other and no one else, shaking their heads, belly laughing, grabbing each other's shoulders, as if they were the only ones in the park.

Meanwhile, park visitors continued to watch their encounter, moving closer, taking photos and videos, waiting to see what would happen next. The president pointed toward a nearby trail, grabbed his companion's arm and began walking in that direction. The Secret Service detail spread out. Two of the agents dressed in hiking clothes started up the trail. Two stood by, waiting to follow.

By this time, most visitors in the park had surmised what was going on and moved toward the president and his companion. As they approached the trail, the president leaned into his friend, whispered briefly and walked to a family, two parents and three children, who were standing nearby. He greeted the parents and bent down to speak with the children. He patted heads, autographed backpacks and told the kids to listen to their folks and work hard in school.

He rejoined his friend at the trail entrance. O'Neill was close, closer than he thought he would be, standing next to a loud couple who appeared to be the only Democrats in the park that morning. "What idiots would vote for a Republican after Trump?" the wife said. "My God, this guy joined the military and wound up in Iraq. How smart can he be?"

O'Neill still couldn't get a clear picture of the friend, whose back was facing O'Neill, which didn't matter because O'Neill wasn't going to get a photo they could use with the hat and sunglasses in place. The day was going to be hot. They would be walking up that hill then coming back down. That hat would come off eventually, if only to wipe a brow.

That's what O'Neill told himself.

*   *   *   *   *

Denis Lenihan was in the situation room, standing at a table with Don Mangini where two of Chief Chiocca's technicians were monitoring their computers. The technicians were receiving the digital photos of faces captured by the camera in the Secret Service van parked at the entrance to Squaw Peak. The photos were being fed to the federal law-enforcement database and those of the thirty-seven states that made their databases accessible to the federal government. The technicians were reviewing the "hits" as they came in. So far, the Secret Service's strategy was working well. The pictures of the drivers and passengers were clear, for the most part. Lenihan had heard of this capability but had never witnessed it. The technology was impressive. Lenihan and Mangini stood behind the technicians, watching as faces popped up on the computer screens.

"There's Manzi," said a technician as Bobby Manzi's face appeared on the screen. "He was a passenger in a car. The next photo is the driver's."

"Wait! I know that face," Mangini said as O'Neill's picture appeared. Mangini moved closer to the table, examining the monitor. "That's Shooter O'Neill!"

"The *Chronicle* photographer?" Lenihan asked.

Mangini nodded and continued to study the photo. "I'm sure of it. Remember they did a photo spread of Senator Warren's family during the campaign?"

"Sure, I remember that," Lenihan said.

"Shooter was the one who took the photos of her sewing moccasins, sharpening arrowheads, skinning a beaver. I'm sure it's him."

As Mangini spoke, the technician fed the two pictures through the Secret Service database. Agents McDaniels and Masters joined them. The technician received identification confirmation and printed out two pages for McDaniels. One was an FBI report on Manzi's connections to New York Italian organized crime activity. The other report identified the driver as Sean Patrick O'Neill. Lenihan and Mangini looked at one another. First PJ's girlfriend and Manzi were linked. Now a *Chronicle* photographer and Manzi were driving together into the park where POTUS was having what was supposed to be a secret outing with a friend.

"What the hell is going on?" Mangini said, which was exactly what Lenihan was thinking.

The group stood in silence. Shortly, however, it dawned on Lenihan that POTUS was not in physical danger. The mob guy was with a *Chronicle* photographer, not a hit man. This had to be Jake Rosen's doing. Hiring Krissy as an intern, setting up PJ with the hooker, sending a *Chronicle* photographer to the president's secret rendezvous with a guy in contact with the same hooker, the revitalization of the Network. There were too many coincidences to ignore. Lenihan calmed down. The calmest he had been since he had arrived in Arizona. Now he understood what they were facing. Whatever DAFFIE's scheme was, this one was different. A plan to embarrass, to humiliate, to neuter POTUS. A plot to undermine the leader of the free world. They wanted photos of Whitcomb with his still anonymous friend. But, at least, this wasn't a plot to kill him.

"Agent Masters, please send the drone operators the photos of Manzi and O'Neill," the chief of staff directed. "Can they pick them out of a crowd?"

"Yes, they can sir," one of the technicians replied.

"Good. Let's keep an eye on them. Also, send them to your team with POTUS. I don't want them picked up. I just want them watched for now."

"Yes, sir, we can do that."

Mangini couldn't stop talking. "Why is Shooter O'Neill hanging out with a mob guy in the park where POTUS is going for a hike?" Mangini continued. Looking at Lenihan, he said, "Who is this friend, anyway?"

"Look," Lenihan began, in the most nonchalant, non confrontational tone he could muster, "let's just say that POTUS and his friend have their reasons for keeping this get together private. And leave it at that." He gave Mangini a look that said "and no more questions on this subject."

"Sure, sure thing," Mangini murmured.

Masters and McDaniels remained mute.

Lenihan looked at Masters. "How long will they be hiking?"

"It should be an hour and a half, two hours, depending on how often they stop to rest, have a drink."

"Okay, that gives us some time."

Just then Lenihan's cell phone buzzed. Moshe Schwartz texted him that he and his girlfriend got in late last night and asked if they could get together with Lenihan for lunch? Lenihan was in deep thought. Moshe and Yael would be at the hotel all day, at the fundraiser that night. Moshe was one of the president's best friends. Loyal, trustworthy and discreet. And Yael was a member of one of the best, if not best, intelligence agencies in the world. And Jake Rosen wanted a picture of the president of the United States with a special friend.

Lenihan began to put a plan together. The first part of the plan was to not let O'Neill get a good picture of the friend now hiking with Whitcomb. Looking at the drone pictures of Whitcomb and his companion talking, Lenihan said to Agent Masters, "Please tell the detail with POTUS to tell his friend to not take the hat and sunglasses off while they're in that park."

"Yes, sir."

*   *   *   *   *

Melinda Katzenberg arrived at CJ's at her normal time. The cake and pastries for the fundraiser at the Arizona Science Center were to be delivered at three o'clock in the afternoon. That would give her plenty of time to switch the cake DAFFIE made that was sitting in the trunk of her car for CJ's cake. Katzenberg had volunteered to help with the delivery of the baked goods to the science center. She would make sure that DAFFIE's cake got on the dessert table. Also, Elle Wentworth had put a diversionary plan together: two DAFFIE members would stage an argument over an order with CJ's staff at the front of the store when the van delivering the desserts was being loaded. *That Elle*, Melinda thought, *what a womyn!*

The cake they had decorated that morning looked exactly like the one CJ's would make for the fundraiser. Wentworth was a masterful tactician. The country and especially the Nazi misogynists in the Whitcomb administration and their lackeys at the fundraiser would be taught a lesson they would not soon forget.

*   *   *   *   *

Cassandra picked up her cell phone. She was in a salon getting her weekly hair, skin and nail treatment.

"Hi, PJ, what a nice surprise! I didn't expect to hear from you this early."

"Yeah, well, I have some down time, so I thought I'd give you a call. Just checking in. How's it going?"

"Oh, everything is fine here. Taking a coffee break from work. Looking at grad schools online." She winked at the girl doing her nails.

"Everything okay, PJ? You don't sound so happy."

"No, no, everything is fine."

"How did the fundraiser go last night? Did you get to meet any important people?"

"No, not really. Some local bigwigs. Nobody you would know."

"Wait a minute, PJ. Today is the hike, right?"

"Yeah, well, they're on the hike right now."

"Are you there?"

"No, I told you I wasn't going."

"Did you get to see his friend? I guess not, if you're not there."

"No, I haven't seen POTUS's friend," Howley said then paused, held the phone to his chest and took a deep breath. Raising his phone up, he said, "I haven't seen the friend yet."

"What do you mean?"

"I'll get to meet his friend tonight."

"Really? You will? How?"

"It turns out that the president and his friend are going to have dinner at the hotel tonight."

"In the hotel? What time? How many restaurants do they have there? Do you know which one?"

"Will you please let me explain?"

"Sure, yeah, sure, PJ. I'm just excited for you, you know?"

"They're having dinner in a private room. They won't be in any of the hotel's restaurants. But they decided they wanted to spend some time in the hotel pool. The outdoor pool."

"There's an outdoor pool?"

Yes, there is. That's the one they're going to."

"Wow. And you know all this?"

"Yup. I had to meet with the hotel manager to set this up. The hotel is going to close the pool to the hotel guests at ten o'clock tonight. POTUS and his friend will jump in the pool at 10:30 or so."

"Oh, PJ, you set it up? That is so exciting. Now I wish I had come out with you."

I bet you do.

"PJ, I have to get back to work. Thanks for letting me know about this. I'm so excited for you."

"Okay. Bye."

Howley threw his phone on the bed.

"Good job, PJ. You did fine," Agent McDaniels said as he picked up Howley's phone and put it in his pocket.

"What's going to happen now?"

"We have to see how this works out tonight. If all goes as expected, you'll be flying to Washington tomorrow morning."

"On Air Force One, with the president?"

"No. You'll be on a separate flight."

"Can I see the president?"

"No, PJ, You can't."

"When can I see him?"

"Let's wait and see how this plays out."

*   *   *   *   *

Shooter O'Neill stood on the edge of the group of park visitors who were waiting for the president to come down the trail. They had been kept back from the immediate area of the trail but were close enough for O'Neill to get a good picture of the president and his friend. As he and Manzi had agreed upon, once the president went up the trail, Manzi started to make his way toward O'Neill. He also stood on the fringe of the group who were hoping to catch more glimpses of the president when he came down the trail. When he saw the two agents coming down the trail ahead of the president, Manzi nodded to O'Neill and made his way toward the park entrance. He casually strolled out of the park and went to his car parked down the road.

O'Neill remained among the presidential watchers, waiting for the commander-in-chief to come down the mountain. A few minutes after the two bodyguard hikers reached the end of the trail, the president and his friend appeared. They were still completely engrossed with each other, oblivious to their surroundings. O'Neill pointed his camera at the two companions, as did everyone else standing nearby. He didn't take any photos, however, since the president's companion was still wearing the floppy hat and sunglasses; he was not going to get useful photos with that hat in the way.

The president and his friend moved toward the car that had brought the friend to the park. They stood by the rear door, their backs to the crowd. They were leaning toward each other, heads almost touching, trying to carry on a private conversation surrounded by government agents, curious onlookers and a world-renowned photographer trying to capture a scene for posterity and an impatient boss in New York.

They embraced, clapping each other on their backs. An agent opened the rear passenger door as the friend stepped toward the car just as the president from one side and an agent from the other moved between O'Neill and the car. O'Neill's sight line was blocked. All he could see was the top of the friend's head as the friend sat in the rear seat. Now the president leaned in to the open window to continue their conversation. A few agents then positioned themselves between the crowd and the car, looking outwards.

O'Neill's view was almost completely obstructed. And he still had that damn hat and the sunglasses on. Shortly, the president left the car and moved to his own. Once he got in his car, the presidential convoy left the park. The car with the friend remained for about fifteen minutes, then headed toward the park entrance. O'Neill took a photo of the rear of the car, including the license plate, and sent it to Manzi. Jake was not going to be happy. Maybe Manzi would have better luck.

*   *   *   *   *

Denis Lenihan walked to where Agents McDaniels and Masters and Don Mangini were standing with one of the communications agency technicians. "Where do we stand?" he asked. "Were we able to locate Manzi and O'Neill in the park?"

The technician replied. "Yes, sir. We synchronized the facial recognition camera with the footage from a drone. We saw the car carrying the two subjects enter the park, drive into the lot and park. We were able to identify the two subjects and monitor their movements."

"Where are they now? Where is the president?"

"The president is almost at the bottom of the trail. O'Neill is standing in a crowd, where he has been for some time, near the presidential party."

"And Manzi?"

"Manzi has left the park."

"He left?" Lenihan asked.

"Yes, he walked out the entrance down the road a half-mile or so and got in a car. He is sitting in that car now."

Lenihan stood motionless for several moments. "Any thoughts, gentlemen?" Lenihan inquired of the group.

Agent Masters spoke first. "He is waiting for something. Or someone. In his own car. He and O'Neill came into the park together but left a car outside the park for Manzi. They planned this."

"Why would they need two cars?" Mangini asked.

Masters answered. "They have a plan that requires that they each have a car when the presidential party leaves the park.

"Manzi is going to follow someone."

McDaniels spoke up. "Why would he follow POTUS? The Internet, the media, they've reported where he is staying, his schedule this afternoon and tonight. No need to follow him."

"Agreed," Agent Masters said. "He's going to follow someone else."

The assembled group turned to Lenihan.

"The president's friend," Lenihan said.

"It would appear so," Masters replied.

"I don't want anyone followed," Lenihan said, looking at the group. "I—we—have to protect their privacy."

"We can detain Manzi," Agent McDaniels offered.

"No, I don't want that. I don't want Manzi and O'Neill to know we're onto them."

The group remained silent as they pondered possible solutions. Masters spoke first. "I have an idea. I have to make a phone call.

Jamal, call the detail. Tell them not to leave with the president's friend until we call them back."

"Understood."

Masters stepped away from the group and began scrolling through the contacts on his phone.

*   *   *   *   *

Manzi was sitting on a side street that was one-half mile from the park entrance. From his vantage he could see about a hundred yards down the road toward the park. He watched the president's party drive past, and waited. He received the text from O'Neill with the photo of the car driving the president's friend. When the SUV finally came down the road, he turned on the ignition. He let another car go by and pulled onto the street.

Soon the road became a two-lane road. The Secret Service guys drove the speed limit. Nobody was in a rush.

This is gonna be a piece of cake.

After a couple of miles, the Secret Service car entered the interstate. They drove ten minutes and exited, took two quick turns onto a local road, then a turn onto a narrow road leading to a guard booth and a gate. Manzi watched the Secret Service vehicle stop at the gate. A guard came out of the booth and spoke to the agent driving the car. He moved back to the booth and the gate rolled back, allowing the car to enter. And the gate closed.

Uh oh, we got a problem.

Manzi drove up to the booth and lowered his window. "Good afternoon, my friend, how are you this fine day?" Manzi restrained his natural New York aggressiveness and spoke in a pleasant tone.

"Good afternoon to you, sir," the security guard, a plump, cheerful Hispanic, responded. "How can I help you?"

"Well, I would like to go in there," Manzi said, nodding toward the closed gate.

The guard, chuckling, said "I am sorry sir, but this is a private community. Only residents and their guests are permitted in here. I didn't see a resident sticker on your bumper. No one has called to give me your name and license number, so you are not a guest either. I'm afraid I can't let you in."

"I see, well, I'm actually moving out here in a few months, and I promised my wife I'd scout out a few neighborhoods." Manzi pulled out his wad of cash and started peeling off fifties. "How about I just go in and take a look around for a few minutes?"

Now the guard was laughing out loud. "Sir, no, please sir, put the money back. I can't let you in. Sorry, I really am, but I can't. And won't."

Manzi stared at the guard, considering what his next step would be.

"What's the name of this place?"

"This is High Desert Ranch, sir."

"High Desert Ranch?"

"Yes, sir."

Manzi, nodded his head, staring through the gate. "Okay."

He raised his window and backed the car away from the gate. He went back to the main road and pulled into a convenience store lot. He looked up High Desert Ranch on the Internet. Established twenty years ago, it offered privacy, security and luxury residences for one hundred seventy residents.

One hundred seventy homes in there. *The Jew ain't gonna be happy.* Just then his phone rang. Cory Chan from DC was the contact name that popped up.

* * * * *

Manzi drove to the Mexican restaurant near the airport where he and O'Neill had met two days ago, as they agreed. He was in the middle of lunch when O'Neill walked in and joined him.

"Fuck me, fuck me, fuck me," O'Neill said, drawing the stares of a few nearby patrons as he made little effort to lower his voice.

"I take it, Mr. Shooter, that you were not successful."

"Yeah, you take that right. The friend had this wide brim hat and oversized sunglasses. I got plenty of photos but I don't think they're going to do us much good. Or Jake. Where does the friend live? Did you get a good look without the goddamn hat?"

Manzi took his second shot of tequila and finished his beer. He looked at Shooter with a smile. "Do you want the good news or the bad news?"

"Oh, screw that, junior. Just tell me what the fuck happened."

"I got your text with the picture of the car and picked them up as we arranged. I followed them for thirty minutes or so and bada bing, they pull into a gated community."

"A what?"

"A gated community. You know, a community that has a gate that they don't let you through unless you live there or know somebody. I tried talking my way in, but it didn't happen."

"Oh shit, Jake is going to blow his stack."

"Hold on, Mr. Shooter, that was the bad news. You didn't ax me what the good news is."

"Okay, Robert, let me 'ax' you. What's the good news?"

"Our girl in DC came through. You know about her?"

"Yeah, I've been told."

"It seems that our man from Washington and his local friend, having spent a few hours in the desert, are taking a dip in the pool tonight."

"Really? At the hotel?"

"Yeah. At the hotel. They're going to close the outdoor pool tonight at 10:00 PM, and the two friends are going to take a dip."

"Well, my boy, it seems that all is not lost. Let's finish up here and swing by the pool and see where I can set up."

They drove over to the hotel. They went through the lobby and followed the signs to the pool. The hotel was open and functioning; only access to the wing where the presidential party was staying was restricted. The pool was located in the rear of the hotel. Off to one side was the hotel's golf course; to the other side were tennis courts.

"Look over there," O'Neill said. On the other side of the tennis courts was a two-lane access road. Beyond the road stood a corporate office park with several buildings facing the hotel and overlooking the pool. "Do you think we can get in one of those buildings over there, say, to the ninth or tenth floor?"

"Let me make a call." Manzi took out his phone and walked toward an unoccupied section of the pool deck. "Carmine, how ya doin' buddy? This is Bobby Manzi. Yeah, yeah, I'm in town. A short trip. Nah, business. Hey, look, Carmine, I need a favor."

Manzi rejoined O'Neill in a few minutes. "We're good to go, Mr. Shooter. See the middle building with the cactus logo and "1600" under it? That's where we're going tonight. A guy from the maintenance workers' union is gonna meet us at the service entrance at 9:45 PM sharp. He'll take us up to the tenth floor. There're a lot of vacant offices up there you can set up in."

"Excellent, Robert, excellent. From there I can get clear shots of whomever is in the pool area, and no one will be wearing a hat and sunglasses at 10:30 at night."

*   *   *   *   *

Lenihan walked into the situation room at noon. He had just spent forty-five minutes briefing Whitcomb on the morning's events. He also discussed and received approval from Whitcomb to implement the plan he had put together. The president then went to the children's hospital for the scheduled visit.

Lenihan approached Agents Masters and McDaniels, who were talking with Chief Choicca and Don Mangini. "So, what's the status?" Lenihan asked.

"I think we're okay," Masters replied. "The head of security at High Desert Ranch was very cooperative. He is a former captain with the Phoenix PD. I worked on a few cases with him before he retired. Good guy. They let our detail with the president's friend in the complex. Mr. Manzi was not afforded the same courtesy. Our detail went out the rear entrance they use for deliveries and contractors. We had another team waiting. The second team took the president's friend home. No one followed them."

"Good. How did the call go with the girl?"

"I think it went fine," McDaniels replied. "Howley followed the script perfectly."

"Okay, good."

"He's wondering what's going to happen to him."

"He's the least of my concerns right now. We'll deal with him when we get back to DC."

Masters continued. "I met with the hotel manager an hour ago. He has no problem closing the pool to guests at ten o'clock tonight. POTUS will have it all to himself. We'll post agents at each entrance. There are only three of them. It shouldn't be a problem. And, lastly, one of our surveillance teams spotted Manzi and O'Neill at the hotel earlier. They were at the pool, looking around."

Chief Chiocca spoke up. "We linked into the hotel's security camera system and were able to locate them. At one point, Manzi walked away from O'Neill, making a phone call. When he came back, he pointed to the office buildings that are across the service road north of the hotel."

Lenihan looked at the assembled group. "Are those buildings close enough to get photos of the pool area?"

"With the right equipment, definitely," McDaniels responded. "Are we going to follow Manzi and O'Neill for the rest of the day?"

Lenihan looked at the group. "I don't see the need to follow them, based on what we just saw. What if they see your people? As I said earlier, I don't want to tip them off that we're on to them."

"What I suggest, Mr. Lenihan," Masters said, "is that we post a few teams near those office buildings tonight. They can conceal themselves and watch the buildings. They can notify us when Manzi and O'Neill show up if you think that's what they intend to do."

Lenihan thought for a moment. "I can live with that. Let's do that."

"We'll set that up. Anything else for now, Mr. Lenihan?" Masters asked

"No, I think we've covered everything."

"I understand Mr. Schwartz and his companion are joining POTUS for dinner."

Lenihan replied. "Yes. They're at the hotel now. They're going to the fundraiser then coming back to the hotel with POTUS."

"Understood. We are all set here."

*   *   *   *   *

"I could not tell who the mystery friend is from the photos Shooter sent," Jake Rosen said to Fran Ritzie as Ritzie entered his office, before Ritzie got a chance to close the door.

"Neither could I. And I don't know if we'll be able to identify the friend even knowing where the friend lives. I called Montanez. High Desert Ranch is a very exclusive gated community. He says he might be able to get a list of the proprietors, but many people in there buy their homes in corporate or LLC names for tax and privacy purposes."

"In other words, Shooter and the Italian have to come through tonight after that fundraiser."

"I know, Jake, I know. I spoke to Shooter. He says if the BAGI girl is correct, he will have ample opportunity to get plenty of photos of Whitcomb and his friend. In bathing suits. Lounging around a pool. Thinking they're all by themselves. Never suspecting that they're being watched. This could be exactly what we're looking for. These pictures could seal the deal for you."

"Yes, I agree. If all goes according to plan. But that has not happened today, has it?"

"No, but it looks like luck is turning our way. We're in a good position, Jake."

Rosen looked at Ritzie, his face rigid, not betraying any emotion. "I told the Italian to call me immediately after this photo shoot. I want to know how it goes as soon as they are done. I want to see these pictures as soon as possible so we can move forward with the plan. Understood?"

"Certainly."

*   *   *   *   *

Melinda Katzenberg and another DAFFIE member were in the back of the van on its way to the Arizona Science Center. So far, Elle Wentworth's plan was proceeding as designed. The shouting match the DAFFIE members had instigated at the front of the store gave Katzenberg the opportunity to switch the DAFFIE cake for CJ's. The event caterer had faxed the schedule to CJ's earlier in the day. A cocktail party went from 5:00 to 7:00 PM, then Whitcomb was to give his speech at 7:15 PM. The timer in DAFFIE's cake was set to go off at 7:25. Even if the Whitcomb wasn't in the immediate vicinity of the dessert table, the effective range of the device exceeded the dimensions of the room where the fundraiser was being held. Everyone in that room would be impacted by Operation Layer Cake.

*   *   *   *   *

President Whitcomb was alone in his room, freshly showered, reviewing the first speech he was giving that night. He crossed the room, reached into one of his suitcases and pulled out a cell phone.

"Hello, how are you feeling?" he said then listened. "Good to hear. It was a lot of fun, a great workout. Yes, I enjoyed it too. Well, yes, we did have a slight change of plans. Did you get home okay?

Good. No, nothing to worry about. I'll explain it to you tonight. Speaking of a change in plans, we have to make a slight one tonight also. You remember my friend Moshe Schwartz? That's him. He and his girlfriend are going to join us for part of the evening. No, not the whole night. I'll explain everything when you get here. We'll still have a great time together. Yes, and some alone time too. Plenty of that. Don't worry, we'll have a good night. Okay, see you in a few hours."

* * * * *

Jamal McDaniels and Denise Mercado were in the situation room discussing the events of the day and the upcoming evening with Steve Masters. McDaniels cell phone vibrated, and he answered the call. "This is McDaniels. No, Tony, I'm sure I'll never guess where you are. You're where?" McDaniels eyes opened wide. "Let me put you on speaker." McDaniels looked at Mercado and Masters and explained: "It's Tony Marinello and Brian O'Toole."

Jerry DeNigris had requested that all the suspected DAFFIE cell members be placed under surveillance while POTUS was in Phoenix. Marinello and O'Toole had been assigned to watch Melinda Katzenberg that day. They drove to CJ's this morning and saw Katzenberg enter the store at her regular time.

"Tony, I have you on speaker with Steve and Denise. Go ahead."

Tony began, "Yes, well, we waited at CJ's this morning and observed Katzenberg arrive at her normal time. She was in the shop all day until about 2:30 PM. She came out the back of the store with another bakery worker. They loaded what looked like several trays of cookies and pastries in the back of the van. Then she came out by herself holding what looked like a big cake box. But instead of putting it in the van, she went to her car, which was a few spaces away. She opened the trunk of her car, put the cake box in there, then took another cake box out of her trunk and put that one in the van. She went back in the bakery, and her and the guy came back out to put a few more trays in the van. After ten more minutes, her and two guys hopped in the van and pulled out of the parking lot."

"Where'd they go?" Masters asked.

"Well, chief, right now we are sitting in the back of the Arizona Science Center, watching them bring those trays into the service entrance to the building. Katzenberg brought the cake in first, by the way."

"That can't be," Mercado exclaimed. She moved to the closest terminal and pulled up the Secret Service file for the science center event. She scrolled down to the "outside food provider" folder and opened the file. CJ's was not listed as a food service provider for the event.

"I checked this list last week, specifically looking for CJ's. Remember, Jamal, I told you there was only one caterer listed, and it wasn't CJ's."

"I definitely remember you telling me that."

Masters spoke up. "There was some kind of screw up then. The caterer must be using CJ's for desserts and didn't tell anyone. We can look into that later but for now . . ."

"For now, Denise and I are heading over there to see what we can find out," McDaniels reached for his jacket. "Tony, you guys hold your position, and Denise and I will be right there."

"Will do."

Masters spoke up as McDaniels and Mercado turned to leave. "POTUS is not scheduled to arrive there for several hours. We have to clear this up well before then. You understand that, Jamal?"

"Yes."

"I'm going to call DeNigris and give him an update. Report back to me when you get to the science center and know what is going on."

"Copy that."

* * * * *

Don Mangini was sitting in the hotel lobby trying to clear the backlog of unanswered emails before his meeting. At the appointed time, Mangini heard a "Hello Donny," reverberate throughout the lobby. The Reverend Josiah Hood would never be accused of being bashful.

Mangini stood up and put his cell phone away. "Hello, Reverend, glad to see you made it out."

"It's good to be here, Donny. I actually love the dry heat. Doesn't suck the life out of you like a hot humid day in Georgia. Y'all know what I mean?"

"I certainly do, Reverend."

"Besides, I never miss a chance to visit with my little girl. Did I ever show you a picture, Donny?"

"No, you haven't Reverend. I'd love to see one."

"Here she is, my little angel, on her wedding day," Hood said as he pulled a picture out of his wallet.

Mangini was handed a picture of a beaming bride and a befuddled looking groom. If Reverend Hood had been a lineman on his college football team, his daughter could have been the tight end. She cut an imposing figure in her wedding dress. As for her new husband—he would have been one of the waterboys. Skinny with thinning, greasy hair and a pasty complexion, he resembled a man being led to his execution.

"Quite a beautiful couple, Reverend. How long have they been married?"

"Two years, three months, and eighteen days, according to my missus. She keeps track of those things. My son-in-law Jesse is a good Christian man and a mighty fine preacher. My daughter is in good hands."

"That's nice to hear. I don't think my father-in-law has ever said that about me."

Mangini's attempt at humor was met with silence. Trying to recover, he launched into a description of the night's upcoming events, concluding by asking Reverend Hood, "Your wife made the trip, didn't she?"

"Yes she did. She's at one of the hotel's fancy spas getting all gussied up. We don't have many of those lady places near us, so this is a real treat for her. It's going to cost me an arm and a leg, but she's a good woman, and she deserves it, you know what I mean, Donny?"

"Yes, I do Reverend. Do I ever. 'Happy wife, happy life,' I always say."

Mangini's continued attempt at humor was met with continued silence. "Well, uh, Reverend, uh, are you going to the speech in the park before the fundraiser?"

"Yes, Don, we will be attending," Hood responded with a sideward glance. "I would like to see the president in action."

"That's great, Reverend. Actually, I've arranged for you and your wife to sit in one of the sections on the stage reserved for special guests of the president. Which you are, of course. You'll get to meet the president after his speech. I know he is looking forward to meeting you and spending some time with you at the fundraiser."

"That will be fine, Donny. I'd like for that to happen. I'd like to share with the president a few of the concerns of members of my congregation."

"Reverend Hood, I can assure you that the president is eager to meet with you and hear what those concerns might be."

"Thank you, Donny, that will be real special for me. Now, if you'll excuse me, I have to find out what stage of beautification my wife is at. Not that she needs much of that."

"I'm sure that's the case, Reverend. I look forward to meeting her tonight."

"Thanks, Donny. I'm looking forward to this evening also."

*   *   *   *   *

Agents McDaniels and Mercado pulled into the parking lot at the rear of the science center. Agents Marinello and O'Toole stood in the lot, leaning against their car.

"Good afternoon, gents," McDaniels said as he and Mercado approached their colleagues. "Where do we stand?"

Marinello responded. "We checked with the security advance team. They're going to shut down the museum in about thirty minutes. They'll do their final inspection of the building, run the bomb sniffing dogs through their routine and close the building until POTUS arrives."

"How about the cake delivery?" Mercado asked.

O'Toole spoke up: "I went inside the kitchen with a uniformed cop, just took a leisurely stroll through the area. The pastries and the cake are set up on their own table. There is one cake. A large three or four-inch-high sheet cake. Looks like it would fit nicely in the box we saw Katzenberg take out of her trunk. Katzenberg is in the kitchen, arranging the pastries on trays. She saw me and the cop and turned her back to us as she was doing her thing. She seemed to be rearranging the pastries on the trays, making herself look busy, so she didn't have to look at us. That was my take, at least."

McDaniels looked at Mercado. "Let's get in there now. We're going to clear this up."

Turning to Agent O'Toole, he asked, "Brian, when will the bomb sniffing dogs get here?"

"I'd say in twenty minutes."

"Okay. Call me when they get here. We'll want them to start in the kitchen."

McDaniels and Mercado walked in the science center back entrance and stopped to study a display of the floor plans of the building. Pointing to the first-floor plan, McDaniels said, "How about you enter the kitchen from the auditorium. I'll go to the rear entrance and wait until you get to the kitchen door. There are only those two ways in and out of the kitchen so we won't miss her."

"Sounds like a plan. I'll text you when I'm in position."

"Okay." McDaniels made his way to the rear entrance of the kitchen. While he was waiting for Mercado's text, she called.

"What's up?"

"We have a problem. This auditorium is full of kids. Twenty, twenty-five, maybe more. Ten-year-olds. I called O'Toole and told him to come here with some uniforms and get these kids out of here. We have to be careful."

"All right, but we're running out of time. I'm going in."

"Fine. I'll keep an eye on the door in case she comes this way. I'll start getting the kids out now. I'll come in as soon as O'Toole and Marinello get here. Jamal?"

"Yes?"

"Be careful."

"Always am." McDaniels entered the kitchen, which was busy with cooks working grills, assistant chefs slicing vegetables, busboys moving stacks of plates-and Melinda Katzenberg off to the side, standing by a table with pastries, cookies and one large sheet cake.

McDaniels walked through the center of the kitchen, casually observing the organized chaos, keeping Katzenberg in his peripheral vision. The workers paid little attention to him; strangers in suits and police uniforms had been in the building for the last several hours. He saw Mercado enter the kitchen at the opposite door. She nodded ever so slightly to him and stopped to talk to one of the workers, speaking fluent Spanish. In response, the staffer pointed to several different workstations as they walked through the kitchen together.

Katzenberg was still rearranging the pastry and cookies trays, her back to the kitchen. She turned and saw Mercado, who pushed the kitchen staffer away and displayed her badge. Katzenberg then saw McDaniels moving toward her, pulling out his government identification. Mercado yelled in Spanish for the staff to leave the kitchen immediately, which they did without needing any additional encouragement.

Katzenberg's eyes opened wide as the two agents converged on her. She moved with surprising agility, given her girth, to the end of the table where the cake was. She picked up the cake and held it over head. Looking at both agents she yelled, "Don't come any closer! I'm not afraid to use this!"

Mercado and McDaniels stopped in their tracks, drawing their guns. "We're Secret Service. Don't do anything stupid, Melinda. Put the cake down and no one gets hurt," McDaniels said in the calmest voice he could muster. Mercado stepped back, whispering into her phone, "O'Toole, get those kids out of here now!"

Katzenberg was stunned. "How do you know my name?"

"We know all about you, Melinda. And DAFFIE," Mercado responded.

The determination in Katzenberg's face drained away at Mercado's reference to the Group. Did they know everything, she wondered. What should she do now? Who was going to save her, she thought, panicking.

Mercado lowered her gun and stepped toward Katzenberg. "Let's talk this through, Melinda. We can work this out together."

Melinda attempted to summon the rapidly diminishing confidence membership in DAFFIE had instilled in her. "The patriarchy needs to fail. We can no longer tolerate this Nazi, fascist, racist, Zionist Republican regime. The social reproduction of patrimony has to end. Womynkind must be released from the shackles of male oppression. Climate change deniers have to be eliminated. All animals must be recognized as free beings," Melinda shouted, swiveling her head to glare at the agents, breathing heavily and sweating profusely.

And the cake was getting heavier.

"Melinda, it seems you have a lot on your plate. Why don't you put the cake down, and we'll try to straighten this out," Mercado said as she holstered her gun and took a few steps toward Katzenberg, extending her hands, palms up. "Melinda, there's no need for this. I understand you. I feel your pain."

Katzenberg turned to Mercado, ignoring McDaniels. "You do?"

"Yes, I do. Look, Melinda, whatever differences we have, we're both women. We may disagree politically, but, baby, I know, you know, we all have issues with all these asshole men who control our lives."

"You feel that way too?"

"Do I ever. I had a father who ordered me around my entire life, boyfriends who beat me up, bosses who gave me crummy reviews if I wouldn't go out with them. You name it, sweetheart."

"Really? I'm not surprised. You're...you're so beautiful. I'm not surprised you had boyfriends and...and men who wanted to date you."

Wow. Didn't see that coming, McDaniels thought. Katzenberg was now solely focused on Mercado. McDaniels moved to the side and behind Katzenberg.

Mercado smiled and tilted her head. "Thank you, Melinda, that's very nice of you to say," she responded as she moved closer to Katzenberg. She took her jacket off, tossing it to the side, leaving her in a simple, tight fitting white tee shirt.

Katzenberg was mesmerized. And the cake was getting heavier.

Mercado spoke in a soft, friendly tone. "Melinda, what say we get out of here. Go someplace quiet. No crowds. You can tell me your story, and I'll see what I can do to help you out. One woman to another."

Mercado got within a few feet of Katzenberg. She continued to smile at the DAFFIE member, saying, "Come on, Melinda, let me help you with the cake. It's getting heavy, isn't it honey?" Mercado then put her hands under her hair at the back of her neck and in one motion flipped her hair up and shook her head, causing her hair to float in the air before landing on her shoulders. Gazing at Katzenberg while she licked her lips, she said one more time, "Let me help you with the cake, then we can be alone."

Could this be Melinda's lucky day?

Actually-no.

As Mercado approached Katzenberg, McDaniels, now behind the cake-wielding terrorist, swiftly closed the space between him and Katzenberg and lifted the cake out of her hands.

"Get the cake out of here, Jamal, there still may be kids nearby!" Mercado shouted as she took out handcuffs and spun Katzenberg around.

McDaniels headed back the way he came, out the rear of the kitchen, away from the auditorium and any remaining children. He reasoned that this cake had been moved multiple times in the last few hours and that whatever device was in it would not detonate on movement. Still he wasn't taking any chances. He saw a large garbage can by the door leading from the kitchen. He put the cake in the can and placed some trays and pans on top. He dragged the can through the rear door and into the hallway. Did he hear a ticking noise coming from the garbage can?

Katzenberg turned to Mercado as she led her out of the kitchen toward the auditorium. "Are we going somewhere quiet, just the two of us, like you said?"

"No, Melinda, not this time. You have the right to remain silent..."

A loud explosion echoed from outside the kitchen. Mercado was stunned and terrified. She pushed Katzenberg to the ground and handcuffed her to the leg of a table. She ran to the rear door and into the hallway.

"Jamal!" she yelled. "Jamal! Where are you?" she cried, covering her mouth as she began coughing. All she could see down the hallway was smoke.

Pink smoke.

Chapter 34

"What's the report from the science center?" Denis Lenihan requested that SAC Masters come to POTUS's room to brief them on the incident at the science center. Lenihan wanted the administration's version solidified before the media found out about it. Don Mangini was in the room with the president; Jerry DeNigris and Diana Surlee were on the phone.

Masters addressed the group. "What we know is that a bomb was baked into a cake, which was delivered to the science center for tonight's fundraiser."

Lenihan, the president and Mangini looked at each other, all thinking *I was going to be in that room with a bomb in a cake?*

President Whitcomb spoke first. "How is Agent McDaniels? Was anyone else injured?"

SAC Masters responded. "Agent McDaniels was next to the bomb when it exploded. He had put it in a garbage can and was dragging it down a hallway out of the building when it went off. No one else was nearby."

"Oh my God!" Mangini exclaimed. "How badly was he hurt?"

"Agent McDaniels will be fine. He received superficial burns to his hands and face. He did himself a favor by putting the bomb in the can, which contained the explosion. There were no other casualties."

Jerry DeNigris spoke up. "Fortunately, this bomb was not meant to kill or maim. Our preliminary investigation indicates that it was very similar, if not identical, to the bomb DAFFIE used to destroy the shipment of furs in Colorado a few months ago. Just a different color dye."

"So, they didn't want to kill POTUS?" Lenihan asked.

"Apparently not," DeNigris responded. "This bomb was intended to leave a pink stain on anyone in its blast radius. The dye used was not caustic or poisonous or otherwise harmful to humans. However, the stain on human skin is extremely difficult to wash off. It takes multiple treatments over several weeks before the stain can be removed."

"So, we would have had a pink president for a couple of weeks," Mangini commented.

"It appears that was their intent," DeNigris said.

"But why?" Mangini asked. "To what end?"

"Why? I'll tell you why," an angry Lenihan vented. "To embarrass the president and this administration. To show their followers, and the country, that they could get to the president." Lenihan was more than relieved that DAFFIE's plot had been averted, but nevertheless he was shaken at what could have occurred. "They wanted to make a name for themselves by humiliating the most powerful man on the planet. If they had succeeded, the president and his supporters at the fundraiser would have been walking around in a pink hue for weeks. I can see all the photos CNN and MSNBC would have broadcast for weeks."

"The progressives' Internet memes would write themselves," Mangini commented.

"Well, thanks to Agent McDaniels, that didn't happen," the president said.

"Yes, for that we can be grateful," Lenihan sighed. "Don, let's get on the phone with Joel. We have to release a statement. Set up a call in fifteen minutes."

"Will do," Mangini replied as he left the room.

"Jerry, what about the woman who was arrested at the science center?" Lenihan asked.

SAC Masters answered: "She ranted for some time about the male patriarchy, global warming and the coming revolution. She asked for Agent Mercado. When she was told Mercado wasn't available, she shut down and asked for a lawyer."

"What about the other DAFFIE members?"

"We picked them all up, except one," Masters said.

"Which one?" Lenihan asked.

"Elizabeth Wentworth. The owner of Elle's Cafe. We suspect she is the leader of the Phoenix cell."

"And she got away," Lenihan said.

Masters continued. "The team who had her under surveillance lost her. Not sure when but about an hour before the bomb went off a van with two men made a delivery to her cafe. The surveillance team now thinks she may have dressed up as one of the delivery guys and left the cafe. They noted the name on the van but can't locate any business in the Phoenix area with that name. We're looking for her now. Not sure when or if we're going to find her."

"And the others?" Lenihan asked.

"They're all following the same script. 'Am I being charged with a crime?' 'Am I under arrest?' 'I want to speak to a lawyer.' It's as if they rehearsed together. We haven't gotten anything actionable from them. We're going to have to release them in a few hours if we don't come up with evidence to tie them to today's incident."

"Understood," Lenihan said, and he did understand. DAFFIE was not a band of idiots just out of college. They devised a meticulous plan, which had almost succeeded. Of course their leader would disappear before their scheme was put into effect, so she would survive and fight another day if things went sideways. And of course they covered their tracks to protect as many members of the cell as possible. Hence the practiced responses to interrogation.

The president stood up, put his hands on his hips and addressed his staff: "Okay, it looks like, Jerry, you guys have some work to do. But, thanks to Agents McDaniels and Mercado, we can go forward with this evening's events."

Jerry DeNigris immediately spoke up: "Mr. President, I strongly urge you to cancel the speech in the park and the fundraiser at the science center. We don't know—"

"Look, Jerry, I understand your concern but you have the entire DAFFIE Phoenix cell in custody except for the leader who scampered away, correct?"

"That we know of, sir."

"Their plan was to attack us at the science center, right?"

"Yes, it appears so."

"That means that there is nothing planned for the speech in the park, doesn't it?"

"Well, sir, we don't know."

"That may be true, we don't know, but, come on, Jerry, what's the likelihood they were planning separate attacks in the park and the science center?" the president asked, and no response came.

"I take from your silence that you agree with me that two attacks on the same day a hundred yards apart are not very likely. Since the science center attack was averted, I see no reason not go forward with the speech in the park and the fundraiser."

Denis Lenihan was silent during the president's exchange with the veteran Secret Service agent. His initial inclination was to cancel the upcoming appearances, but as he listened to his friend's debate with DeNigris, he saw where this exchange was headed, and he was not surprised.

"Look, Jerry, you know I have the utmost respect for you and your people. But this administration does not let terrorists dictate its actions. Given what we know about DAFFIE and today's attack, I'm confident that DAFFIE took its one shot at me and missed. I see very little chance of any further attacks against us today. The speech in the park and the fundraiser are going forward as planned," the president said, looking at Lenihan and Masters and moving closer to the speaker phone. "Consider that an order. It is now up to those in this room and on the phone to execute it. This meeting is over. I have to get ready for the rest of the day. Thanks to all."

"Yes, Mr. President," DeNigris and Surlee said before they hung up. As Masters went to leave, the president said, "Steve, please send Don Mangini a text at the end of the night and let him know how Agent McDaniels is doing. He can let me know."

"Yes, sir, Mr. President. I'll do that."

"Thank you."

After Masters left, the president sat down in a chair, extending his legs, his head hanging over the back of the chair.

"Jeez, Denis, we dodged a bullet today. Not a real bullet, I know, but being pink for a couple of weeks? That would have really sucked."

Lenihan also sat down. "I'm just stunned. These asshole lesbians. And you know lesbians don't bother me. I know a few. But none like these wackos." He looked at his friend and asked the question that he purposely had not asked in front of the staff moments ago, "Look, Jim, are you sure you can go through with this? Can you make the speech and then hang out with a bunch of strangers for a few hours?"

"Denis, I've been shot at before by people who wanted me and the Marines I was flying around dead, not just a different color. I'll be fine. As far as those lesbians, I have a few stories, but never mind. Look, I have to get ready for tonight. Why don't you take off. I'll see you downstairs when we leave for the park."

"Yes. All right. I'll see you then."

"We good for my late-night swim?"

"Yes, we're all set."

"Good. We're going to get through this, Denis. I know we will."

"I know you do," Lenihan walked out the room, nodding to the two agents standing immediately outside the door. *One attack on the presidency down. One to go.*

*   *   *   *   *

The president's speech in the park went well. He was able to put the DAFFIE attempted attack to the side and made an excellent presentation. The administration released a statement immediately prior to the speech that a nonlethal explosive device had been discovered in the Arizona Science Center several hours before the president's scheduled appearance. The device had been detonated in the science center while being removed. One Secret Service agent received non-life-threatening injuries and was expected to be released from the hospital the next day. The Secret Service and state and local police were investigating the incident and, as of that night, were questioning several persons of interest but had not made arrests or identified the attackers.

Since the threat had been eliminated, the president had been determined to continue evening's festivities. The press release included a statement by the president: "This administration will not be intimidated by criminal acts, whether by individuals or organized groups."

So, a half an hour after his speech, the president was at the fundraiser in the Arizona Science Center, surrounded by a group of local GOP donors when Don Mangini grabbed his elbow, made apologies and guided POTUS to the Reverend Josiah Hood and his wife.

"Mr. President, I'd like you to meet the Reverend Josiah Hood and his wife, Rebecca," Mangini said as he introduced the president.

"Good evening, Mr. President, it's a real pleasure to meet you," Reverend Hood said as he rose to his full height, stuck out his chest and gripped the president's hand. The president immediately remembered Mangini's description of shaking hands with Hood at their first meeting. Don hadn't exaggerated.

"Reverend, it's a pleasure to finally meet you. I've followed you for the past several years and have read several of your sermons." Turning to the reverend's wife, the president smiled and said, "It's a pleasure to meet you too, Mrs. Hood," as he made eye contact with her, conveying his warm personality without being too intimate, a skill he had picked up during his presidential campaign.

"Oh, Mr. President, thank you so much," she responded, grabbing his hand with both of hers. "And please call me Becky. All my friends do."

"Okay, Becky. I really appreciate you making the trip out here too."

"Well, Mr. President, I can tell you that both Josiah and I are thrilled to be here and to meet you. My husband has been telling anyone who will listen that we were coming out here to meet you."

The president laughed, looking at the good reverend. "I hope he goes back to those same folks and tells them some nice things about me."

Now it was Reverend Hood's turn to speak up. "Well, Mr. President, I sure like what I see coming out of your administration. Like many, I supported President Trump while holding my nose. I wasn't surprised when he decided not to run again. I didn't know you—I don't think I know anybody from New Jersey—but, so far, I like what I see."

"I'm glad to hear that Reverend, very glad."

"Now, mind you, I'm not saying I agree with you on everything," Reverend Hood said and stood a bit taller and seemed a little more imposing as he looked at the president with a stern face. "I wish you were a stronger on the killing of unborn children and would loosen the government's purse strings when it comes to religious schools building playgrounds, fixing their roofs, that sort of thing. Many of my followers would like their children to say a prayer to start the school day or before their high school football game without some ACLU attorney running to court to sue the school district."

"Well, Reverend, as I'm sure you know, many issues like the ones you just raised are more often than not decided by the courts not the executive branch," the president responded in a calm but firm tone.

"Mr. President, I understand that completely. In fact, I have told that to many of my congregants who complain to me about various issues, asking me what can be done to make this government more responsive to people who don't work in Hollywood or New York or sit on one of those liberal cable news desks. And do you know what I tell them, Mr. President?" Hood continued, smiling all the while and now winking at Don Mangini, who was anxious to hear the reverend's answer to his own question. "I tell them two things. The first is that it takes a moral, honest and trustworthy leader to navigate the complex cultural and political issues that modern America faces. A God-fearing leader who can be relied upon to make the right choices for America. And, Mr. President, I also tell them that we have to be realistic about our system of laws in this great country of ours. I tell them," Reverend Hood continued as he stepped closer to the president, bending down so that their eyes were level, "exactly what you just mentioned. That the men and women who sit as judges throughout this country will make decisions that impact all Americans across all walks of life for generations to come. That, Mr. President, is one of the reasons I came down here to meet you. So you can look me in the eye and tell me you will nominate men and women to the bench who us people in 'flyover country,' as those talking heads in the media call us, know won't let the government stop us from practicing our religion, telling us who we have to do business with or take away our guns."

President Whitcomb listened intently to Reverend Hood, giving him his full attention. He recognized that Hood represented a significant block of voters who were frustrated at being mocked, ignored and disregarded by many on the left. He intended to assure Hood that he was a politician who was ready, willing and able stand up for the deplorables across the country.

"President Trump did a pretty good job of that. We would like to know if you intend to do the same, sir." Reverend Hood stepped back, looking at the president, trying to gauge the effect his little speech had on the nation's chief executive.

"Reverend, I couldn't agree with you more. As President Trump showed, one of the most significant moves a Republican president can make is to ensure that the federal judiciary, and I am including the district and appellate courts, not just the Supreme Court, that the entire federal judiciary is staffed with judges who will interpret the law, and not make it themselves by adding principles to the Constitution that were not intended by the founding fathers."

"Well said, Mr. President, well said," a beaming Reverend Hood replied.

"I think we are on the same page, Reverend."

"I think so too, Mr. President. And rest assured that I will let my congregants know about our conversation today. And our agreement about what is good for America."

At that point, Denis Lenihan approached the group with Moshe and Yael in tow. The president made introductions as the parties shook hands and exchanged pleasantries.

Lenihan then spoke up. "It's a pleasure to meet you, Reverend. I hope you and your wife are enjoying the evening."

"We sure are, Denis. Donny here has been a great spokesperson for your administration. The evening has been everything we expected."

Turning to Moshe, the Reverend said, "And Mr. Schwartz, it is certainly a pleasure to meet you. I've heard of you and your stores. They're some kind of high-end hardware stores, aren't they?"

"Yes, Reverend, you could call them that."

"If you're ever thinking of opening one in the Atlanta area, we could use you. We have plenty of need down there, especially out in the country where I am, of good quality tools, building supplies and the like. And Yael, you have a beautiful Biblical name. Where might you be from?"

"I am from Israel, Reverend. Moshe is a family friend."

"It is always a thrill to meet a true daughter of Israel. And one as lovely as you I might add." At that comment, Mrs. Hood rolled her eyes and looked at her now empty wine glass.

"And Moshe, may I call you Moshe? I've read that you are strong supporter of Israel, isn't that correct?"

"You are correct, Reverend."

"Yes, well," Reverend Hood continued, smiling at Yael again, "so am I. We may differ in some respects, but Jews and Christians should always be on the same side when it comes to the State of Israel and its continued existence." Reverend Hood turned to Don Mangini. "Donny, would you be so kind as to take my wife over to the buffet line. See that she gets a couple of those fancy sandwiches they're serving." Looking at his wife with raised eyebrows, he said, "She's had two of those white wine spritzers. I don't want her drinking wine on an empty stomach. No telling what she might say about me."

"Oh, Josiah Hood, you stop that right now," Becky Hood said.

"Get along, darling."

Ever the dutiful wife, she walked with Mangini toward the nearest buffet table, laughing the whole time.

After Mangini and Mrs. Hood left the group, Reverend Hood said to Yael, "May I escort you to the bar, young lady, so we can have a drink? I would love to get your take on Israel and the current state of its relations with its Arab neighbors."

Yael moved toward Reverend Hood, winking at Moshe as she put her arm in the crook of Reverend Hood's arm. "Reverend, that is a wonderful idea. I am happy to share what little I know of Middle East politics if you can explain to me, what is it called? The red state and blue state divide in this country?"

Reverend Hood shook his head, grinning at the rest of the group as he led Yael away, in the direction opposite his wife and Mangini. "My dear, I don't know if we have enough hours in the day to describe that. But I'll try. By the way, what did you say you do for a living?"

Yael cocked her head slightly sideways, looking at Reverend Hood with a subtle but nevertheless enticing smile. "I didn't."

"You didn't what?"

"I didn't say what I do for a living."

The reverend was taken aback by the directness of Yael's reply. But she reeled him back, squeezing his arm and giving him a playful look. "I am an international business consultant. In the import and export field." She reached into her purse and handed the reverend a business card.

Reverend Hood examined the card. "'Senior Executive and Managing Director, Universal Exports. Offices in Tel Aviv, Brussels, Paris, Geneva, London.' Quite impressive. May I keep this?"

"Of course, Reverend. It is yours. Do you ever travel to Europe?"

As Hood and Yael sauntered away, the president and Denis Lenihan looked at Schwartz, both trying not to laugh at what they had just witnessed.

"What can I say? She's a friendly girl. She likes to meet people," Schwartz said, shrugging while grinning at his two friends.

A local Republican Party official interrupted, asking the president if he would be willing to meet some of the donors. Nodding to Lenihan and Schwartz, he walked to a group standing nearby and began to shake hands and slap backs.

After the president left, Lenihan and Schwartz were alone in the crowded room. "Is she ready for tonight?" Lenihan asked.

"Yes, she's ready. More than ready. And she is happy to do this for you. But Denis, you know that someday, somewhere, somehow, she's going to want this favor returned. Or, more likely, her bosses will."

Lenihan looked at Schwartz and then turned to watch the president meeting and making new best friends. They had devised tonight's scheme somewhat on the fly. They didn't have much time to put it together. The plan was simple; only a few moving parts, less to get screwed up. Lenihan and Whitcomb hadn't thought about payback for Yael when they put the plan together. But, given for whom she worked, of course, there would be some type of compensation extracted by her superiors at some point. Lenihan couldn't worry about that now. They had to move forward. They had no choice. They'd deal with Yael's recompense later.

Lenihan could hear above the din one of the donors saying to the president, and anyone else who would listen, that "President Trump's wall never made it to my ranch. Are you going to finish it, sir? I mean, what are you going to do to stop those goddamn illegal immigrants from trespassing on my land?"

Lenihan started toward the group. Another fire to put out.

*   *   *   *   *

During the fundraiser, Jerry DeNigris, Diana Surlee and Steve Masters had a strategy session via conference call. "We're all set with the hotel," Masters reported. "They'll clear the pool area out by 10:00 PM. If anyone asks, they'll say they have some emergency maintenance that they have to complete. They will not attribute the closing to POTUS."

"Very good," DeNigris responded. "Steve, your local guys who are assisting tonight will maintain security in the lobby, parking area and the perimeter of the hotel. The presidential detail people will handle the security of the pool area and POTUS's route through the hotel. Understood?"

"Yes, sir. Understood."

"Good. We're all set."

Chapter 35

Bobby Manzi and Shooter O'Neill met their contact at the appointed time. He led them into the building and to a service elevator that took them to the tenth floor. He then took them to a vacant office with an unobstructed view of the hotel's pool area. He showed Manzi how to lock the door when they left. As he went to leave, Manzi pulled out his wad of cash and peeled off two $100 bills. "You never saw us, comprende, amigo?"

"Si, senor, si. Nada," his eyes opening wide at his unexpected windfall. "I see nothing."

"Excellent, mi amigo," Manzi said as he closed the door.

"Well, Robert, we are in business. If your information is correct, I should have some excellent photos for Jake by the end of the night."

"You sure? At night? At this distance?"

"Robert, see all the lights along the road? The lights of the tennis courts next to the pool? The hotel itself? With the film I'll be using, we'll have plenty of light to get Jake his pictures."

"That's good. It makes my life a lot easier if he's happy."

"I hear you laddie, I hear you."

*   *   *   *   *

Denis Lenihan walked into a small room outside the auditorium where the fundraiser was being held. He dialed Steve Masters. "Steve, this is Denis Lenihan."

"Yes sir. About twenty minutes ago our team at one of the buildings saw Manzi and O'Neill enter the building. They were met at the service entrance by a male who was waiting for them and had keys for the entrance. He just came out and left. The surveillance team is remaining in position and out of sight."

"Okay, so our plan is working so far," Lenihan said.

"It seems so," Steve confirmed. "We moved another team to that building. Both teams will wait for them to come out. They will not enter the building or engage the subjects when they come out."

"Good. Let them do what they came to do. We can't let them know we're on to them."

"Understood, sir."

*   *   *   *   *

At eight o'clock Don Mangini, accompanied by two Secret Service agents, approached the president and told him, loud enough for everyone in the immediate area to hear, that it was time to leave so that he could take the scheduled overseas call. As the president said his goodbyes to the donors surrounding him, Mangini grabbed his arm and led him to the nearest exit. With the two agents clearing a path through the crowd, Mangini was able to make it seem that the president was being involuntarily removed from the reception when he would rather stay to chat. They had perfected this routine through the earlier road shows.

Denis Lenihan, Moshe Schwartz and Yael met the president and Mangini outside the auditorium at a designated location. The group then left the science center in the presidential motorcade to return to the hotel, leaving Mangini to oversee the end of the fundraiser.

Once they pulled away from the science center, Lenihan looked at Schwartz and Yael, but mostly Yael. "We certainly appreciate your assistance in...this."

"Assistance in this charade?" Schwartz volunteered.

Whitcomb chuckled at his friend's comment but not very loudly or very long. Typically unflappable, the president, notwithstanding his earlier expressions of confidence to his chief of staff, was more hopeful than resolute that the plan Lenihan had crafted would succeed. He could only hope that this whole charade, as Schwartz called it, turned into a successful double cross as in a John le Carre thriller rather than a Shakespearean tragedy.

The president's retinue arrived as planned. They were met at the rear of the hotel by a team of agents. They were escorted through the kitchen to a freight elevator that took them to the seventh floor. They then walked through the serpentine passageways used by the housekeeping and room service staffs to the wing where the presidential party was staying. The group said goodbye for now and dispersed to their rooms.

The president opened the door to his suite as his Secret Service detail took their stations in the hallway. The president took off his jacket and tie, tossing them on a nearby chair as the door to his bedroom door opened.

"So, how was the fundraiser?" his friend from hiking asked.

"Not terrible. Actually met some nice people. I get pat on the back a lot at these things. Good for the ego," the president responded, smiling all the time as he moved toward his waiting friend. "Come on, let's go inside so I can change." They walked into the bedroom arm in arm. "We have some time to kill before dinner gets here."

*   *   *   *   *

"You all set, Mr. Shooter?"

"Yes, Robert, thank you for asking."

"You want a bite of this sandwich?"

"No, Robert, I'm fine."

"I got some water and soda here. You want something?"

"No, Robert, I don't need anything."

"How's the pool look?"

"It looks fine. They seem to be chasing people out of there."

"Yeah, well, it's almost ten o'clock. Cory said they're closing the pool to the guests around then."

"Yes, well, it appears that they are keeping to their schedule."

"That's good."

"Yes, it is. Say, Robert, do you have anything to do?"

"You mean right now?"

"Yes, right now."

"Nah, the only thing I have to do is make sure you don't get interrupted."

"Wonderful."

*   *   *   *   *

Shortly before 10:15 PM, Denis Lenihan knocked on the president's door. He waited a minute and heard a muffled "hold on I'll be right there." In another minute or so, Moshe Schwartz and Yael joined him outside the president's suite. The president opened the door, stuck out his head, and asked for a few more minutes. After he closed the door, Schwartz and Yael exchanged glances and looked at Lenihan. He didn't acknowledge them and looked straight ahead. In a few more minutes, Whitcomb opened the door and ushered his waiting friends into the room. The door to his bedroom was closed. The president was wearing a bathing suit and a Rutgers baseball shirt and holding a bourbon.

"How was dinner, Jim?" Schwartz asked.

"Excellent. The chef did a great job."

Lenihan looked at his phone. "We have to get going soon."

"I'm ready," the president replied. The three men then looked at Yael. "Let me change, and I'll be ready too." Yael grabbed her bag and headed toward the bathroom. As she opened the door, she turned to the group. "Mr. President, would you like me in a bikini or a one-piece?"

The president's eyes opened wide as he looked at Yael. Schwartz held his hand over his mouth, suppressing a grin. Lenihan looked bewildered. Another decision to make?

"Yael," Whitcomb responded, "whatever you feel most comfortable in will do fine, I'm sure. Right, guys?"

Lenihan and Schwartz murmured their agreement.

As she was changing, Lenihan called the agent in charge of the protection detail. "We'll be ready in a few minutes." When he got off the phone, he began to run through the evening's plans one more time with the president. After a few minutes, Yael came out of the bathroom in her one-piece suit. Schwartz, even though he had seen her in the suit before, and up close, admired her appearance once again. The president also took the time to study his new companion, at least for this part of the evening.

"Very nice, Yael, very nice," Whitcomb said.

"Thank you, Mr. President. And Denis, do you think this will do?"

"I, uh, yes, uh, Yael, I, I think it will do fine."

Yael took a swim suit cover out of her bag, slipped it on and sat down. "I am ready whenever you are, Mr. President," she said, definitely the calmest person in the room.

A knock sounded on the door, and Lenihan opened it. It was agents from the protection detail. "They'll be right out," Lenihan said as he closed the door.

The four in the room looked at each other. "Game time," the president said as he moved toward the door, gesturing for Yael to join him. "Are you ready for a dip in the pool, Yael?"

Yael rose from the chair and walked to the president's side. "I certainly am, Mr. President. It will be my pleasure."

"Good luck, Jim," Schwartz patted Whitcomb on the back.

"Thanks, Moshe. Thanks for all your help."

"Anytime, buddy. Give 'em hell!"

The president smiled at his friend and gave him a thumbs up sign.

The president put on a windbreaker. Lenihan knocked on the door and opened it to find four agents from the protection detail waiting. Whitcomb guided Yael out of the room, and the entourage headed down the hallway led by two of the agents. The other two waited to follow the president and Yael. One of them spoke into a microphone concealed in his hand: "Leatherneck is on the move."

Lenihan closed the door. He walked over to the bar that was set up. "You joining me for a drink, Moshe?"

"You bet, Denis. I'm sure you need one. But I think everything is going to work out tonight. It's a good plan."

"I could use one of those, boys, if you don't mind," the voice of the president's friend came from the other side of the room.

Lenihan and Schwartz turned toward the door leading to the adjoining bedroom. Lenihan had forgotten about the president's friend; he quickly recovered. "Of course, Kerry, forgive me for not inviting you. What would you like? And have you met Moshe Schwartz?"

"No, but I've wanted to for some time. How are you, Moshe? Jim has told me a great deal about you."

*　　*　　*　　*　　*

Jake Rosen pushed the plate with his late-night snack to the side. He was only able to eat half of the sandwich. He got up from the conference table to get him and Fran Ritzie another scotch. He wasn't very hungry tonight, but he could use another drink, even knowing it was going to be a long night. Rosen had been unable to concentrate since he arrived in the office this morning. He kept running various scenarios in his head, imagining all the things that could go wrong tonight, based on all the things that had gone wrong in the last few days. At 7:00 PM he instructed his assistant to hold all his calls and to tell anyone who asked that he was unavailable for the rest of the evening.

Ritzie could see the strain, anguish and fear in Rosen's face. "Come on Jake, we're in a good position. Thank God you had the foresight to develop that source in the White House so close to Whitcomb. It's been a goldmine these last few weeks, especially since they've been in Phoenix. Your plan is going to work. We're going to have Whitcomb by the balls."

Rosen handed Ritzie his drink. "I know Fran, I know. That is what you continue to tell me. But I need to see actual results, not receive a pep talk."

"Jake, we'll know soon enough. Shooter is in a great position. He'll get the pictures we want with no floppy hats, sunglasses or bodyguards in the way. After tonight, Whitcomb will be putty in your hands."

"From your lips to God's ears."

*   *   *   *   *

"Well, Robert, it looks like your girl in DC came through. Unless I am mistaken the president of the United States just entered the pool area." Shooter O'Neill was looking through his camera, setup on a tripod.

"Bingo! I knew Cory and her girl would come through." Manzi moved to the window, standing next to O'Neill. He couldn't see much from this distance. "Can you see the friend? Can you get a good shot of the friend?

O'Neill leaned back from his camera eyepiece and looked at Manzi with a puzzled expression. He then leaned in to the camera. He was silent for close to a minute. Manzi looked at the pool and could barely make out figures moving about.

"What is it, Mr. Shooter?"

O'Neill didn't answer. After a few moments he let out a string of expletives. He moved back from the camera. "We've got a problem."

"We do?"

"Yeah, we do. Take a look."

Manzi moved up to the camera, leaning into the eyepiece. He saw Whitcomb dive into the water and swim underwater to the middle of the pool. He rose to the surface and turned to face the area of the pool deck from which he dove. Manzi swung the camera ever so slightly to see a strikingly beautiful woman moving to the edge of the deck. She waved at Whitcomb, who was motioning for her to join him. She dove toward the nation's chief executive and commander in chief. She swam into his arms and they embraced, obviously enjoying their private swim.

She hopped up into his arms as he laughed, throwing his head back. She wrapped her legs around his hips and lowered the top half of her bathing suit, giving Whitcomb (and Manzi, even at this distance), quite a view. She leaned back, floating on her back as he swung her around in the water.

"Madonna mia! This is not good! What's he doing with a broad like that?"

O'Neill moved toward the camera. "Step aside, Robert. I have to get some pictures for Jake. Although he is going to be quite surprised when he sees who Whitcomb's swimming partner is."

The president and Yael continued laughing, hugging and splashing each other for several minutes, putting on quite a show for Manzi and O'Neill.

"He's not going to be happy."

"I know, Robert. But our assignment is to get pictures of the president in the pool with his special friend. And that is what we're doing."

"Does she look anything like the person he went hiking with?"

"I never got a look at her face. As for her body, the clothes she was wearing today were baggy and layered so I really couldn't judge what type of figure she had.

"Seeing who's in the pool with Whitcomb, I would have never guessed the lovely creature we are looking at now and the person hiking with Whitcomb this morning are one and the same. But your girl said they would be at the pool tonight."

"Maybe, Mr. Shooter, just maybe, there's another friend? Maybe that friend is on the way down? Maybe we should wait and see?"

"Sure, Robert, sure. We can do that. I'll take a few more pictures of the happy couple." O'Neill then looked into his camera. After a few moments, he said, chuckling, "Look at that: I didn't know the female body could bend that way."

O'Neill handed Manzi another camera with a long-range lens, so he could see the evening show. After fifteen minutes, the president and Yael got out of the pool. They grabbed towels and took turns drying each other off from head to toe, then sat in nearby lounge chairs. They had a continuous conversation, gazing at each other, laughing at their respective comments, and periodically stroking an arm, shoulder or thigh.

"Wow," was all Manzi could muster.

Two old friends enjoying some alone time together. At least, that's what it looked like to Manzi and O'Neill. And O'Neill captured it all digitally. The last picture O'Neill took was of Whitcomb and Yael, almost directly facing the camera, as Whitcomb helped her pull the straps of her bathing suit over her shoulders. The president put on his shirt and windbreaker and his companion her cover. With their backs to the camera, they strolled across the pool deck toward the hotel. After a few steps, the woman leaned into Whitcomb and slipped her hand into his. They reached the door leading from the pool. The door opened, and they disappeared into the building.

"No one else is coming, Robert."

"Yeah, I guess not. It was a longshot, I know."

"Help me pack my gear. Let's get the hell out of here."

"When are you sending Jake the pictures?" Manzi asked as they were gathering the equipment.

"He wants the pictures as soon as possible. I'll do it from the car. I don't want to get caught in here by some late-night worker or janitor."

"You're right. Let's get out of here. If Jake knew what was coming, though, he wouldn't be in such a hurry to get the photos."

"I still can't believe she's a girl."

*　*　*　*　*

Lenihan, Schwartz and the president's friend, Kerry, were on their third round of drinks, enjoying themselves as Schwartz regaled them with some of his and Whitcomb's escapades while they had been deployed in Iraq. Some of the stories were new to Lenihan.

"You know, we don't see each other that often, but Jim doesn't talk much about being over there. He's never told me any of your stories, Moshe," Kerry said.

"I told you the funny ones," Moshe said. "There are some that are not so funny. I can tell you, from personal experience, if you've been in combat, seen people killed, sometimes friends; that's not something you want to relive. You just want to get out of there and go on with your life. It's hard for people who have not experienced combat to understand."

Kerry leaned forward, saying "Yes, I've read that several times, or words to that effect. I would help him if he needed it, and he let me."

"I'm just suggesting to you to not take it personally. Believe me, it's not you. It's him."

"Oh, I don't, I really don't. But thank you for explaining."

The door to the suite opened, and the president walked in, thanking his protection detail. "Hello, gentlemen. You got one of those for me?"

"Certainly," Schwartz responded, hopping out of his chair and moving over toward the bar.

"How did it go?" Lenihan asked.

"Swimmingly," the president replied, earning a groan and a sideways glance from Schwartz as he brought him his drink.

"Where's Yael?"

"She went to her room to change. She'll be here shortly. And your evening?" he said, surveying the room.

"I can't speak for Denis, but Moshe and I had a wonderful time. Mostly sharing stories about you. Didn't we Moshe?" Kerry said.

"I know I did," Schwartz responded.

"Is that so?" the president said, now giving Schwartz his own sideways glance. "So, what's the most interesting thing about me you heard tonight, Kerry?"

Whitcomb was interrupted by a knock on the door. Schwartz opened the door to let Yael in. "Hello, all," she said. "Moshe, dear, I could use one of those."

"Of course. Would you like a whiskey or champagne?"

"I would love some champagne. We're celebrating, aren't we?" Yael said, looking around the room.

"I think so," Whitcomb said.

"So, it went okay?" Kerry asked.

"I think it went better than okay. We gave them a pretty good show; wouldn't you say Yael?"

"Yes, Mr. President, I think we did. If they were in the building they were supposed to be, they got some nice pictures of us."

"Action photos?" Moshe asked, which led to him receiving a punch from Yael. The group roared in laughter.

Moshe raised his glass. "I propose a toast. To the success of Operation—we never named your plan, Denis, did we?"

"No, we didn't. And let's not," Lenihan replied. "The last thing we need is the name of a supposed secret operation floating out there for someone to leak. The next thing you know, a Network member is slinking around the White House, asking questions."

"Okay," Moshe said, winking at Yael. "To Operation No Name."

"To Operation No Name," the group repeated, as Lenihan rolled his eyes at the celebrants and downed his drink then went to the bar to pour himself another.

Whitcomb followed Lenihan. "Any report from Steve Masters?" he asked as Lenihan filled his glass too.

"Masters sent me a text. They're sitting in their car. O'Neill has a laptop out and is fiddling with it," Lenihan said.

"Most likely sending some photos to....?" Whitcomb didn't finish his sentence.

"Yes, I assume so. To somewhere."

"I think there are going to be some very unhappy people in New York tonight," Whitcomb ventured.

"I certainly hope so," Lenihan answered.

The group had a few more drinks and chatted for another hour. The president then stood up. "Okay, folks, the party is over. This was an interesting day and night, I guess, but I'm bushed."

"Me too," said Moshe as he stood up. "Come, Yael, let's repair to our room and get settled in for the night."

"As you wish, Moshe," Yael said; she walked to Whitcomb, extending her hand. "It was a pleasure to be of service to you, Mr.

President. As unusual as it was," she said, smiling at Whitcomb. "I hope Operation No Name is a success."

"I can't thank you enough for your help, Yael. You were wonderful. I hope you come down for a visit to the White House with Moshe the next time you are in the U.S."

"Thank you very much, Mr. President. I will take you up on that offer, as you Americans say."

"I look forward to it."

The president and Schwartz hugged each other, each pounding the other's back. "You really came through when I needed you, Moshe. I can't thank you enough."

Schwartz let out a big belly laugh. "Well, thanks, good buddy, but Yael did all the work. I'm glad we were here and able to help out. If there is anything you need, give me a call."

"I will, Moshe, I will."

"It was a pleasure to finally get to meet you, Moshe," Kerry said.

"Thank you, Kerry. Hopefully, we'll see you again sometime soon."

"That would be great."

Lenihan put his drink down, getting ready to leave. "Kerry, wonderful to see you."

"You too, Denis. This was great. Certainly, an eye opener for me. I hope all goes well with your plan."

"So far, so good."

"And Yael, it was certainly a pleasure to meet you. If you don't mind me saying, you are a lovely creature," Kerry said.

"Thank you, Kerry. I hope to meet you again," Yael said, then she and Moshe left the room.

Lenihan turned to Whitcomb. "If I hear anything noteworthy from the Secret Service, I'll let you know. Otherwise, no news is good news."

"Agreed. I'll see you in the morning."

"Thanks again for all your help, Denis."

You're welcome, Jim. Good night, Kerry."

"Good night, Denis."

Now, finally alone in the suite, Whitcomb said to his remaining friend, "I think, I hope we won't be disturbed the rest of the night."

"Let's get one more drink and into the bedroom and relax. You've had a long day, Jim."

"Kerry, that's the best idea I've heard today. Let's do that."

The president made two drinks. He and Kerry then walked into the master suite, arms wrapped around each other.

* * * * *

"What did Manzi say?" Jake Rosen asked Fran Ritzie, his voice barely audible.

"He said the information was correct, Jake. Whitcomb and his friend went swimming in the hotel pool after 10:30 PM."

"And these are Shooter's photos?"

Ritzie had already gone through the photos. He stood beside Rosen as Rosen scrolled through the photos O'Neill had sent. "This doesn't look like the friend we were expecting, Fran." Rosen was outwardly calm, but Ritzie could see the vein throbbing in his temple and his face getting redder as he repeatedly clicked the pen in his left hand.

"I thought we had him in our sights this time," Fran said.

Rosen did not respond as he went through the photos one more time.

"What about that incident in the museum before the speech?" Rosen said.

"Some type of bomb containing colored dye, you know, the type of dye they put in bags of cash when bank robbers do their thing."

"I see. Who did it?"

"The White House has not announced who planted the bomb. Montanez says his sources in the Phoenix PD say it's a domestic terrorist group named 'DAFFIE.'"

"Never heard of them."

"They're a group of radical vegan lesbians," Ritzie said.

"Oh. They are the worst kind, or so I have heard."

Ritzie continued. "Anyway, the only casualty was the Secret Service agent who discovered the bomb. He was not seriously injured."

"Good for him," Rosen replied.

Ritzie paused. He had never seen Rosen so morose. He wasn't even this upset when the Pennsylvania, Wisconsin and Michigan voting results came in on election night in 2016. The only sound in the room was that of Rosen clicking his pen.

"And what about the Native American protests? Did the Antifa element show up? Did the alt right groups make an appearance?" Rosen asked.

"They did. But the Arizona State Police and local police kept them separated. There were no significant confrontations."

"So, no Charlottesville?" Rosen said.

"No, Jake, I'm afraid to say. No repeat of Charlottesville."

Rosen went back to his silent mode, except for the clicking pen, with a melancholy look on his face.

"Do you want me to summon the Council in the next few days?"

Rosen was staring straight ahead, no longer looking at the photos of the presidential swim mates. "Why? What is there for the Council to do?"

"We can find out who this woman is. I've asked Montanez to dig up what he can."

"To what end? He was with a woman. We sent O'Neill halfway across the country to get photos of Whitcomb in a pool with a half-naked woman. That was not what we were led to believe was happening tonight."

"I know. I'm just trying to help, Jake," Ritzie said.

"I know you are. But right now I do not know if any help, by anyone, can be rendered." Rosen let out a plaintive sigh and became silent (except for the pen).

Epilogue

Two months later, the president and his staff had just returned to the Oval Office from the press conference in the Rose Garden at which the president formally announced his intent to seek reelection; the event had gone well. The timing of the announcement was Don Mangini's idea. The GNP was at its highest level since President Trump's third year in office. The numbers for employment, the trade deficit and inflation were also very favorable. Coupled with the Israeli-Egyptian-Jordanian peace accord, the Whitcomb administration was riding high. Mangini's suggestion had been seconded by Denis Lenihan, and the president had agreed.

Of course, Whitcomb's popularity ratings received a boost when the details of DAFFIE's plot were made public. His growing number of supporters marveled at the composure he exhibited during his speech in the park once they learned that DAFFIE's attack had been disrupted only hours before. After a brief meeting, the staff dispersed to their offices and cubicles to continue the day's work. Joel Hirsch and Denis Lenihan remained in the Oval Office.

"We've had a good day, gents," the president said.

"Yes, we did, Mr. President," Hirsch responded. "Even Jim Acosta had nothing to yell at you about. Poor Jim," Hirsch continued, "he went to all the road shows, waiting to be attacked by your supporters. Cameraman in tow, ready to get it on video. And no one did."

The three men chuckled.

"Speaking of the road shows," Lenihan said, "we're planning another five, starting in two months."

"Great. I think that is great. I've had enough time back here. It will be good to get out of DC again," the president responded.

"Jerry DeNigris, in light of what happened in Phoenix, asked that we make some modifications to our procedures this time around," Lenihan continued.

"Such as?" the president asked.

"Such as not announcing the cities at which we plan to appear so far out, not announcing the venues we are going to use until the week before. Some other things."

"Doesn't sound unreasonable, Denis."

"No, it isn't. We'll work it out," Lenihan replied. "Oh, by the way, I got a call from Carl Winthrop. His security people confirmed that Soros did fund that camp for the Native Americans outside Phoenix."

"Better late than never," the president responded.

"Do you want me to let someone friendly, someone at Fox, know?" Hirsch asked.

"At this point, I don't know if it is such a big deal, especially since the local police were able to contain those groups. I was thinking that we should just keep this in our back pocket in case something similar happens at one of the future road shows. We might find it useful. What do you think, Mr. President?" Lenihan said.

"Yes, that make sense to me. Let's hold onto this," the president directed.

"Okay. And Joel, I saw Maura O'Reilly's column yesterday. It wasn't as bad as you thought it was going to be," Lenihan said.

"No, no it wasn't. I sat down with her two weeks ago and was able to talk her down a bit." He didn't mention that O'Reilly pressed him on the Phoenix trip. She seemed to know more about what had gone on out there than he did. The president went for a swim one night in the hotel pool with a young, beautiful woman? Just the two of them? That was news to Hirsch.

He knew that Moshe Schwartz, an old friend and supporter of the president, made the trip and brought an Israeli woman friend or relative, Hirsch wasn't sure which. Was that who the president went swimming with, Hirsch wondered? He had told O'Reilly what he knew but hadn't looked into it any further.

"In any event, we got some interesting comments from the two focus groups we ran after the road shows," Hirsch reported. "Based on that feedback, there are a few new topics we think you should talk about. I'll get together with Mangini, and we'll run them by the campaign staff."

"Thanks, Joel," the president said.

"Joel, could you excuse us?" Lenihan asked.

"Certainly. I was leaving anyway for my next meeting."

"Thank you," Lenihan responded.

After Hirsch left the office, Lenihan stood looking at the president, arms crossed, feet spread apart, a grimace on his face.

"Yes, Denis? You look like a man ready for a fight."

Lenihan took a deep breath, then exhaled. "I received a letter from the Israeli ambassador today. Personal and confidential."

Whitcomb stared at Lenihan. "And?"

"And Ambassador Erdan has politely but firmly stated a case as to why the United States should sell them, at a steep discount, 65 of those new fighter jets."

The president smiled, scratched his head and sat down at his desk. *And so it begins.*

Whitcomb and Lenihan looked at each other for a moment, both men waiting for the other to speak. The president stood up, and moved to one of the windows, watching White House gardners trimming some bushes. He turned to face Lenihan and spoke first.

"I guess I...we...shouldn't be surprised."

"No, we shouldn't."

Smiling, the president said, "I wonder if this has anything to do with Moshe's invitation to come to Livingston in two weeks."

"I didn't know about that."

"Yes, well, I neglected to mention that to you. Yael is going to be visiting. Moshe thought I might like to come up for the night, spend some time with them, get away from here. You're invited too."

"I see. In that case, this letter makes perfect sense. The timing, at least."

The two old friends looked at each other again without speaking.

Now laughing and rubbing his face with both hands, the president said, "Doesn't Senator Hopkins on Armed Services owe us a favor?"

"He owes us big time."

"Looks like we're going to have to call that marker in."

Lenihan moved closer to the president and picked up his tablet to make some notes. "I'll start loosening him up. We'll have him over for cocktails next week. He's very close to the vice president. I'll include her. I'll also reach out to Political-Military Affairs at State to start that process."

"Good. Let's get this done, Denis.

"Moshe, Moshe, Moshe…."

*　　*　　*　　*　　*

Denise Mercado lightly rapped on the door to Jamal McDaniel's office, which was partially open, and walked in. "Hello, stranger."

"Ms. Mercado! How are you? How did the interviews go?"

"I'm great, and I think they went fine. I met with one agent, then a team of three agents, and then DeNigris and Surlee. It all seemed to go well."

"That's a good sign that you made it to DeNigris. Not everyone makes it that far."

"I may have you to thank for that. They all said you gave me a glowing recommendation."

"Hey, I just told the truth. We can always use someone like you on the protection detail."

Mercado was in Washington to interview for a position on the presidential protection detail. She had accumulated enough time on the job, and after working with McDaniels in Phoenix, decided she wanted a change of pace and scenery.

"I do have to say, Jamal, you're looking good. The last time I saw you, you looked like a chocolate Easter bunny that got rolled around in crushed pink peeps." Mercado tried not to laugh at the memory of McDaniel's appearance after the exploding cake at the Arizona Science Center.

She failed.

"Damn, I'll tell you, I didn't think that pink crap was ever going to come off. I had seven, eight treatments. I still see some in my pores when I shave," McDaniels responded, shaking his head.

"How about the burns?" Mercado asked seriously.

Holding his hands up, he said, "They're fine. Had some blistering and swelling. But that went away in a few days. The burned skin eventually peeled off. No scarring."

"I am so relieved for you. And you got a promotion?"

"Yeah, I'm a team leader now."

"That's great! Congratulations! You deserve it," she said.

"Yes, well, we know why I got it."

"Yes, we do, but come on, Jamal. You dragged that bomb out of there, away from those kids in the next room. You didn't know there was only dye in that cake. What if they had used real explosives?" Mercado shuddered at the thought. "You're a hero. A pink hero, for a few weeks. But a hero nevertheless."

This time Mercado laughed out loud, pleased with her joke, but McDaniels didn't seem to enjoy it as much. Seeing that, Mercado switched gears: "You're still taking me out to dinner tonight, right?"

"Yes, I certainly am. We're going to a new place, near Dupont Circle, that has gotten good reviews."

"That sounds great. You know, Jamal, I'll be here for a few days. You are also going to give me a tour of the nation's capital, aren't you? I haven't been here since junior high."

"Yes, Denise, yes, I said I would do that. I have some time coming so we can explore the District together."

"Excellent! I'm going to go back to my hotel to change. Why don't we meet at the hotel bar? We can have a few drinks."

"Sounds like a plan," he said.

Mercado stood up and saluted McDaniels. "Aye, aye, team leader, sir!"

*   *   *   *   *

Elizabeth Wentworth pulled herself out of the warm water of the hot tub and dove into the chilly water of the adjacent kidney shaped pool. She was at the bed and breakfast she and her DAFFIE compatriots visited periodically. She was here by herself, after traveling across the Northwest, using false identities and making her way down the coast. She was confident that her trail had been lost and none of the jackbooted fascists in the government had any idea where she was.

Several of her DAFFIE sisters were due to arrive over the next few days. They would undertake an exhaustive review of Operation Layer Cake to determine what had gone wrong. Wentworth wasn't sure. She had racked her brain the last two months, mentally replaying the plan over and over again. Was the DAFFIE Phoenix cell somehow infiltrated? Did one of the Group members say the wrong thing to a friend or relative or get roaring drunk in a lesbian bar and start bragging about their plans to free oppressed womyn? (it wouldn't be the first time). Did Melinda Katzenberg somehow screw up?

The authorities had not released any significant details of the bombing at the science center or their investigation. All she knew was that the feds had somehow discovered the cake with the bomb baked inside it and were taking it out of the building when it exploded. One government agent was injured. Collateral damage. Shit happens in war. But Wentworth was undeterred. This was a temporary setback. DAFFIE would regroup and continue its operations and ultimately succeed.

Wentworth got out of the pool and went to her lounge chair. Her chilled wine was waiting. She was halfway through Sarah Jeong's new book, *The Destruction of the White Cisgendered Patriarchy: A Beginner's Guide*. *That girl sure can write,* she thought.

*   *   *   *   *

The weekly meeting of the *Chronicle*'s senior staff concluded. Jake Rosen was, at best, disinterested. He had been that way since the Phoenix road show. As the attendees trickled out of the conference room, Fran Ritzie hung back. After the last person left, Ritzie closed the door and sat next to Rosen. "How are you doing, my friend?" Ritzie asked with genuine concern.

"I am fine, Fran. What can I do for you? I am about to leave for the evening."

"I had a long chat with Tony Montanez this afternoon."

Rosen looked at Ritzie, not responding.

"Montanez did a little digging into High Desert Ranch. Spoke to some of the staff and to a few residents he was able to identify. No one knew of anyone living there having a connection to Whitcomb."

Rosen did not respond.

"Montanez also found out who Whitcomb's swimming partner was."

"Who is she?"

"Her name is Yael Meir. She is a family friend of the Schwartz brothers, particularly Moshe."

Rosen curled his lip. He hated the Schwartz brothers almost as much as the Koch brothers. Goddamn right wing Zionists.

"She is a consultant or sales person, something like that, for an Israeli import and export firm. They have offices all over the world," Fran said.

"And?"

"That's it. I don't have anything else from Montanez right now."

Rosen pondered Ritzie's report for a few moments. "I do not believe you will ascertain any useful information, Fran. You are spinning your wheels, as they say." Rosen looked intently at his lieutenant. "We failed. We had our one chance to score, and we failed. The opportunity to take control of the White House has passed us by."

Both men sat still. Ritzie was waiting for Rosen to say something. Anything. Rosen had nothing to say. A knock sounded on the door, and Harry O'Rourke, the deputy executive editor, entered the room holding a folder.

"Yes, Harry, what is it?" Rosen asked.

"Jake, I thought you would want to know that Kathy McDonough is the new staff reporter we hired from *The Atlantic* a few weeks ago."

"Yes, I recognize the name."

"She, well, she's finished a story that she began at *The Atlantic*, which, I guess, kind of explains why she left there."

"What is the story?" Rosen asked.

"It's about the number of abortions black women in the United States have had in the last decade."

"What?" Rosen said. "What the hell kind of a story is that? Why would we print a story like that?"

Ritzie leaned back from the conference room table. He didn't want to be in Rosen's line of fire.

"I said the same thing but, uh…but she insists that the story is a good one and should be run. She says *The Atlantic* wouldn't print it, and if we don't print it, she'll get it printed somewhere else. Or just throw it up online."

"Did we know about this in the interview process? Did she disclose that she was working on this story? Is she a Catholic?" Rosen asked.

"Well, not to me. No. I don't think she told anyone. And yes, she is Catholic," Harry approached the conference table, gingerly placing the folder on the table. "Here's the article." He stepped back, eyes downcast.

Rosen, by now biting his knuckles, remained seated, shaking his head and muttering to himself. He dismissed O'Rourke with a wave of his hand.

O'Rourke was happy to leave. After several minutes, Ritzie broke the silence. "Do you want me to do anything?"

Rosen, looking at but not touching the folder O'Rourke had put on the table, shook his head. "I will take care of this myself."

"Okay. Then I'll be leaving. Good night, Jake."

"Good night."

Rosen sat staring at the folder. He eventually reached for it and was about to open it, but tossed it to the side. He walked to his desk and sat down. He pulled a cell phone out of the lower right drawer. He dialed a number and was sent to voicemail. Irritated, he left a message. "Robert, meet me in the garage tomorrow at 5:30 PM. I have a job for you. Please be punctual."